The
Twelve
Little Cakes

THE
TWELVE
LITTLE CAKES

Dominika Dery

RIVERHEAD BOOKS

a member of

Penguin Group (USA) Inc.

New York · 2004

RIVERHEAD BOOKS
a member of
Penguin Group (USA) Inc.
375 Hudson Street
New York, NY 10014

Library of Congress Cataloging-in-Publication Data

Dery, Dominika.
The twelve little cakes / by Dominika Dery
p.   cm.
ISBN 1-57322-283-6
1. Dery, Dominika—Childhood and youth.
2. Authors, Czech—20th century—Biography.   1. Title.
PG5039.14.E78Z476   2004   2004046757
891.8'6354—dc22

Printed in the United States of America
1   3   5   7   9   10   8   6   4   2

This book is printed on acid-free paper. ∞

Book design by Stephanie Huntwork
Cake illustrations by Beth Krommes

For my mother, Jana, my father, Jarda, and Barry

ACKNOWLEDGMENTS

I would especially like to thank my agent, Theresa Park, and my editor and publisher in one person, Julie Grau, for their humanity and professionalism. They were my guardian angels, who helped me to overcome the most difficult times of my life. Without them, this book would not have been the same.

THE
TWELVE
LITTLE CAKES

THE LITTLE DELIGHT

A YEAR BEFORE I WAS BORN, I started turning up in my mother's dreams. She would go to sleep and I would appear before her: a happy little girl in a time of great unhappiness. It was the mid-seventies and Czechoslovakia was at the mercy of the Russians. The borders had been closed, the Soviet Union had taken control of our government, and the hope of the sixties had been crushed by the Cold War. Things were so bad, in fact, that my parents had resolved not to bring another child into the world.

And then I turned up.

My mother remembers the first time she dreamed me. She was standing in the middle of a blossoming garden and a little girl came running through the trees.

"Ahoj!" the girl exclaimed, which is the informal way of greeting someone in Czech. She took my mother's hand and smiled hopefully.

"Will you come with me?" she asked.

"Yes," my mother replied, and the little girl led her to a swing that hung from the branch of an apple tree.

"Push me!" she cried.

She climbed onto the swing and my mother began to push it. "Higher!" the girl demanded, and my mother pushed her until her feet touched the sky. The sun broke through the morning clouds and my mother's heart was filled with happiness. When she woke up, she could still hear the little girl's laughter. She pressed her body against my father's back and sighed. What a beautiful dream, she thought. And then the alarm clock went off and she had to get up and catch the 7:15 train into Prague.

My mother worked as an analyst at the State Economic Institute. She wrote books that her Communist bosses took credit for, and had to support her family on a meager wage, as my father had difficulty keeping a job. He had worked for the Czech government during the sixties, and was blacklisted by the Russians after the 1968 invasion. An engineer by trade, he would occasionally find work shoveling coal into a furnace, driving a garbage truck, or mixing concrete on a construction site, but the second his political records reached his employers, he would be fired. There was also a real threat that he might be thrown in jail, as it was forbidden to be unemployed under communism, and my mother's biggest fear was a late-night phone call from prison.

The first time the little girl came running through the trees, my mother thought of her own happy childhood. It wasn't until the third or fourth dream that she suddenly understood that the girl was her daughter. Night after night, the girl would appear in the garden and lead my mother to the swing, and she would squeal with delight as the sun broke through the clouds. It had been a long time since my mother had heard such innocent laughter, and she would wake up each morning with a strong feeling that things were going to get better. She hoped until she believed, and then she believed until she knew. She would have another child, and that child would be the little girl from her dream.

She told my father about the girl on the swing, and he eventually agreed that they would have another child. My sister, Klara, was nine at the time, and excited to learn that she would have a baby sister. Neither she nor my dad were the slightest bit fazed by my mother's decision to give birth as the result of a dream. My mother's dreams had a habit of coming true. She came from a long line of people who had premonitions, and the way she remembers it, the little girl was not only demanding to be born but also insisting that my parents snap out of their depression and come to terms with what had happened to their country. Life under communism was difficult but not impossible. The system was unfair but the human spirit triumphed on a daily basis, and if there was one thing my parents knew for certain in a time of great social and political upheaval, it was this: they loved each other with all their hearts. It was spring in the garden of my mother's dreams, and the girl's laughter took her back to the days when she and my father were unafraid. Their love was still strong, so maybe the dream was telling them that the time had come to try and live without fear. In 1974, my mother went off the Pill and tried to become pregnant. And the moment she decided to do this, the little girl vanished from her dreams.

"She was a messenger," my mother tells me now. "But it was definitely you. Everything was the same, especially your voice. I had to wait all those years for you to start talking, but when you did, your voice was exactly the same as I remembered it."

The little girl's disappearance upset my mother very much. It was as though a light had snapped off at the end of a tunnel, and her faith was tested every month as her early attempts to get pregnant were unsuccessful. She and my dad kept an eye on the calendar, changed their diets, and made love regularly, but nothing happened. They consulted the top specialists in Prague, but it was only when she sat down with an old and wise factory worker that the answer presented itself. The factory worker had been a respected gynecologist in the forties. He had lived through the German and Russian invasions and had been reeducated by the Communists in the time of Stalin. He had seen a lot of terrible things in his life but maintained a strong belief in the basic goodness of people, and when my mother told him about the little girl in her dreams, he took her hand and smiled.

"You want your child too badly, Jana," he told her. "The best things in life usually come along when you least expect them. If you really want to become pregnant, my advice would be to stop trying so hard and leave it in the hands of the little god."

In Czech fairy tales, the little god is a benign but powerful character who turns up in times of conflict. He is depicted as a kindly old man who watches from a distance and smiles approvingly when a problem resolves itself, or sighs and shakes his head when it doesn't. Occasionally, he will turn people into bears (if they're wicked), but most of the time he seems content to let his subjects sort their problems out themselves. One of the nicest things about the little god is that he really does seem genuinely happy when things turn out for the best.

My mother considered the factory worker's advice and decided to leave my birth in the hands of the little god. From that moment on, she and my father made love for the joy of making it instead of out of desperation to conceive, and of course the moment they did, my mother became pregnant. Things were difficult as a result of my father's struggle to keep a job, and my parents really couldn't afford another child, but their faith was rewarded by a sudden upswing of circumstance. My father managed to get hold of a license to drive taxis, and because of the independent nature of the taxi companies at the time, it would be many years before the secret police could take this job away from him. He worked at night most of the time, ferrying customers across Prague in the hours when the secret police had clocked off. The great irony about his taxi-driving years was that he earned a lot more money than he ever would have as an engineer. My dad was not only an excellent driver, he was also very chatty and charming. He made a point of taking the most direct routes to his customers' destinations, and quickly built up a small but devoted clientele who not only trusted him but enjoyed listening to his stories. He told everyone he drove that he would soon be the father of a second child, which is how he met the obstetrician who delivered me.

Unless you were a high-ranking member of the Communist Party, you didn't get to choose which doctor or hospital you went to. Under the state health system, you had to go to the medical center that was closest to your place of residence. If the doctors there were ill-mannered or incompetent, there was nothing you could do about it. When my sister was born, my mother was sent to the Karlov Hospital, which was a cold and oppressive building in a desolate yard, with crows perching ominously in the trees outside her window. My mother was very unhappy giving birth there, and told my father that she would do anything to avoid delivering another baby in "The Crow Hospital." Shortly afterward, as luck (or the little god) would have it, my dad struck up a conversation with a pretty young doctor who had just been transferred to the nicest hospital in Prague. The woman's name was Dr. Raclavska, and she was taken by my father's story about the little girl his wife had seen in her dreams. The young doctor also needed driving lessons, so my dad quickly cut a deal. He taught her in exchange for her accepting my mother in the delivery room when she was due. It was against all the hospital regulations, of course, but communism was full of people making private arrangements, which is how I came to be born in the exclusive Podoli Hospital on March 7, 1975, the same month Dr. Raclavska passed her driving test with flying colors.

The Podoli Hospital was a lovely, cream-colored building that stood beneath the Vysehrad Castle on the south bank of Prague's Vltava River. It overlooked a place where the swans traditionally nested in winter, and was so nice it was almost impossible to get into. Prague was full of places that ordinary citizens weren't allowed to visit, and one of the saddest things about the Soviet occupation was that it forced the formerly civilized Czech people to become very adept at cutting under-the-table deals.

From 1948 to 1989, the people who profited most under communism were those with the moral flexibility to say one thing and do another. With the exception of a very small percentage of overly idealistic or stupid people, everyone in Czechoslovakia saw communism for what it was: a deeply flawed and corrupt system in which a wealthy elite were able to oppress their fellow countrymen in the name of equality. This moral flexibility dates back to the Russian liberation of Prague in 1945. One of the first things the Red Army did was use Gestapo archives to identify all the Czechs who had secretly collaborated with the Nazis. Instead of punishing these people, the Russians coerced them into joining the secret police, which played a major role in the 1948 putsch, in which the Czechoslovakian government was overthrown by the Communist Party. A reign of terror ensued until the death of Stalin in 1953, by which time the status quo was firmly in place. party officials paid lip service to Marxism and the myth of the worker while systematically stealing the assets of the state; the result being a small elite of the superrich overseeing a country with serious economic problems.

In the mid-sixties, when my father worked briefly for the government, there was a lot of disillusionment about Soviet-style communism. People accepted the ideology because they were afraid, but their fear didn't prevent them from seeing the wealth that was flaunted by the party elite. In the spirit of the times, many idealistic young people wanted to change the way their country was run, and this led to the emergence of a humanist faction within the party. This faction wanted to implement a progressive brand of socialism and, more important, sever the ties between the Czech and Russian governments. In 1968, much to its own amazement, the faction found itself controlling the majority of votes in the Czech parliament, and wasted no time in trying to dismantle the old Soviet infrastructure. Censorship laws were loosened, KGB agents were sent back to Moscow, and rich Communists from the Stalinist era suddenly found themselves on the receiving end of a progressive new movement that was called the Prague Spring.

The old guard's response was simple and treacherous. They accused the government of "counterrevolutionary activities" and sent a petition to the

Soviet Union, inviting the Red Army to invade Czechoslovakia. Happy to oblige, the Russians rolled into Prague on August 21, 1968. The old guard was reinstated, and people like my dad found themselves shoveling coal or mixing concrete. The most dispiriting thing about the 1968 invasion was the ease with which the Russians brought our country to heel. We capitulated without a fight. With only one exception, every single member of the Prague Spring cabinet signed a "normalization agreement" that authorized the Soviet Union to take control of our affairs, and our brief flirtation with idealism was over. For the next twenty years, a particularly cynical regime of socialism would prevail, in which favor-trading and petty scamming were the order of the day, and young doctors in need of driving lessons would cheerfully agree to sneak a dissident's wife into a Communist hospital.

ON THE MORNING OF MY BIRTH, the usual contradictions of the system were in place. Despite its exclusivity, the Podoli Hospital was over-crowded with patients, and the doctors and nurses were drinking on the job. It was a Friday, a day before the International Day of Women, and the hospital staff were celebrating in advance. While Czechoslovakia was nowhere near as poor as Russia, we had quickly embraced the Commu-nist calendar and work ethic, which consisted of many public holidays and lots of cheap booze. The International Day of Women was particu-larly notorious, as it provided men with an opportunity to get roaring drunk without the usual fear of reprisal from their wives, and my mother had spent the entire week before my birth trying to hurry her contrac-tions along. Having a daughter on the International Day of Women may have sounded like a romantic notion, but it was dangerous as well. By the mid-afternoon, the entire hospital would be operating in an alcoholic haze. It was therefore with great relief that on the morning of March 7, with Dr. Raclavska in attendance, she managed to push me out while the hospital staff was still relatively sober.

"Is it a girl?" my mother panted.

"It's a girl," Dr. Raclavska smiled. "You have a beautiful baby daughter."

My mother let out a huge sigh of relief.

At that precise moment, the sun broke through the clouds and flooded the maternity ward with light, and the door to the delivery room flew open and a crowd of doctors and nurses rushed in.

"Hezky Mezinarodni Den Zen!" they exclaimed, presenting Dr. Raclavska with a big bunch of flowers.

The nurses crowded around my mother and complimented her on such a healthy-looking child. Everyone was dressed in hospital white, and my mother says it was like we were surrounded by angels. Then the head nurse wrapped me up in a blanket, snapped an identification tag around my wrist, and whisked me away to the nursery before the party in the hospital became too wild. She placed me on a large communal trolley that was crowded with other loaf-sized bundles, and locked the door behind her.

My mother contacted my dad via the taxi dispatcher, and spent the rest of the morning waiting for him to arrive. Because she was an unofficial patient, Dr. Raclavska had not been able to secure her a bed. So while the young doctor had hurried off to see whether a bed was available in one of the other wards, my mother lay on a bench in the delivery room, listening to the clinking of glasses and popping of champagne corks in the distance.

Eventually, my father and sister appeared. They had been delayed at the front gate by a hospital guard who refused to let them in until they bribed him with a carton of cigarettes, and when they finally arrived at the maternity ward, no one knew anything about my mother or me. My dad had to search for Dr. Raclavska, who had become sidetracked in a distant wing of the hospital. But after he presented her with a bottle of cognac, she resumed her mission to find my mother a bed. While she did this, a nurse escorted my dad and sister to the maternity ward and wheeled me out into the lobby in an oversized pram. It was here that my father and sister saw me for the first time. My eyes were closed and I wriggled around in my blanket, clenching and unclenching my fists.

"Hello, Dominika," my sister cooed, trying out the unusual name she had talked my parents into giving me.

The doctors and nurses congratulated my father, prompting someone to open yet another case of champagne. Then Dr. Raclavska appeared with the news that she had found my mother a bed, and brought my dad and sister into the delivery room.

My mother smiled wearily at their arrival, and looked very pretty in spite of her ugly hospital nightgown. My dad knelt beside her and smothered her with kisses while Dr. Raclavska cracked the bottle of cognac and poured herself a celebratory drink. She had been lucky to find a bed. The maternity ward was overcrowded, because Prague was full of women like my mother who had decided that the best way of coping with the Socialist state was to try and find happiness through their families. It was a protest, but an acceptance as well. Unlike the West Germans, who rebuilt their country in the postwar years by investing and believing in the concept of the nation, we learned to abandon our nation and concentrate on ourselves. We followed the teachings of Marx and Lenin every day, but the biggest irony of communism was that it taught the working class to look out for Number One. In the "normalization era" of the seventies and eighties, Czech families did whatever it took to survive, and the more we pretended to go along with the system, the less frightening the system became. By the mid-eighties, communism was like an old dragon that would occasionally crawl out from its cave and eat someone for dinner. As long as it wasn't you the dragon was eating, you could live with the sound of screams in the distance. Which was precisely what we did until the Velvet Revolution.

THREE DAYS AFTER MY BIRTH, my father collected my mother and me from the Podoli Hospital and drove us home to our village on the outskirts of

Prague. We crossed the Vltava River and followed it southwest until the baroque skyline was replaced by smoking chimneys and Communist tower blocks. After a while, the Vltava turned into the smaller Berounka River, which snaked its way into a lush valley where the small township of Cernosice nestled into the hillside. This would be my home for the next eighteen years.

Our house was at the very top of the hill. It was a charming, Art Deco villa that had once belonged to my mother's grandparents but was now subdivided into collective housing so that three families could live there. My parents and sister occupied the first floor, and a friendly old bachelor lived in the basement, but the other family that shared the house was far from friendly. They were the Nedbals, and they were professional informers. Mr. Nedbal had been a policeman in the fifties, and, after his retirement, he and his wife secured themselves a very nice place to live by volunteering to keep my dad under surveillance. My father's previous quiet but important work in the Ministry of Foreign Affairs had been such that the old-guard Communists never forgot him, even after the revolution. It would be many years before I would learn why, but the first half of my life was spent watching invisible forces work actively against him. The old Communist dragon was forever sniffing around outside our front door, but it never ate us for dinner. What didn't kill us made us stronger, and I remember my childhood with a lot of fondness and joy.

One of my earliest memories is of the family sitting around the TV on the day before Christmas when I was three, watching our dog, Barry, star in a famous Czech film. Barry was an enormous Saint Bernard with a comically sad face. He had saved my parents in the hard years following the Prague Spring by being a natural in front of the camera. While my dad was struggling to find and keep a job, Barry appeared in five of the biggest films of the early seventies. He was a good-natured beast who towered above me as I took my first steps, and my father made a little sled for me to sit in so that Barry could pull me through the streets when they were covered with snow. We never failed to draw huge crowds, as Barry was without question the most popular dog in Czechoslovakia. He was even more popular than Laika, the dog the Soviet Union launched into space in the fifties. Whereas Laika was an alert, if somewhat panic-stricken animal, Barry was the perfect model of laziness. He was quite sneaky and would do anything to get out of work, and was the antithesis of all things the Soviet propaganda stood for.

In those early years, Barry was my favorite member of the family. From the moment I learned to walk and talk, I was forever running through the house in search of someone to play with. While my enthusiasm may have warmed my parents' hearts, it also created a lot of problems. My family knew that the Nedbals were listening through the walls, so they had developed a habit of talking at low volumes whenever they were inside the house. My sister, Klara, was particularly good at this, but I was the opposite. My voice was bright and strong, and I used it so much, my mother dubbed me her "little trumpet." Whenever she and my dad were trying to be discreet, I could be counted upon to repeat whatever they were saying at the top of my lungs, so every time my parents had something important to discuss, they would send me outside to play with the dog.

"Why don't you go outside and play, little one?" my mother suggested that December afternoon. "Put on your red jacket and take Barry with you. Klara and I have to get a few things ready for Christmas."

"Barry's a good boy!" I exclaimed. "Come outside, Barry!"

"I was thinking of taking Dominika with me when I picked up the carp," my father growled. "Would you like to come for a drive?" he asked me. "We'll only be a few minutes."

"Yes, please!" I said excitedly.

My father was a short but handsome man with prematurely gray hair and hazel eyes that sometimes turned yellow. With his gray hair and yellow eyes, he looked like a wolf. He had a strong voice, like me, except it was deep and raspy from smoking lots of cigarettes, and whenever he talked, it sounded like he was growling. From the moment he woke until the minute he went to bed, my dad was constantly in motion. He ate on his feet and worked very hard to keep the dragon from our door, and as the years passed and time finally caught up with him, he would lose his angular, wolflike physique and end up looking like a big gray bear. Only his deep, growling voice and big heart remained the same. Despite the constant disappointments and frustrations, he carried us through the hard times with an almost impossible sense of optimism, and was constantly dreaming up crazy schemes to keep us going until the Soviet regime was finally deposed.

"Where are we going, Dad? Are we going to the shops?"

"We're going to buy a fish," my father said. "You'll need your jacket and boots."

I followed him into the living room, which was where my sister and I slept, and he helped me put on my jacket, boots, and gloves. Then we walked upstairs to the garage. The hill we lived on was very steep, so our villa was on three levels. The garage was right at the top, and then you walked down a garden path to the main floor, where my family lived in two rooms next to a third room that was permanently locked. The Nedbals lived on the second floor, with the bathroom, and Mr. Kozel lived in the basement next door to the kitchen. As a toddler, I spent a lot of time running up and down the stairs, and quickly learned where the friendly parts of the house were. Going to the bathroom was never much fun, whereas the kitchen was a safe zone, the one place in the house where we could speak freely. Mr. Kozel was both slightly deaf and disinclined to gossip, so we spent most of our time in the kitchen, which was constantly filled with the most wonderful smells. My mother was an excellent cook, and the stove and boiler kept the room nice and warm in winter.

Up in the garage, my father opened the big wooden doors that led out onto the street, while I scrambled inside the car and wedged myself into the space behind the gearbox. The roads in our village were terrible, even though we lived in one of the nicer areas in Greater Prague, and my dad often complained that it would be easier to drive on the moon than across the potholed streets of Cernosice. But the bad roads made the trip down the hill very exciting. I would wrap my arms around the rubber gearbox mounting, while my father eased the car out of the garage, and then we would rumble down to the foot of the hill where there was a little row of shops and a beauty salon. Shopping with my dad was always an adventure. His pockets would be full of crumpled taxi-driving money, and he would often manage to talk the local shopkeepers into producing hidden goods from behind their counters. Unlike my mother, who was scrupulously honest and would turn a crown twice in her hand before spending it, my dad was more of a wheeler-dealer, and he would use me shamelessly to warm the hearts of the women who worked in the bakery.

On this occasion we parked in front of the grocery store and walked around the corner to the Hotel Slanka. In front of the pub, three men in plastic aprons stood behind two large tubs the size of miniature wading pools. Water sloshed from each tub, and behind the men stood a low bench that was covered with blood. My father picked me up and carried me over to the tubs.

"See the fish?"

Both tubs were full of big, gray carp. They swam slowly in circles, lazily opening and closing their mouths.

"Which one would you like?" my father asked me.

"The big one!"

"They're all big," my father said. "Which big one do you mean?"

"That one!" I cried, pointing to a silvery carp with long whiskers.

One of the men took a net and scooped the fish out onto a scale.

"Three kilos twenty," he said. "How do you want it?"

"We'll take it as it is," my father told him.

He put me on the ground and gave the man twenty crowns. Then he pulled a canvas bag out of his pocket and held it open while the man deposited the carp inside it. It was a huge fish with bulging eyes, and I liked it immediately.

We put it in the trunk and drove back up the hill.

"Hello, Mum!" I called out as we unlocked the front door. "Come quickly! We have a fish!"

My mother and sister came running, and we followed my dad upstairs to the bathroom. He filled the bath and dropped the gasping fish into the tub. The water quickly revived the carp and it started to swim around the bath like a torpedo, slapping the surface of the water with its tail.

"What's his name?" I asked.

"It doesn't have a name," my mother explained. "It's a special carp for Christmas."

I stood on the tips of my toes and peered over the rim of the bathtub.

"Hello, Mr. Carp!" I said, making my father and sister laugh. "Don't be afraid, we'll take good care of you!"

"Come on everyone, lunch is ready," my mother smiled.

She took me by the hand. "You can help me if you like," she said, running her fingers through my hair, and I followed her down three flights of stairs to the kitchen. I watched as she sliced some bread and put it in a basket, and then I carried the basket to the kitchen table, where we ate all our meals.

MY MOTHER WAS SLIM and pretty and mysterious, with the eyes (and smile) of the Mona Lisa. She had her dreams and premonitions but was also extremely well read. My father viewed life as a day-to-day struggle, but my mother saw things from a greater perspective. She was the granddaughter of a founding member of the prewar Communist Party, and after the Communists took control of the country, she had watched her parents misuse the power they inherited. My mother's parents were members of the Communist elite that had invited the Russians to invade Czechoslovakia. They were fabulously wealthy, but as a little girl my mother couldn't help noticing that the families of her friends were very frightened of her mother. At a time when women took great care to dress and act as plainly as possible, my grandmother was widely known as the "Red Countess." Back in the fifties and sixties, rich party members really did behave like the kings and queens of Prague. My mother, who had read all the Communist texts as a child, was appalled by the way her parents and their friends not only manipulated the system for their personal gain but also destroyed anyone who spoke up against them. In the end, she rebelled by marrying my father, a factory worker's son from the mining town of Ostrava. In one of those great ironies of life, my mother's parents, who had built their fortune in the name of the working class, hated my father on sight. The common man was great in theory, but under no circumstances was their daughter going to marry one, so, in 1968, my mother found herself on the opposite side of the political fence from her parents, and two years after the Russian invasion they officially disowned her. She and my dad were expelled from the party and ended up sharing a house with a family of informers.

While my father was outraged by the old guard's betrayal, my mother was heartbroken, having watched her parents evolve into the kind of people who would want to stop their country from becoming independent. My mother's parents had everything except moral integrity, and the more they profited under the Communist regime, the more cynical and bitter they became. As a result, my mother had resolved at an early age to try and be as morally upright as possible. It wasn't easy. Soviet-style communism demanded a lot of moral latitude, and my father was particularly good at finding loopholes in the system. If they hadn't married each other, it's possible that my dad might have succumbed to political temptation or my mother might have been crushed by the State. But together they had a rare combination: incorruptibility and a willingness to fight. My parents had many opportunities to sacrifice their ideals, but they never did. And while life may have been a lot harder than it needed to be, it was the life they had chosen, and they had few regrets.

WE HAD A LOVELY pre-Christmas lunch, and then my dad and Klara took Barry for a walk in the forest while my mother led me upstairs for my afternoon nap.

"But I'm not sleepy!" I protested as she tucked me up in bed.

"You're never sleepy," she smiled. "But if you close your eyes, I'll read you a story."

"A story! Will you read me *The Grandmother*?"

"Certainly," my mother agreed. "If you get it down from the shelf, I'll read you the first chapter."

The Grandmother was one of my favorite books. It was a memoir by a Czech writer called Bozena Nemcova, who had lived in the last century when our country was part of the Austrian empire. Ms. Nemcova's grandmother was a wise and loving woman, a constant source of inspiration to her family. She had a very simple outlook on life, which was that people should look after each other as much as possible, and whenever there was a problem, the grandmother always managed to solve it in a positive way.

I liked Ms. Nemcova's grandmother very much. I had never met my real grandparents, so I thought that the grandmother in the book was a magical character, like the Fairy Godmother from *Cinderella*. When my mother read, I would close my eyes and imagine that the grandmother was sitting next to my bed, smiling at me as I drifted off to sleep.

When I awoke from my nap, my mother and the grandmother were gone. The living room was dark, and the trees outside were whispering in the wind. I climbed down from my bed and tiptoed over to the door. I had recently discovered that if I stood on the very tips of my toes, I could reach the handle and open the door by myself. I was very proud. I didn't have to call my mother to let me out, and I could surprise her by appearing in the kitchen unexpectedly.

I pushed the door open and walked down the hall into the stairwell, where I could hear my mother and sister laughing. I decided that before I went down and joined them, I would go and say hello to Mr. Carp. I climbed to the second floor and tiptoed into the bathroom. The Nedbals' door was slightly ajar, but the house was quiet and I hoped they might be out. The Nedbals were very old and they smiled all the time, but I never had a good feeling when I saw them. They didn't seem like nice people, and Mrs. Nedbal smelled like old sheets.

There was a rusty metal bucket beneath the sink, and I pushed it over to the tub and climbed on top. The fish was floating motionlessly in the bath. His back was close to the surface of the water, and I reached down and gave him a pat.

"Hello, Mr. Carp," I said softly. "Are you asleep?"

He squirmed at my touch but eventually got used to my patting. I followed his long, slick body with my hand, stroking him from head to tail.

"You're a good boy," I told him.

There was a faint creaking behind me, and I turned to see Mrs. Nedbal in the doorway. She was a plump and wrinkled lady who always dressed in faded tracksuits and cardigans.

"Hello, Mrs. Nedbal!" I said. "Look! There's a fish in the bath!"

"So I see," Mrs. Nedbal said pleasantly. "This is a communal bathroom and there's a fish in the bath, and yet no one has bothered to ask me or my family if we wanted to use it."

She gave me a tight-lipped smile that sent a shiver down my spine.

"Do you want to take a bath?" I asked.

"Not at this moment, no," she replied. "But if I wanted to, I wouldn't be able to, would I?"

She took another step toward me and broadened her smile into a grimace. Her hair smelled like she hadn't washed it in months.

"And you're standing on my bucket." Mrs. Nedbal sighed. "It's my private property and you've taken it without asking. I do hope you haven't broken it."

I climbed off the bucket, and she made a show of checking its rusty bottom for damage.

"Dear, oh dear," she said tartly. "An apple never rolls far from the tree, does it? You start taking people's things without asking, the next thing you know, you'll be stealing the very beds they sleep on. It's no wonder your grandmother keeps her room locked downstairs."

I looked up at Mrs. Nedbal in surprise. "My grandmother?" I exclaimed. "Do you know her?"

"Oh, yes," Mrs. Nedbal smiled. "This is your grandmother's house. She used to live here before your father drove her out."

"She did?"

"Yes. This whole house was hers. Now all she has is that one room downstairs, which she keeps locked because your parents were very cruel to her. Such a terrible shame."

I thought about the locked door opposite my parents' bedroom.

"Is she still there?" I asked.

"Your father drove her out before you were born. Imagine! His own mother-in-law!" She leaned down and lowered her voice confidentially. "It's all in the courts, you know. I wouldn't be surprised if you found yourselves looking for a new house next year."

"But I don't want a new house!" I cried. "I like this one!"

"So did your grandmother," Mrs. Nedbal said quietly.

She put the bucket back under the sink, shaking her head and smiling bitterly as I fled. I ran for the safety of my parents' bedroom, but stopped in front of the locked door on the opposite side of the hallway. In the whole time I had lived in the house, my grandmother's door had never been opened. It was a high, white door with a shiny brass handle and a large keyhole that I was too small to look through. I pressed my ear to the door and wondered whether my grandmother was still inside. The room was very quiet, so I lay on the floor and peeked under. I was able to make out the legs of what looked like a bed, but I couldn't see any sign of my grandmother. Maybe she was asleep. I didn't want to wake her, so I got back up and ran down to the kitchen where my mother and sister were baking Christmas biscuits.

"Hello!" I called out. "I'm awake!"

"Yes you are," my mother laughed.

"I went and said hello to the fish!" I told her. "And then Mrs. Nedbal came and took the bucket and told me that we might have to find a new house!"

"Really?" My mother stopped laughing.

"Yes! And she said that the grandmother lives in the room next to yours, and this is really her house. We don't have to leave here do we, Mum?"

A look of sadness passed across my mother's face.

"Come here," she said.

She picked me up and hugged me tightly to her chest.

"We're not going anywhere," she said. "We're going to stay here and have a lovely Christmas. Don't worry about the house, and don't you listen to the Nedbals. If anyone is going to find themselves looking for a new house next year, it will be them."

She sat me down on my special place at the counter. There was sugar and cocoa and flour everywhere. Several trays of biscuits sat cooling on the floor and the smell of vanilla wafted sweetly from the oven.

"We're making strudel. Would you like to help?" my mother asked.

"Yes!" I said. "Can I have a biscuit?"

"Of course you can," my mother smiled.

She rolled a sheet of dough while my sister peeled and chopped some apples, and I crushed cinnamon and cloves with a mortar and pestle. Outside, snowflakes fell from the sky like feathers. By the time the sun had set, the garden was covered in white. My dad came in with a box of wood for the stove, and we huddled in the kitchen, talking and laughing as we baked the strudel and spread jam on the biscuits. I could hear Mr. Kozel's radio playing Christmas carols in the next room, and an owl began to hoot in the forest. The forest was full of owls and badgers and pine martens, and the nights were very noisy with the sound of them hunting. As part of the old winter-solstice tradition, my mother filled a large wooden bowl with water and put it on the table. She put four little candles inside four walnut shells, lit them, and floated them together in the middle of the bowl.

"One candle for each of us," she said.

We switched off the lights and watched the candles as they slowly drifted apart and burned out, which is the way it goes in life. On this night, they seemed to stay together much longer than usual, and I went to sleep feeling happy and safe.

The following morning, I leaped out of bed and raced into my parents' room. I dove beneath their blanket and snuggled up between them.

"Hello, Dad," I whispered in my father's ear. "Wake up! It's Christmas!"

"*Ježis Marja!*" my father growled. "What time is it?"

"Shhh, little one," my mother said softly. "Pretend that you're a biscuit in an oven and you have to bake for another fifteen minutes before you're ready to be eaten."

I loved this game. My parents threw their arms around me and I squirmed happily between them, imagining myself turning brown and crispy in a big warm oven. They would try to keep me in the oven for as long as possible and would sometimes overbake me by accident. My dad loved to pretend he was asleep. He would snore theatrically and make his arms very heavy, and I would have to yell and wriggle like a fish before he would wake up and let me out of the oven.

"Is the Baby Jesus coming?" I asked excitedly.

"Of course he is," my mother replied. "He'll be here this afternoon and he'll bring the Christmas tree with him."

"Will we see him?"

"We'll try," my mother smiled. "He's very shy, you know. But we'll definitely hear him. He always rings a bell when he comes to visit."

In Czechoslovakia, Christmas is celebrated on December 24, which is when families eat a big dinner and open their presents in front of the tree. When I was growing up, the Christmas season began with the arrival of Saint Mikulas on the "Angels and Devils Night" of December 5, and would climax with the Baby Jesus visiting each house on December 24, bringing not only presents but the Christmas tree as well. During the day, children watched fairy tales on TV (fairy tales were the mainstay of the Czech film industry during communism, as they were politically harmless and a lot of fun to make), and then the family spent the late afternoon waiting for the Baby Jesus to arrive.

The magical appearance of the Christmas tree was one of the things I loved most. My parents would get my sister to take me for a walk, and as we made our way around the village, I would see Christmas trees in all of the neighbors' windows. The Baby Jesus was obviously in the area, so I would beg Klara to take me home in time to see him, but she would always be too slow and we would arrive at the house at the exact moment that he was ringing his bell to signal his departure. I would race through the house trying to find him, but of course he would be gone, and then I would see the tree for the first time: all decorated and surrounded by presents. Each year, the tree would turn up in a different place in the house, so a big part of the fun was checking each room to see if it was there.

Waiting for the Baby Jesus was so exciting, it was hard to sit still for the fairy tales. I loved all the Czech fairy tales, especially *The Terribly Sad Princess, Cinderella,* and even the Russian classic, *Grandfather Frost,* but it was difficult to concentrate when every sound in the house made me think that the Baby Jesus might be sneaking in upstairs. My parents were in the kitchen and my sister was reading a book in the living room, and I was afraid that we might not hear the bell and he would come and go without us seeing him. Every time I heard a noise, I would run to the front door. After I had done this a few times, I decided to go up to the bathroom and say hello to Mr. Carp.

I trotted up to the second floor and snuck into the bathroom, this time closing the door behind me. I walked over to the bath and stood up on my tiptoes.

"Hello, Mr. Carp!" I said.

I peeked over the rim of the tub and discovered that the bath was empty. The water had been drained and I could hear the Nedbals laughing in the room next door. My eyes welled with tears and I ran downstairs to tell my parents.

My mum and dad were standing in front of the kitchen counter, and I dashed into the room and stopped dead in my tracks. My father's sleeves were rolled up and his hands were covered in blood, and the carp was lying on a sheet of newspaper with its head cut off and its belly slit open. Its bulging eyes stared blankly at the ceiling as my dad took a knife and started to scale its headless body. I thought that the Nedbals had stolen the fish, but I couldn't imagine that my parents had killed it. I turned around and ran back upstairs, finding myself in front of my grandmother's door. I pressed my cheek against it and started to cry.

"Granny, are you there?" I sobbed.

I knocked but nobody answered, so I tried to talk through the keyhole.

"Please, come out," I said. "Please?"

I imagined that Grandmother was standing on the other side of the door, and I closed my eyes and pictured her kindly face and happy smile. I talked through the keyhole for a long time, then sank to my knees and curled up on the floor. After a while, my mother came up to find me.

"What are you doing?" she asked.

"I'm talking to Grandmother." I sobbed. "I want her to come out."

"You want her to come out of this room here?" my mother asked. "She's not here, little one. She lives in Prague. Did Mrs. Nedbal tell you that she lives in this room?"

"I think so," I sniffed.

"Oh, Trumpet," my mother sighed. "This is your grandmother's room, but she doesn't live here. She just keeps her furniture in it. My parents live in a big apartment in Prague. This used to be their summer house until they were forced to give it up."

"Did Daddy make her go away?"

"No. My parents owned too many houses and the housing committee made them give some of them up. They gave this one to me so that we could keep it in the family, and then we had an argument. My mother and my sister are trying to get it back."

"Can't they just come and live here?" I asked.

"I don't think they want to," my mother said sadly. "It's very hard to explain, but your father and I aren't friends with my parents anymore. We think they did a bad thing, and they don't like us because we tried to stop them."

"You killed Mr. Carp!" I said accusingly.

"Ah, so that's why you're crying," she smiled. "We killed him so that we could have a traditional Christmas. If you kill a carp and dry some of his scales and put them in your purse, it means you'll have lots of money next year. Besides, if we didn't kill him, he would have died anyway. Once you take a fish out of its pond, it doesn't last very long."

"But I liked him."

"Well, we'll be having him for dinner," my mother explained. "And he'll taste very nice, because he was fresh. Fresh fish always tastes better than the fish you can buy at the market." (The only fish you could buy at the market was the kind that came in cans.)

My mother pulled a handkerchief out of her pocket and made me blow my nose. She ruffled my hair and talked to me until I cheered up, and then she took me into the living room where my sister was sitting with her book.

"Why don't you take Dominika for a walk?" my mother asked her. "You could go to the river and feed the swans."

"Now?" my sister frowned. "Isn't it early? What time is the Baby Jesus supposed to come?"

"I think he might be a little early this year," my mother said. "Dominika's a bit restless and a walk might do her good."

"Can we take Barry?" I asked.

"Yes, take Barry with you," my mother agreed. "He's alone in the garden, looking miserable."

I glanced out of the living-room window and saw Barry's huge head sticking out of his kennel. His face was sad and the bags around his eyes seemed even bigger than usual.

"*Ahoj*, Barry!" I called out.

Barry immediately cheered up. He emerged from his kennel, wagging his tail.

"We're going to feed the swans!" I told him.

Klara let out a deep sigh and went to put on her jacket and a scarf. She was thirteen now, and the novelty of having a little sister had worn off. She had become quiet, because I did enough talking for both of us and the older I got the harder it was for her to get a word in edgewise.

"What time do you want us to come back?" she asked.

"Let's see." My mother checked her watch. "It's two-thirty now, so keep her out until five."

"Five?" My sister sighed. "Okay. Can you give me some money to buy bread for the swans?"

"We won't miss the Baby Jesus, will we? He won't come while we're away?"

"No." My mother opened her handbag. "He never comes before six, and he has to visit all the other houses in the street first."

"Do you promise?" I asked.

"I promise." She patted me on my head.

She zipped me into my red skiing outfit and helped me into my boots. Then she sent me outside, where Klara was struggling to get Barry on a leash. Barry never listened to Klara. My sister wasn't very good with dogs, but I could get Barry to do anything. He never failed to come when I called, and I could even make him sit and shake hands.

"Come on, Barry!" I cried as we waded through the snow. There was at least a foot of snow at the top of our garden, and I had to lift my legs very high to step through it. My skiing outfit had a pointy hood that was lined with lamb's fur, but my cheeks stung in the cold. It was one of those bright, freezing days where the sky was blue and clear, and the neighbors were outside their front gates, shoveling the snow off their driveways.

"Hello!" I called out. "We're off to feed the swans!"

"*Ahoj*, Dominika and Klara!" they chorused. "And here comes Bohousek, looking fatter than usual."

"His name is Barry!" I said proudly. "He was on television!"

"We know. We've seen him," the neighbors smiled.

"Doesn't she look like a little garden gnome?" Mrs. Simkova from across the road chuckled. "Maybe we could plant her at the foot of our garden."

"No!" I told her. "I have to be home in time to see the Baby Jesus!"

The neighbors laughed and I followed Barry and my sister to the end of the street. Just before the bend, we turned into the little pedestrian laneway that zigzagged down the hill. From here we could see the entire Cernosice valley. The windows of the houses were dusted with frost, and icicles hung from every gutter. We walked all the way down to the little row of shops, which were still open, as December 24 wasn't a public holiday. We went to the grocery store and tied Barry to the bicycle racks outside the front door. The windows were decorated with flickering Christmas lights and tinsel, and there was a long line of people waiting to get in.

"They've probably sold all the rolls by now," my sister muttered.

"Sit, Barry! *Sedni!*" I said as we joined the line.

We always stood in line when we went to the shops, but it wasn't because there was a shortage of food. There was plenty of food in Czechoslovakia; what we didn't have was variety. The shelves were full of packages of rice and flour and butter and sugar, but they were plain-wrapped and there was only one brand. The practice of arriving early and standing in line was caused by the slowness of the shopkeepers, who made a point of talking to everyone. Favored customers would be told what kind of under-the-counter goods were available and when they were expected to arrive, and shopping could be infuriatingly social. Maintaining a good relationship with the local shopkeepers was very important, so no one complained. But it was very frustrating. Bread and milk sold out quickly, and we often waited in line for half an hour, only to find crumbs in the bread box and sour puddles where the bags of milk had once been. Still, I loved going to the shops, because there were lots of little cakes in the bakery, and many different kinds of sausages in the delicatessen. If there were three things every shop in our country could be counted upon to have in abundance, they were beer, sausages, and little cakes.

Czech beer is world-famous, of course, but we also have a big pastry-and-sausage tradition. When I think of my childhood, I think of little cakes and sausages, because they were symbolic of the way we lived under communism. Before the Second World War, we were similar to the Germans and Austrians in that we had a town mentality. Local businesses survived because of neighborhood goodwill, and communities were tight-knit and civic-minded. When the Communists took over, they destroyed our town mentality by coercing neighbors, friends, and even families into denouncing each other for anti-Communist activities. In the early years, the punishments handed out were sufficiently harsh to destroy any kind of trust between neighbors, forcing communities to live in a constant state of fear. After a while, this fear was replaced by a numb compliance in which neighbors would greet each other as "comrade" and profess great admiration for the Socialist state. For forty years we did this, watching with weary resignation as our buildings fell to pieces and our roads went unrepaired. We talked the nonsense of the system, and the system rewarded us with cheap booze, public holidays, and little sausages and cakes. No afternoon tea at the local Politburo was complete without an array of little cakes wrapped in pastry-shop paper; no cigarette break at the local pub was truly satisfying unless there was a fat sausage in mustard to accompany the several pints of beer one knocked back in quick succession. For the majority of the Czech working class, a boring but easy state job and a barbecue every weekend was enough to keep them going through the hard times of communism. Which was something the people in power were counting on.

Standing in front of the pastry counter, I could see over twenty different kinds of little cakes. My favorites were the marzipan fruit, the swan, and the little indian. All the cakes were homemade and they were very cheap. My mother had given Klara ten crowns to buy some bread rolls for the swans, but there was no question that she would buy us some little cakes as well.

"Which one would you like?" she asked me.

"A marzipan apple and a swan?" I said hopefully.

My sister nodded at the pastry-shop lady, who used a long spatula to scoop the cakes out of the display case.

"Anything else?" the lady asked.

"And a Little Indian! Because it's Christmas! Please?"

"Okay. Just this once," my sister sighed.

We bought our bag of bread for the swans, and then walked outside to find Barry surrounded by his usual crowd of admirers feeding him their Christmas groceries. He ate everything they gave him, without even bothering to look and see what it was. He just opened his mouth and rolled his eyes like he did in the movies, making everyone roar with laughter.

"Let's go, Barry!" I grabbed his collar to let everyone know that I was his friend. The crowd was very impressed. We untied Barry and led him down the street, past the Hotel Slanka and across the railway tracks to the Berounka River. There was a weir and a mill directly opposite the station, and a pedestrian bridge between the weeping willow trees. We crossed the bridge to the middle of the river, and Klara lifted me up onto the railing so that I could see the swans beneath us.

"Hello, swans!" I cried. "We've brought you some bread."

In the old days, the Berounka River was very clean and full of beavers. Now the beavers were gone and the water was brown, but it was still very picturesque. The water was frozen solid on the far side of the bridge, but the fifty-meter stretch between the bridge and the weir remained unfrozen and was a favorite nesting place for ducks and swans. There were at least a dozen swans and they were very elegant, vaulting their necks gracefully to catch each piece of bread we threw. The ducks were quick and rude and tried to steal the bread from the beaks of the swans. They beat their wings and ran on the water, while the swans clacked their beaks in anger. The commotion grew so loud that Barry decided to get in on the act. He was a good-natured dog, but he also knew how big and powerful he was, and when he decided to bark, it could be quite frightening. He towered above my sister and me as he stood on his hind legs and barked at the ducks.

"Sit, Barry!" I said. "*Sedni! Sedni,* Barry! Shhh!"

Barry looked down at me and began to lick my face. He stopped barking, but continued to lean on the railing and look out across the river as though he was contemplating the mysteries of life.

When we had finished throwing bread to the swans, Klara looked at her watch and announced that it was time to go home. The sky had turned dark as we walked back through the town, and the street lamps snapped on with a buzzing sound. We zigzagged up the hill, exhaling clouds of steam and stamping our boots to keep our toes warm.

There was a Christmas tree in a window overlooking the path, lit up and glowing through the frost-encrusted glass.

"Oh, no!" I cried. "The Baby Jesus is here already!"

I grabbed Barry's leash and tried to make him run through the snow, but he wasn't very interested in running. Neither was my sister. They both continued to plod up the hill, and I was very upset by the time we got home. I was sure that we had missed the Baby Jesus. I dashed inside the front door and kicked off my boots, and then my heart began to pound with excitement as I heard the sound of a bell ringing downstairs. I raced down to the kitchen, then back up to the living room and into my parents' bedroom, where I found myself standing in front of the most wonderful tree. The room smelled of pine needles and potpourri, and it was dark except for the Christmas lights and candles. "Silent Night" crackled softly from the radio, and I was so overwhelmed I almost burst into tears. Then my parents switched on the lights. *"Vesele Vanoce!"*

"Merry Christmas!" I ran to the window. "Thank you, Baby Jesus! Thank you for such a lovely tree!"

The sky outside the window had just turned black, and I waved at the stars and vowed that I would thank the Baby Jesus properly next year. My mother cleared a space in front of the tree and we all sat down to open our presents. Each package was wrapped in colorful paper and was tied with a ribbon with a little name tag attached. I knelt in front of the gingerbread "Bethlehem" my mother made every year, and wondered what the Baby

Jesus had brought me. I couldn't read yet, so I handed all the interesting-looking packages to my sister and asked if they were mine.

"This one! What does this one say?" I demanded, pointing to the biggest box in the pile.

"It says . . . Dominika!" Klara smiled.

She placed the big present in front of me, and I untied the ribbon and tore the box open.

"It's a pair of skis!" I squealed. "The Baby Jesus has brought me my very own pair of skis!"

The short yellow skis were unbelievably nice. They were decorated with two little rows of cartoon ducks, and even came with a pair of matching ski poles. I ran and put on my shoes, and then strapped myself into the skis and spent the rest of the evening walking around the house in them.

"I can ski!" I called out. "Look! I'm good at it already!"

I tried to steer myself with the poles, but it wasn't very easy. The skis kept getting tangled up and I kept falling on my bum until my mum and dad took me by the hands and swung me off the ground. They carried me between them and I skied through the air into the living room, where the table was set with our best plates and glasses.

"Here's the Christmas carp," my mother said, uncovering a tray she had brought from the kitchen. "It's very tasty, but be careful, it's full of bones."

She put a piece of fried carp on my plate, along with a scoop of potato salad. Savory ham rolls and soup with liver dumplings were the traditional Christmas appetizers, and after that we would devour the fried carp. My mother's Christmas dinners were always delicious, but my favorite part was dessert, when we ate the biscuits we had baked. We had made enough biscuits to keep us going through the New Year, and I sat in front of the tree with a little basket of biscuits and felt very happy in my little yellow skis. After that, my mother played Christmas carols on the piano and we all sang.

"Hurry up to Bethlehem, doodleai, doodleai, doodleai day," my father growled in his deep voice, while my sister and I tried to harmonize above him. Klara had a good ear for melody, but she always sang quietly, whereas I always sang as loudly as possible, making the words and melody up as I went along. My mother didn't sing at all, because she wasn't very good at it, but she was an excellent pianist and could sight-read all the carols in the book. I took off my skis and stood on the piano stool and turned the pages for her. She smiled at me to let me know when she was ready. We sang with gusto, ignoring the Nedbals as they banged on the ceiling with a broom.

"Shut up!" they yelled. "We can't hear the television!"

My father smiled like a wolf and began to sing even louder, and soon I was singing at the top of my lungs. My mother signaled me to turn another page, and then she looked at me with tears in her eyes. The little girl who had demanded to be born. I stood on the stool and sang along with my family, unaware of how much hope I had brought into their lives.

THE ROOF

 MRS. NEDBAL'S SLY REMARKS in the bathroom were more serious than I ever could have known. The following April, my parents went to the Supreme Court to try to stop the Red Countess from throwing us out. Even though one-third of the house legally belonged to my mother, the Red Countess had used her political connections to scare a number of judges into ruling in her favor.

She hired two expensive attorneys to build a case against my parents, and employed the Nedbals to eavesdrop on their conversations, both on the phone and through the walls.

The Red Countess maintained that my parents were conspiring against the Socialist state, and wanted to disinherit my mother from the property her Communist grandfather had left her. It was a long and ugly battle. My parents had already lost in the district, regional, and city courts of Prague, and knew that if their appeal to the Supreme Court was unsuccessful, not only would they be evicted but they would also be ruined by their obligation to pay my grandmother's legal expenses. Realistically, my parents had no chance, and everyone knew it. Mrs. Nedbal's smile was even sharper than usual, and my parents took to whispering in the house and sending me outside to practice my skiing. I became very good on my little yellow skis, but my parents were too distracted to watch me.

We needed a miracle, and a miracle appeared out of the blue one evening as my father was driving his regular taxi route through Prague. He was hailed by an old man outside Charles University. The man turned out to be the legendary attorney Dr. Safranek, who was known as the "White Fox" in legal circles, due to the fact that he hardly ever lost a case. He was very old and didn't accept clients anymore, but he listened to my dad's story and gave my father his card. The following day, my parents went to his office in a desperate attempt to persuade him to represent them. After their last appeal, their lawyers had resigned and told them that their attempt to keep the house was hopeless. Dr. Safranek knew exactly who the Red Countess was, and he wasn't very optimistic. But he took another look at my mother and saw her lovely Mona Lisa smile and, against his better judgment, he decided to defend her.

"Come back in a week. I'll sniff around and see what I can come up with," he told my parents.

Dr. Safranek had no illusions about Communist justice. He knew that the only way to win the case would be to play the same kind of game my grandmother was playing. The Red Countess was a big fish, and the best way to get rid of a big fish was to find an even bigger fish to eat her. Through his private information network, he discovered that Comrade Pastorek, the judge who had thrown my parents' appeal out of the city court, was a man with a lot of powerful enemies, and he came up with a cunning strategy that had nothing to do with the legal merits of the case.

Comrade Pastorek had been a judge in the time of Stalin, and had sent thousands of people to Communist "reeducation" camps in the late forties and fifties. Back in those days, it was not only dissidents and intellectuals who were sent to these camps, but also important Communist officials who were routinely purged to destabilize their power. Many of these officials were rehabilitated after Stalin's death, and a few of them even regained their political status. The most famous rehabilitated politician at the time (and who happened to have been sent to prison by Comrade Pastorek) was none other than Comrade Gustav Husak, the president of Czechoslovakia.

When my mother returned to Dr. Safranek's office the following week, the White Fox suggested that she write a letter to the president explaining the situation and pointing out that the judge who had ruled in the Red Countess's favor was the same judge who had sent him to prison twenty years earlier.

"But will the president read my letter?" my mother asked doubtfully.

"Oh, yes. I think so." The White Fox smiled.

As well as being a successful litigator, Dr. Safranek had also been a successful ladies' man. He had maintained good relationships with his ex-lovers, and the information network he built up over the years was largely made up of the women he had slept with. It was no coincidence then that one of his old lovers now worked as the president's personal secretary. Dr. Safranek had already contacted this woman and told her to look out for my mother's letter. The plan was for the secretary to give the letter to the president when he was in a particularly bad mood.

My mother wrote the letter and delivered it personally to the secretary, and, as Dr. Safranek hoped, Comrade Husak was enraged. He ordered the general prosecutor to investigate the case, and then forwarded it to the Supreme Court, where it was discovered that Comrade Pastorek had overlooked eight paragraphs of Socialist law when he overturned my parents' appeal. His judgment was not only overruled by the Supreme Court, but Comrade Husak made sure that he was forced to retire in disgrace. The case was then returned to the district court, which cheerfully authorized my parents to buy out the remaining two thirds of the house and saddled my grandmother with a massive legal bill.

The Red Countess was shocked and furious, but she was also very frightened. She had always been afraid of my father, and the fact that he had been able to get the president to intercede on his behalf made her suspect that he still had powerful friends from the old days. She knew nothing about the White Fox or his ex-lover, but she was sufficiently intimidated by the outcome of the case to never bother my parents again.

We had won, but the victory broke my mother's heart. Deep down, she had always hoped to reconcile with her parents, but the court case was too big and too public, and the humiliation the Red Countess suffered was too great. It was almost ten years since the Soviet invasion, and Comrade Pastorek's dismissal was seen as a major crack in the old guard's armor. Many important party members were angry at my grandmother for allowing a private dispute to resolve itself so badly, and her untouchable status in Prague high society was revoked. Dinner invitations were refused, theater tickets stopped coming, and the Red Countess never forgave my mother for this. All contact was severed, and she and my grandfather whiled away their remaining years in their luxurious apartment in Old Town Prague. All the letters my mother wrote were returned unopened, and on the rare occasions when they would meet in town, my grandparents would walk away in silence.

A few weeks after we had won the case, I was playing with Barry in the garden when I heard the sound of a truck in our street. Our street was very narrow, so the truck had been forced to turn around at the bottom of the hill and reverse all the way up the street to our house. Barry and I ran to the front gate and watched as two men in overalls jumped out of the cab and unlatched the flatbed door. One of them tooted the horn while the other lit a cigarette, and after a while Mr. and Mrs. Nedbal came outside. They were carrying big canvas bags filled with clothing, which they hauled over to the truck while the two men in overalls stood around and watched.

"Hello, Mr. Nedbal. Hello, Mrs. Nedbal," I said. "What are you doing?"

The Nedbals didn't smile. They didn't say anything. They threw their bags into the back of the truck and glared at me as they returned to the house. I cautiously followed them in. I could hear my mother in the kitchen, but I went upstairs and pretended to go to the bathroom to see what the Nedbals were doing. Both of their doors were open and I could see inside their apartment for the very first time. Their living room was very messy, and I was startled by Otik, the Nedbals' son, who was helping them move out. I was very frightened of Otik. He was in his mid-twenties and had a glass eye that always seemed to glare at me, no matter where I stood. He picked up a chair and headed toward me, so I dashed into the bathroom and waited for him to go away.

"Are you really leaving?" I asked Mrs. Nedbal, once Otik had disappeared downstairs.

"That's right," she replied bitterly. "We're out on the street. Who knows or cares what will happen to us? Certainly not your father. He won his case. That's all that matters to him."

She picked up a cardboard box and carried it briskly from the room.

I hovered around the bathroom and watched until Otik eventually announced that they were ready to leave, and when I poked my head around the bathroom door, the apartment was empty. I slipped into the Nedbals' bedroom and stood on my toes to look out of their window. They had a much better view of the valley than we did. Their two rooms were slightly smaller than ours, but I thought they were actually much nicer, even though they were very dirty. There were cockroaches in the kitchen cupboards, and the walls were brown with grease. I picked my way through the trash on the floor and found a brand-new oven mitt in the corner of the kitchen. I examined the mitt and slipped it on my arm. It was bright green and came all the way up to my elbow. Suddenly, I heard the sound of the truck again in the street, and I ran to the window and watched the Nedbals drive away. They were sitting on their couch in the back of the flatbed and they didn't look very happy. I waved good-bye with the mitt, but they didn't wave back.

I decided to take the mitt downstairs and ask my mother if I could keep it. It was like a big green puppet, and if I moved my thumb and fingers, I could make the mitt talk.

"Hello!" I said to the mitt.

"Ahoj!" the mitt said in a funny, high-pitched voice.

I ran out of the Nedbals' apartment and was trotting down the stairs, when I stopped in amazement on the first floor. The big door opposite my parents' bedroom was open, and I could hear the sound of someone moving around inside. It was as though our house was slowly coming to life. I tiptoed nearer and listened. The heavy shuffling definitely didn't belong to any members of my family, and my heart leaped to my throat as I realized that my grandmother must have come back for her furniture. I summoned up all my courage and peeked around the door.

My grandmother's room was lavishly furnished. There were three large, elaborately framed paintings on the walls and plush red carpet on the floor. Most of the furniture had been covered with sheets, but I could tell that everything was expensive and nice. It was as though I had discovered a secret room in a castle.

At the far end of the room, an old, plump woman was removing some dusty books from an even dustier bookcase and packing them into a cardboard box. Her gray hair was rolled up in a bun, and she was humming quietly as she worked. She was the spitting image of the grandmother from Ms. Nemcova's book. After a while, she turned and saw me in the doorway.

"You must be Dominika," she said gently.

The old woman had blue eyes and a melodic voice, and I ran into the room and threw my arms around her knees.

"Are you my grandmother?" I asked her.

The old woman looked down at me with astonishment.

"No," she said. "I'm your Auntie Mary. But I know your grandmother very well."

"Do you?" I asked. "What is she like? Is she nice?"

"Of course she's nice," the old lady smiled. She bent down to rummage in one of the boxes, and pulled out a leather-bound album.

"Here," she said. "This is your grandmother Kveta in front of the National Museum."

The photograph was a black-and-white image of a lady wearing a fur coat and a hat. She looked very dignified and important, but her face was quite fat and she had a double chin. Her mouth was set in an imperious smile, but she didn't look very happy, even though she was well-dressed and standing on the steps of a beautiful building.

"That's my grandmother?" I said incredulously.

Auntie Mary must have heard the disappointment in my voice, because she closed the photo album and put it back in the box. There was a little antique table next to the bookcase, and on top of the table was a pink Duralex glass. Auntie Mary picked up the glass and showed it to me.

"This is a very special glass," she said. "It will never break, even if you drop it on the floor. Would you like to have it?"

"Yes, please," I nodded enthusiastically.

She gave me the glass, then she took my hand and led me downstairs. She knocked on the kitchen door and my mother opened it. There was a long, embarrassed pause.

"Good afternoon, Auntie," my mother said. "Would you like a cup of tea?"

"No, no," the old woman replied, and I noticed that her voice was trembling. "I just came down to tell you that it would be better if you could keep your little girl out of our room until I finish packing. I have a lot of work to do, and I'd really like to finish before it gets dark."

"Of course," my mother said.

Auntie Mary nodded, and went back upstairs to my grandmother's room. My mother watched her leave, and a look of longing appeared on her face.

"Look what I've got!" I tried to cheer her up. "I have a big green glove and a special glass that will never break!"

"Where did you get the glass?" my mother asked.

"Auntie Mary gave it to me!" I said. "Is she really my auntie?"

My mother sighed heavily. She sat down on a chair and pulled me into her lap.

"No, she's not your real aunt," she told me. "Auntie Mary isn't anyone's aunt. She's my mother's servant. She spent her whole life working for my parents, but because people aren't supposed to have servants in communism, we had to call her Auntie Mary in public."

"She's nice," I said. "She's just like The Grandmother!"

"Yes, she is." My mother's eyes welled with tears. "Auntie Mary took care of us when we were little and looked after us when we were sick. She was more of a mother than my mother ever was, and I really loved her—" she choked back a sob and her chin began to tremble.

It was terrible to see my mother cry. I threw my arms around her neck and patted her hair with Mrs. Nedbal's mitt.

"Don't cry, Mummy!" I pleaded.

"I'm all right, little one." My mother wiped her eyes and smiled weakly. "Don't worry."

She took the mitt and inspected it. "Did Auntie Mary give you this as well?" she asked.

"No, I found it in the Nedbals' kitchen," I said. "It was lying on the floor but it's very clean and green! Mrs. Nedbal says that they have to go and live in the street because nobody cares for them. Do they really have to live in the street?"

My mother laughed and shook her head.

"Of course not," she said. "We gave them and Mr. Kozel some money and helped them find a new apartment. Don't you worry about Mrs. Nedbal. She likes to try to make people feel sorry for her, but when other people are having a hard time, she always seems rather happy."

"Is that why she smiles all the time?" I asked.

"Maybe it is," my mother said wistfully.

"What are you doing?" I asked, looking around the kitchen. "Are you cooking something?"

"Yes, I am," my mother smiled. "We're having some people over to help us celebrate getting the house back, so I'm baking a cake and making some strudel. Would you like to help?"

"Okay!" I said. "Can I sit up on the bench?"

My parents threw a party to celebrate their victory, and the house filled with people laughing and talking at normal volume. My mother was dressed in a fashionable outfit my dad had bought her as a present, and she looked very pretty. My father was in high spirits, and I could hear his booming laugh. There were at least ten people in the living room, but the only person I really knew was Tomas Glatz, my father's best friend. Mr. Glatz was a Jewish intellectual who came from Slovakia and spoke many languages. He and my father had met when my dad was working for the government and, after the Soviet invasion, he and his wife, Helena, had stayed friends with my parents in spite of their expulsion from the party. Whenever my father needed to make a phone call without the Nedbals listening on the other line, he would drive to Prague and visit the Glatzes. They were a lovely couple and I liked them very much. According to my mother, they had been inspired by her decision to have me, and Helena had recently given birth to their own baby daughter, Monika.

My dad was a good host and made sure that everyone was enjoying themselves, but the real star of the party was the glamorous Mr. Poloraich, an elegant man who had once been a famous spy in America. Mr. Poloraich had striking features and tufts of hair sticking out of his ears and nose, which gave him the look of a puppet stuffed with straw. He had also known my father in the old days and, after the invasion, he would often turn up with a bottle of scotch and spend the evening in the kitchen talking politics with my dad. He was a very good storyteller, and I couldn't help noticing that in spite of his hairy nose and ears, a lot of ladies seemed to congregate around him. He stood in the middle of the room with a cigar in one hand and a glass of scotch in the other, and regaled the crowd with amusing stories from the West. Midway through one of them, he was interrupted by a series of loud exclamations in the hallway, and we turned to see a well-dressed lady rushing into the room.

The lady must have been in her sixties, but she wore a tight-fitting purple suit with a plunging neckline that accentuated her enormous cleavage. She was short and energetic, and the first thing I noticed was the bright orange lipstick she was wearing. She also wore a thick bracelet with lots of clanking charms, and I watched with fascination as she rattled across the room and threw her arms around my dad, stamping his face with her orange lips.

"Jarda! My boy!" she exclaimed, in what I would later learn was a North Moravian "short beak" accent. "I am so very please for you! You have win this most difficult court case and now the house has been return to your family!"

She stepped to the side and smiled radiantly.

"And I don't believe you have meet my fiancé, Mr. Doskar?"

A balding man with a deeply wrinkled face appeared behind her and blushed as he shook my father's hand. "How do you do?" he nodded bashfully, and I noticed that his teeth were yellow and brown.

"Klara! Come here my darling!" the woman shrieked, abandoning the men and rushing over to my sister. Before my sister could protest, the woman grabbed her head and pushed her face between her breasts. "How much I have miss you!"

Her enormous bosom heaved with emotion while my sister struggled to catch her breath, and then the woman's eyes widened as she saw me hiding in the corner. She pushed Klara briskly to the side, then came over and swept me up off the floor. She plastered my face with orange kisses.

"Aren't you a pretty little girl!" she told me. "Almost as pretty as I, when I am your age." She put me back on the ground, nodded in my mother's direction, and went to say hello to Mr. Poloraich.

"Who was that?" I asked my mother.

"That's your grandmother," my mother said. "Her name is Hilda."

"My grandmother? I thought her name was Kveta!"

"Kveta is my mother," she told me. "Hilda is your father's mother. She's your other grandmother."

"I have another grandmother?" I shook my head in amazement.

"I'm afraid so," my mother sighed.

"But why didn't anyone tell me about her?" I asked. "I want a grand-mother! I want someone to tell me stories."

"I don't think Hilda has time to tell you stories, Trumpet," my mother said. "She's very busy and doesn't even have much time for your father these days. This is the third time we have seen her since you were born. She doesn't come to visit very often."

"Why not?" I asked.

"I think she's having too much fun," my mother replied.

MY FATHER'S FAMILY came from Ostrava, one of the ugliest and poorest cities in Czechoslovakia. My grandmother had been so poor when she was young, her biggest dream was to have curtains in the windows. She had been a great beauty, but had quickly married a man she didn't love, to get away from her brutal, drunken father. The man's name was Emil, and he was a quiet fellow who worked as an accountant in the State Iron Works. He and Hilda had two sons, and after thirty years of proletarian life in Ostrava, he died and my grandmother moved to Prague and reinvented herself as a Socialist businesswoman. She ran a popular buffet at the Florenc bus station, and made a lot of money selling little cakes and sausages and watered-down booze. She was very popular in the transport community, dating many bus and train drivers in the years following my grandfather's death. But my dad had a hard time dealing with all her boyfriends and fiancés.

Strong and capable as he was, my dad had a turbulent relationship with his mother, perhaps due to the fact that they were so similar. Hilda was also a wheeler-dealer, and she was used to getting her own way by any means necessary. I watched as she circulated through the party with old Mr. Dos-kar trotting behind her. Before long, she had disappeared upstairs and was making a thorough inventory of the house. My father shadowed her nervously and I followed at a distance, trying to imagine this loud and flamboyant woman reading me bedtime stories. Her hair was jet black and curly in the Bohemian style, and it was obvious that she had been very pretty as a girl, but with her colorful suit and accent, she looked and sounded a bit like a parrot. I could hear her chattering excitedly as she tramped through what had been the Nedbals' apartment, and at which point my father intercepted her and took her to the kitchen for a chat, leaving Mr. Doskar in the living room, helping himself to sandwiches. My mother and sister were standing nearby, watching my father lead Hilda downstairs.

"She doesn't want to live with us, does she?" my sister whispered.

"I have no idea what she wants. I didn't even know she was coming," my mother whispered back.

"And I can't believe she brought that man with her."

"Neither can I," my mother agreed.

"His name is Mr. Doskar!" I exclaimed. "He's very old and his hands keep shaking all the time."

Mr. Poloraich, who had regained control of the party, made a suave joke that saved Mr. Doskar from embarrassment, and my mother smiled gratefully as she whisked me from the room.

"Why don't you go outside and see if Barry would like to eat the leftover chicken?" she said. "There's a plate in the fridge. Get your father to help you."

"Okay." I was always happy to go and see Barry.

I went down to the kitchen and looked at the fridge. The handle was too high for me to reach, but I was actually more interested in listening to my dad and my grandmother talking in Mr. Kozel's old apartment. My father was trying to keep his voice down, but my grandmother's voice became louder and louder, and after a few moments the apartment door crashed open, and she stormed up the stairs with my dad right behind her.

"How dare you!" my grandmother was shrieking. "Where the sun doesn't shine, the doctor comes knocking! I catch my death of cold in this apartment! To even suggest that I live in such condition! You should be ashame of yourself, Jarda! Ashame!"

"But Mum," my father growled as he followed her upstairs. "We have to reconstruct the house. We're months away—"

"I hear enough!" Hilda roared as she waved at her fiancé. "Come, Mr. Doskar! We leave!"

She strode to the front door and made a huge show of putting her boots on. Poor old Mr. Doskar looked up from the couch, where he had been happily nursing a glass of Mr. Poloraich's scotch, and seemed very confused. He handed the glass to my mother and mumbled his thanks, then he hurried over to the door to help my grandmother into her coat. His hands were shaking very badly, and it took them a long time to leave, but when they did, Hilda made sure that she slammed the door behind them. The mood of the party was definitely ruined, and my dad was quiet and sad for the rest of the day.

"You know, I'm not really sure that I would like Granny Hilda to be my grandmother," I confided to my mum as we were doing the dishes. "I would rather have a grandmother like from the book. I would much rather have a grandmother like Auntie Mary."

"One of the first things you learn in life is that you can choose your friends, but you can't choose your relatives," my mother informed me gently. "Once you've got them, they stay with you forever."

"But that's not fair," I complained. "When you're writing your books, I have no one to play with. Dad's busy all the time, and you're both too busy to read me stories."

"That's true," she agreed. "We have to work very hard now to try and fix the house before winter, but maybe we can find you a nice babysitter who could read to you during the daytime. Would you like that?"

"Maybe," I said. "But I like it most when you read to me."

"I know," my mother sighed.

JUST BEFORE THE COURT APPEAL, my mother had come to an arrangement with her bosses at the Economic Institute: she was allowed to write her books at home as a small compensation for them taking credit for her work. My mother hated writing these books. There was a great deal of pressure to alter her statistics and make the Soviet economy look better than it was. But she refused to do this. Instead, she presented the statistics and her analysis in such a way that if you weren't reading closely, you might think that the numbers were favorable, but upon careful inspection, you would see the statistics for what they really were. (In April 1985, an American journal called *Soviet Studies* quoted several of her books, referring to them as some of the most reliable sources of information about the Soviet economy on record.) Writing these books was very hard work, and whenever a deadline loomed, my mother would become too busy to look after me. Klara was at school, and the local kindergartens were overflowing with baby-boom children, so my parents started looking around for someone to babysit me. They eventually found an old Austrian woman who agreed to take care of me for not much money.

The old woman's name was Mrs. Habova, and I was very excited when she first appeared at our house, because she looked a little bit like Auntie Mary. She was tiny and wrinkled, with gray hair, thick glasses, and an even thicker accent, and she seemed as enthusiastic about having me in her life as I was about having her in mine. Her husband had recently died and her children had all grown up, so she was delighted to have a little girl to look after. The problem was, she was terribly strict. I had to call her *Oma*, which means "Granny" in German, and she would turn up at nine o'clock every morning and cook me a runny egg for breakfast. I didn't like runny eggs and I didn't like speaking German, but Oma Habova seemed determined to try and raise me the same way she had raised her own children, which was with an emphasis on discipline and timing. Every day was carefully planned, and every mouthful I ate and every breath I took seemed to be incorporated into Oma's schedule.

"Mein Zwergelchen, es is zu spät!" she would fret while I poked my egg with a spoon. *"Los los, du musst schneller essen!"* ("My little dwarf, it is too late. . . . Hurry up—you must eat faster.")

I would screw up my face and force myself to eat the egg, and then we would go outside for a walk. I loved going for walks, especially in the spring and especially when I could persuade Oma to take me into the forest. Our street ended in a cul-de-sac at the very edge of the forest, and there was a lovely walking track that Oma would sometimes take me down. The forest was completely untouched, so, along with the owls and badgers and pine martens, there were also deer and foxes. The smell of rotten oak leaves and pine sap was wonderful, and we could walk for about a kilometer before the track curved around the side of the mountain and there was a steep ravine on one side. Whenever we came to the ravine, Oma would take my hand and lead me back to the street.

"But can't we keep going?" I would protest. "I like it up here. I'll be careful, Oma, I promise!"

"I know you will, *Zwergelchen*," she would say. "But we can't go any farther because of the wolf."

"The wolf?" I would ask.

"The wolf who lives in the ravine," Oma would tell me. "He's very hungry, and he likes nothing more than to eat little girls and boys who disobey their grandmothers."

"Is he the same wolf as the wolf in *Little Red Riding Hood*?"

"Yes, I think he is," Oma would agree.

"Well, then he eats grandmothers, too," I would point out.

"Maybe he does." Oma would smile. "In which case we had both better get out of here, *nicht wahr?*"

By the time we arrived home, Oma would usually be so tired that all she wanted to do was sit in front of the TV and knit—her favorite activity. In the early weeks of our time together, she asked me if I would like to help, and when I said yes, she wound a ball of wool around my hands, handcuffing me to whatever scarf or sweater she was knitting. Then I had to sit on the floor and watch an incredibly boring arts-and-crafts show until it was time for my nap.

"What are you going to read to me today?" I would ask. "Will you read me *Prince Bajaja?*"

"That depends on whether you'll be quiet," Oma Habova would answer.

"But I like talking," I would cry. "And I like to know what's going on."

"If you listen, you'll find out," Oma would say.

"Yes, but I like it when you tell me!" I would insist.

Before Oma came along, I always looked forward to my afternoon nap, because my mother would sit on the edge of my bed and read me stories until I fell asleep. She was very patient and would answer all my questions about the characters in the books, probably because she understood that the best way to put a talkative child to sleep is to let her talk until she's tired herself out. Oma's own children must have been very quiet, because she simply couldn't fathom the idea of talking during nap time. And once she started to read, she would simply increase her volume to drown out my questions, mispronouncing the words in her thick Austrian accent.

"Once upon a time, there was a handsome ponce," she would say. "And one day, he rode out to look for a poncess . . ."

After a few months of being babysat by Oma, I began to notice that there were a lot of old ladies in our street who were even more like The Grandmother than she was. Three of these ladies lived quite close to our house—Mrs. Liskova, Mrs. Noskova, and Mrs. Sokolova. They were very old and kind, and whenever Oma and I walked past their front gardens, they would wave and say hello. They seemed much more relaxed and friendly than Oma, and I secretly imagined they were the three fairy godmothers from *Sleeping Beauty*. Whenever it was sunny, the ladies could be found working in their gardens, and I would look forward to seeing them weeding their flower beds or sitting on their front steps with peaceful smiles on their faces.

"Hello, Mrs. Liskova!" I would call out as we made our way down the street. "How are you today?"

Mrs. Liskova was a tall and bony woman in her eighties, who lived in a villa near the bend in the road.

"Very well, thank you!" she would reply, shading her eyes with her hand. "I'm just sitting here with my roses, having a bit of a think."

"What are you thinking about?" I would ask.

"Don't be rude," Oma Habova would whisper. "It's none of your business what she's thinking."

"I was just remembering the good old days before the war," Mrs. Liskova would sigh. "There are so many stories I could tell, but nobody has the time to listen these days."

"I do!" I would exclaim. "I'd love to listen to your stories!"

"Another day perhaps!" Oma would call out, nudging me with her stick. "We have to be home in time for lunch!"

"No hurry," Mrs. Liskova would laugh. "I'm not going anywhere."

The house next to Mrs. Liskova's had a bright green coal shuttle in the garden. It was the home of Mrs. Noskova, a tiny, birdlike lady who walked on crutches but always seemed to be in a good mood.

"Hello, Mrs. Noskova." I would wave. "We're going for a walk."

"I wish I could come with you," she would smile.

"How's your dog?" I would ask. "Is Corina feeling better?"

"She's just old," Mrs. Noskova would reply. "There's no cure for old age, I'm afraid."

Oma would shiver at the thought and bustle me down the road to the next lady's villa, which was a gray cube with a small balcony on the first floor. This was Mrs. Sokolova's house. She was the nicest of the three, and she would sometimes even wait for me in her garden. My mother told me that Mrs. Sokolova had lived a very difficult life. Her husband had been the director of a bank but had committed suicide after the 1948 putsch, because he knew that the secret police were coming for him and that by killing himself he would spare his wife and children from persecution. Like so many women whose husbands had been killed or imprisoned by the Communists, Mrs. Sokolova had to support her family by working a physically demanding job in her later years. Twenty years as a railway porter had destroyed the circulation in her legs, but she wasn't angry or bitter about her life. She would wait for me near her front gate whenever it was sunny, and would sometimes give me biscuits she had baked for me herself.

"Hello, Mrs. Sokolova!" I would cry, shaking Oma loose and running through the gate.

"Careful, you'll knock me off my feet!" Mrs. Sokolova would laugh. "I made these biscuits from an old recipe my mother taught me when I was your age."

She would pull a paper bag filled with biscuits out of her apron and press it into my hand.

"Say thank you to Mrs. Sokolova," Oma would prompt.

"Thank you very much. The last ones were delicious!"

"You're very welcome." Mrs. Sokolova would smile.

Oma and I would continue down the road, and after I had eaten a couple of biscuits, she would confiscate the rest of the packet, telling me that they would ruin my appetite for lunch.

"But I'm hungry!" I would protest. "All I've had to eat is a runny egg."

"Hunger is the best cook in the world," Oma would say wisely. *"Wenn du nichts ʒu essen hast, alles schmeckt gut!"* ("When you have nothing to eat, everything tastes good.")

"Yes, Oma," I would sigh. *"Jawohl."*

As the midsummer weekend approached, I found myself looking forward to having my mother take care of me instead of Oma, and I was disappointed to discover that my dad had hired a crew of tradesmen to work *melouch* on our house instead. Working *melouch*, or "on the side," was the Czech equivalent of moonlighting, except the moonlighting took place in broad daylight when the people concerned were supposed to be at work. The practice of taking off from work (for weeks at a time) and earning cash on the side was so commonplace, a sophisticated system of bribes had evolved where workers would routinely cover for each other in exchange for reciprocal favors further down the line. The problem, of course, was that this was illegal, so the people doing the work were able to hold their employers to ransom. My father not only had to pay his crew handsomely to repair our house, he also had to indulge their whims, which invariably consisted of a never-ending supply of beer until they were too drunk to keep working, usually by mid-afternoon.

As a result, the early part of our summer consisted of my mother cooking sausages in the kitchen all day, while my sister ran up and down the hill to the Under the Forest pub, ferrying beer to the workers as they stood around and watched my dad demolish the Nedbals' apartment. The men would arrive early and make an impressive show of rattling their tools. It was like an army of termites was eating its way through our house. Under my father's supervision, the workers knocked down the Nedbals' walls and ceiling and then moved up to the roof, cutting the rafters with their chain saws and throwing the terra-cotta tiles onto the ground, making a tremendous racket and filling the house with clouds of red dust.

It was obviously not a safe environment for a little girl, so my parents asked Oma if she would mind taking care of me at her apartment. Two months of babysitting had taken its toll on both of us, but she graciously agreed. Every morning she would collect me at eight and we would walk to the opposite side of the hill, where she lived in the basement of a small art deco villa. We would climb down a steep flight of steps from the road to her garden, and Oma would unlock her front door with one of the many keys she carried on a big safety pin. Her apartment was dark and cold, and the plaster on the ceiling kept peeling off and falling onto the carpet. She also lived right next to the cellar, so everything smelled like old potatoes and coal. We weren't allowed to sit in the garden, because it was her landlord's private property, so Oma would switch on an electric heater and position me in front of the TV. Her television set was broken, so she would spend a lot of time fiddling with the aerial and sticking it out of the window to catch what little signal there was, but the screen was always grainy and it was always the same boring arts-and-crafts shows. Every day, I would carry my big book of fairy tales to her apartment, but the basement was so quiet and grim it made the scary parts of the stories even more scary than usual, and I was always too frightened to ask her to read to me.

After lunch, which would usually consist of *Kartoffeln* and some kind of meat, Oma would ask me to help with her knitting. Lately, this was all we did in the afternoons. We were having the most beautiful weather outside, and I grew more and more frustrated in Oma's damp apartment. Every morning I would walk to her house as slowly as I could, savoring the sunshine and the smell of fresh lawn clippings, and I would say hello to the old ladies and wish that they were my grandmothers instead of Oma. It didn't seem fair that there were so many nice ladies and lovely gardens in our street while I had to be babysat by someone who wanted to spend all her time indoors.

The summer holidays passed incredibly slowly, and after two weeks, I was bored to the point of tears. It was a crucial week on the construction site. They were at the point of dismantling the truss, and my father was paying six roofers twenty crowns an hour each (a lot of money in those days). He needed them to work quickly, because the weather forecast had predicted rain in a week, and it was important to have the roof up by then. My mother and sister were exhausted, and my dad was tense and short-tempered, and even though I didn't understand what was going on, I was in a sulky mood as well. I didn't want to go to Oma's apartment, so I started to behave badly the moment she came to pick me up.

"Can't we go to the forest? Just for a little while?" I wheedled as she helped me into my jacket.

"Not today," she said distractedly. "I need to buy a few eggs so I can cook you your breakfast."

"I don't want eggs for breakfast!" I cried. "I want to go to the forest! You always say 'not today,' and we never end up going. Why can't we eat here and then go to the forest?"

"You know very well why we can't," Oma told me. "Your kitchen is full of dust. Now come along, put your jacket on and I'll make you a nice breakfast at my place."

"I don't like your place!" I said angrily. "It's cold and dark and it smells funny."

"Little dwarf, you are trying my patience," Oma snapped. "Get ready, or I'll tell your mother you're being difficult."

"I don't have to do what you tell me all the time," I blurted. "You're not my real grandmother!"

Oma's eyes widened and she looked very hurt. Without saying a word, she left the living room and went down to the kitchen. I knew that she was going to complain to my mother, and I wished that I could stop her, because I didn't really mean what I had said. I knew that Oma was doing her best to look after me, and I also knew that my mother would take Oma's side and make me apologize for being rude. I felt guilty, but I also felt angry, because I didn't want to spend another lovely day indoors. Before I quite knew what I was doing, I ran to my cot and collected the green mitt from under my pillow, and then I put on my boots and dashed out the front door, turning left and running into the forest.

"I don't want to go to Oma's apartment," I told the mitt.

"Me, neither!" the mitt agreed.

"Oma's mean and she doesn't like Barry," I sniffed.

"Poor Barry!" the mitt replied. "He's very lonely now that you spend all your time in Oma's stupid apartment."

"I wish Barry was here," I said. "If the wolf came along, Barry would bite him."

"I wish Barry was here, too," the mitt said. "He's much bigger than the wolf, isn't he?"

"He's much bigger," I said. "The wolf would be afraid to come near us if Barry was here!"

"Well, we won't go very far then, will we?" the mitt said nervously. "We'll just go in a little way."

"Okay," I agreed. "We won't go very far."

The oak leaves crunched beneath my feet and the trees sighed gently in the wind. I talked loudly to the mitt to stop myself from being afraid. After a while, we came to a crossroads in the path, and I knew from my walks with Oma that the little track that crossed our big one led back to Cernosice. The track was steep, but it leveled out into a dirt road that ran behind Mrs. Liskova's and Mrs. Noskova's back gardens.

"I think we should go up this path here," I told the mitt.

"I think so, too," the mitt agreed.

"I'm very sad that I made Oma upset," I said. "Oma's not so bad, is she?"

"No, she's not so bad," the mitt agreed. "Do you think that the wolf lives nearby?"

"I don't think so," I said. "I think he lives a long way away, on the other side of the mountain."

"I'm not afraid of the wolf," the mitt whispered.

"I'm not afraid of the wolf, either!" I said loudly. "The wolf is just a big and nasty dog who lives in the forest, and if he comes along, I'm going to tell him to go away."

I clutched the mitt and quickened my pace.

"Hurry up," the mitt whispered. "I can see Mrs. Liskova's gate."

The path curved through the trees to the back of Mrs. Liskova's house, and I dropped the pretense of bravery and ran for the safety of her garden. I shut the gate behind me and sighed with relief. The forest didn't look half as scary as it did from the other side of the fence. I walked around to the front of the house, where I found Mrs. Liskova tending her roses.

"Hello, Mrs. Liskova!" I called out to her. "I've come to listen to your stories."

"Why, it's Dominika! How very nice to see you," the old lady smiled. "Do your parents know you're here?"

"Yes," I lied. "I've been in the forest all by myself!"

"Really?" Mrs. Liskova said, brushing the dirt from her knees. "That sounds rather dangerous."

"I was a bit frightened," I admitted. "But I'm very glad I'm here."

"Are you now?" she laughed. "And what's that you have there? It looks like an oven mitt."

"It is a mitt," I said. "Sometimes he talks, but he's feeling a bit shy at the moment."

"I see," Mrs. Liskova smiled. "And what kind of stories would you like me to tell you?"

"You were going to tell me all about how nice things were when you were a little girl," I said.

"Was I now?" Mrs. Liskova sat down on a bench and folded her wrinkled hands in her lap. I sat down on the grass in front of her, using my mitt as a cushion.

"Well, let's see. When I was your age, Cernosice was a popular holiday town that people from Prague used to come and visit on the weekends," Mrs. Liskova said. "The river was clean and there were many excellent hotels and restaurants to go to, and the forest was full of mushrooms you could pick yourself and eat."

"That sounds very nice," I said.

"It was nice," Mrs. Liskova sighed. "Back in those days, Prague was one of the most civilized and influential cities in Europe. Lots of great writers and musicians and artists lived here. Did you know that Mozart wrote *Don Giovanni* while he was living in Prague?"

"I know who Mozart is," I said proudly. "My mother has his records."

"He was a very great composer," Mrs. Liskova agreed. "Many people think that if he had stayed in Prague instead of moving back to Vienna, he would have lived longer and written more music."

"I like it here in your garden," I told Mrs. Liskova. "It's very noisy at my house at the moment."

"So I can hear," she said. "And look, here comes Mrs. Noskova." She pointed to the villa next door, and I saw her neighbor limping slowly through her garden.

"Hello, Mrs. Noskova!" I called out. "What are you doing?"

"I'm gathering strawberries," she replied, leaning heavily on her crutches. "Mrs. Sokolova is baking a cake and I promised to bring her all the ripe strawberries I can find."

"Would you like some help?" Mrs. Liskova asked. "Maybe Dominika could give you a hand."

"I love strawberries," I said excitedly. "I'll help you!"

There was a low hedge separating the two gardens, and I noticed that Mrs. Noskova's garden was slightly nicer than Mrs. Liskova's. There was a row of cherry trees and a little strawberry patch, not to mention the bright green coal shuttle that looked like a miniature train. Mrs. Noskova waited for us by her strawberry patch, leaning on one crutch and using the other to turn the leaves and see if there were any ripe strawberries beneath them.

"I can help because I'm small," I told the two ladies. "I can find all the strawberries that are hiding."

I knelt down and started to look through the patch. There were lots of strawberries, but only a few of them were red and juicy. I crawled on my hands and knees and carefully inspected each of the clumps, and whenever I found a ripe strawberry, I put it in Mrs. Noskova's basket. Many of the nicer-looking strawberries were already half eaten.

"I keep telling my son to put a scarecrow in the garden," Mrs. Noskova said. "The starlings are really bad this year. They always get to the strawberries before I can pick them."

"The hawks and falcons have left the forest," Mrs. Liskova pointed out. "A lot of the big birds have moved on. Remember when the owls were so noisy it was impossible to sleep?"

"That was a long time ago," Mrs. Noskova said wistfully. "I actually love the chirping of the starlings and swallows. I just wish they wouldn't eat all my strawberries."

"Don't worry," I said. "I'm doing a good job down here."

I filled the basket with as many strawberries as I could find, and then we went over to Mrs. Sokolova's apartment. All three ladies lived on the ground floors of the villas their families owned, but Mrs. Sokolova's apartment wasn't damp and claustrophobic like Oma's. It was warm and cozy, and smelled of cinnamon and vanilla. The door was open, and in the living room there was a little round table with a hand-embroidered table-cloth. Mrs. Liskova and Mrs. Noskova leaned their walking sticks and crutches against the wall and eased themselves into the chairs. Mrs. Soko-lova was brewing a pot of tea, and I helped her carry the milk and sugar to the table.

"Would you like to help me wash the strawberries?" she asked.

"Yes," I said. "I found all the ones the starlings didn't eat."

"Well, aren't you a good girl," Mrs. Sokolova smiled. "We'll wash the strawberries and then maybe you can help me put them on the cake."

"Okay!" I said happily.

We washed the strawberries, and then Mrs. Sokolova put on her own oven mitt and removed a baking tray from the oven. I put my mitt on, too, and watched as she transferred the cake from the tray to a plate. We cov-ered the cake with strawberries and topped it off with a big squirt of whipped cream. Then she gave me the plate and I carried it carefully to the table while Mrs. Liskova and Mrs. Noskova smiled encouragingly.

"It's a good thing I brought my mitt!" I said. "Normally he sleeps un-der my pillow. My mother doesn't let me use him in the kitchen."

"She probably doesn't want him to get burned," Mrs. Noskova said.

"But that's what he's for," I pointed out.

"Do you have other dolls or toys to play with?" Mrs. Liskova asked.

"I have my sister's teddy bear, but mostly I play with Barry in the gar-den," I told her.

"Barry must be getting old now," Mrs. Noskova remarked. "Your par-ents got him around the same time I got Corina."

"He's on television every Christmas!" I said proudly. "And when it snows, he pulls my sled."

"Who would like a piece of cake?" Mrs. Sokolova asked. "I'll slice it, and maybe Dominika can put it on the plates."

She cut the cake into pieces and directed me to put a large slice on my plate and very small slices on everyone else's. Mrs. Liskova and Mrs. Noskova ate like birds, pecking away at their portions with their forks. I finished my slice very quickly and Mrs. Sokolova gave me a second piece, which was something my mother would never have done.

"It's good to see someone with a healthy appetite," she smiled.

The afternoon drifted lazily by and the shadows grew longer outside the kitchen windows. The three ladies may have moved and talked slowly, but it was obvious that they had known each other for a long time, and it was fun watching them laugh and tell childhood tales as though they were still young women. Their stories were wonderfully enchanting, and I felt hypnotized by the slow rhythm of their speech. We finished the cake and were on to our third cup of tea, when Mrs. Sokolova's middle-aged daughter appeared at the door.

"Mum, Klara Furmanova's here looking for her sister," she said. "Dominika ran away from home this morning and her family has been searching for her all day."

"Good heavens!" the old ladies exclaimed. "Is it true? Did you really run away from home?"

"I didn't mean to," I said softly. "I just didn't want to go to Oma's apartment."

My sister joined Mrs. Sokolova's daughter in the doorway.

"We've been looking for you everywhere," she said in a stern voice. "Dad had to get his workers to search the forest. We were afraid you might have gone to the ravine."

"I went to visit Mrs. Liskova," I whispered. "I've been here all afternoon."

"We're awfully sorry, Klara," Mrs. Liskova apologized. "We thought your parents knew she was spending the day with us."

"They didn't," Klara said grimly. "Mrs. Habova is in tears, and Dad had to pay his workers to search the forest instead of working on the roof. The day has been a complete disaster."

"Well that's unfortunate, but the main thing is that Dominika is safe," Mrs. Sokolova said firmly. "She's been keeping us company and we've enjoyed having her, haven't we?"

Mrs. Liskova and Mrs. Noskova agreed heartily, and Mrs. Sokolova shot me a sympathetic smile.

"You're welcome to visit us any time, Dominika, but you must ask your parents first," she said. "Next time I see your mother, I'll have a word with her, but in the meantime you must tell them that you're very sorry for running away. Will you do that?"

"Yes," I said sadly. "I am very sorry."

"Very well," Mrs. Sokolova nodded. "You had better hurry along now so that everyone will know that you're safe."

Klara took me by the hand and led me out of Mrs. Sokolova's apartment, and as we walked up the street to our house, I could see a crowd of people outside our front gate. My mother was comforting Oma, and my dad was talking to the roofers and Mr. Hasek from next door. Everyone seemed anxious until one of the roofers spotted Klara leading me home. My father was particularly relieved, but the brief glow of happiness that crossed his face was quickly replaced by anger. The sun had started to sink through the forest, and the shadow of the crowd stretched a long way down the road. I walked slowly through the shadow until I reached my father's feet. When I looked up into his eyes, they were yellow and bright with concern.

"We were sick with worry," he growled. "Do you understand what you have done?"

"I'm very sorry, Dad," I whispered.

"I'm going to have to spank you," he said. "You must never, ever run away again. Do you hear me?"

Big and strong as he was, my father had always taken the greatest care to be gentle with his daughters. I had never been spanked before, and I could tell that he was very reluctant to do it, but the neighborhood had become involved in my disappearance and it was important for him to discipline me while everyone was watching. As the roofers stood around and nodded approvingly, he bent me over his knee.

I clutched the mitt and looked up at my father.

"Okay, Daddy," I said tearfully. "But *malinko a pomalinku.*"

The Czech language is full of diminutives. What I had meant to say was, "Not too hard and not too fast," but by diminishing the sentence, what I ended up saying was, "Only a little bit and very slowly."

My father's hand wavered above my bum, and then his knee started to shake as he spanked me.

"What can you do with a kid like this?" He laughed.

The punishment was over before I knew it, and my dad set me back on the ground. The roofers and Mr. Hasek were roaring with laughter and even my mother and Oma were smiling. My father, of course, had given me the lightest spanking he could manage, and the whole ordeal was more theatrical than harsh, but I learned my lesson and never tried to run away from home again.

The next morning, Mrs. Sokolova had a chat with my mother and told her that I was welcome to visit her and the other ladies whenever I wanted. My dad somehow managed to put together enough money to hire the roofers for one more day, and, once the difficult work was over, Mrs. Habova retired as my surrogate grandmother. From that time on, whenever I wanted someone to read to me or feed me biscuits, I would get my mother to phone Mrs. Liskova, and then I would carry my big book of fairy tales down the street to her front gate, where my three fairy godmothers would be waiting.

I never got to know my real grandparents very well, but in those early years of my life, the three old ladies who lived in my street did a wonderful job of making me feel loved.

three

THE LITTLE COFFIN

THE DAY OF WORK we lost when I ran away from home turned out to be a major setback for my dad. At the end of July, all the tradesmen he had hired went back to their real jobs, and we spent the rest of the summer living in a house without a roof. The walls on the second floor were unfinished, and the naked truss looked like a skeleton picked clean. From the street, the exposed floor made our villa look like a doll's house, and my mother was particularly upset by the fact that our neighbors could see us using the bathroom. We hung up sheets to try and make it more private, but I actually loved having a bath in a bathroom with no walls. We would wait until the sun had set, and then we would take turns in the bath, sharing the water, because our boiler was broken. I would always get to go first, while the water was still hot, and there was nothing nicer than sitting in a warm bath, feeling the breeze against my neck and looking up through the rafters at the night sky overhead.

As the end of summer approached, my father had no choice but to finish the house by himself. He drove his taxi in the evenings, and his days were spent sourcing and transporting material (bricks and tiles were hard to come by), to rebuild the roof and attic on his own. My mother raced against time to complete her book, and the moment she finished, my dad conscripted her to mix mortar in his old cement mixer. Klara carried buckets of mortar up the scaffolding to where he was frantically laying bricks, and the remarkable thing was that he got his walls up faster than a six-man team of *melouch* workers. I was the only one who didn't have to work, until my dad saw me playing near the cement mixer one day and decided that I was old enough to help.

"Come with me," he said. "I have something for you to do."

He led me to a pile of old bricks from the demolished walls of the Nedbals' apartment.

"I'm running out of bricks and I don't have money to buy any more," he growled. "But these old bricks are good. They're just covered with a bit of mortar. What I want you to do is try and knock the mortar off the bricks with a hammer, like this."

He pulled a hammer out of his carpenter's belt and tapped off a chunk of mortar.

"Now you try," he said.

He handed me the hammer and I gave the brick an enthusiastic bash, splitting it in half. My father took the hammer from me and gently demonstrated the best way to clean the brick.

"See? *Malinko a pomalinku*," he smiled.

I made myself a seat using a piece of timber, and selected a brick from the pile. It took me a while to work out a good technique, but I eventually got the hang of it. By the time my mother called me in for my bath, I had a small pile of clean bricks to show her.

"I cleaned these all by myself," I said proudly. "Look, I can do it with only one hit."

I expertly tapped a brick with my hammer, making the mortar fall away like the shell off a walnut.

"Very impressive," my mother smiled. "Dinner's nearly ready, so why don't you go up and get your father to run your bath?"

I trotted upstairs and found my father at work on the bathroom wall. He was smearing the last of his new bricks with mortar and tapping them into place with the handle of his hammer.

"Hello, Dad! I cleaned a lot of bricks."

"Aren't you a good girl," he laughed. "If I were the captain of a ship, I would sail the stormy seas with you as my first mate."

I blushed with pride as he started my bath. A splutter of brown water exploded from the taps and my dad wearily sponged clean the bottom of the tub. Once the water had cleared, he plugged the bath and we waited a long time for the broken boiler to fill it. Dusk seeped through the valley. My father pulled a handkerchief out of his pocket and laid it across a dusty pile of cement bags.

"Here. Sit on this," he told me.

He sat on the cement bag next to me and lit himself a cigarette.

"Are you going to drive the taxi tonight?" I asked him.

"Yes," he yawned. "But I'm going to try and finish this wall first."

"Why did you want to make the roof more higher?" I asked. "I thought the house was nice as it was."

"I'm not just making the roof more higher," he replied. "I'm adding another floor to the house so that you and Klara can have your own bedrooms."

"I'd like my own bedroom," I told him.

"Well, you'll have one," he said. "And it will have big windows you can look out and lots of space to play in. And in time, when you grow up, your children will have a place to live in as well. You see, I'm really building this house for you and Klara."

"Did your parents build you a house, too?" I asked.

"No. They couldn't afford it," my father replied. "They were very poor, but there was also a war going on and we spent many years living in a cellar. Have I told you this story?"

"No." I loved it when my father told me stories.

"Well, we were invaded by the Germans before the start of the war, and they made a lot of their weapons in Czech factories," he said. "So when the Allies started dropping bombs on Germany, they dropped a lot of bombs on us as well."

"Did they drop bombs on you?" I asked.

"Not on me personally, but they dropped a lot of bombs on Ostrava," he explained. "Your grandparents and I lived right next to a factory that the Allies were desperate to destroy. It was the Ritkers chemical plant that produced fuel for the German V1 and V2 missiles, and it was so full of rocket fuel and explosives, the Allies would have wiped out half the city if they had hit it."

"You would have been blown up!"

"We were incredibly lucky," my father said. "Whenever the sirens went off, the workers would set fire to a dozen barrels of tar, sending a cloud of black smoke above the factory. The English planes would arrive half an hour later, and they wouldn't be able to see anything, so they just dropped their bombs in the middle of the cloud. They must have dropped thousands of bombs above Ritkers, but for some reason they always missed."

"Where did the bombs end up falling, Dad?" I asked. "Did they fall on anyone's house?"

"They fell on a middle-class neighborhood on the other side of the factory," my father told me. "I'm sure the Allies didn't want to hurt these people, but hundreds and hundreds of families were killed. That's what war does, you see. It kills innocent people."

He turned off the water and helped me take off my clothes. The evening breeze was cold, and my teeth chattered as he lowered me into the bath.

"How's that?" he asked.

"It's lovely and warm!" I squealed.

My father sat on the rim of the tub and lit another cigarette. His hands were dirty and he looked very tired.

"When I was growing up, my parents used to take me to Pisek for holidays every year," he said reflectively. "We would catch the train from Ostrava to Prague, and then take the local train out to Pisek, passing through Cernosice along the way."

He crumbled some dry mortar from his fingers.

"Every time we came through, I would look up at these hills," he sighed. "I would stand next to the window and press my face against the glass. It seemed like such a nice place, especially compared to Ostrava, which was destroyed by the war and then ruined by the Russians. When I was a little boy, Cernosice looked like Heaven. From the moment I saw it, this was where I wanted to live."

"What was Ostrava like?"

"It's a coal-mining town. There was a lot of coal in the ground that the Russians wanted, so they made our factories and mines work hard to produce it for them. After a while, it became unbearable. The trees and buildings would be covered in coal dust, and the streets would be so hot in summer, the tar would melt and stick to your shoes. You couldn't swim in the river because it was full of chemicals, and you couldn't walk across a bridge without holding your nose."

"That doesn't sound very nice," I said.

"It wasn't. It was a rough town full of poor people like my parents. You had to be strong to survive, and even stronger to get out. If there was one thing I knew when I was growing up, it was that I was going to get out as soon as I had the chance."

He finished his cigarette and sent the glowing embers floating out into the darkness.

The sky had turned inky black, the moon and stars smothered by clouds. Dishes and cutlery clattered in the distance, and I could smell the sausages the Haseks were cooking next door. My father put a washcloth on his hand and gently soaped my back, and then he rinsed me, shook me dry, and wrapped me up in a towel. He helped me into my pajamas as my sister came up to take her turn in the bath. Then he went back to his wall, continuing to lay bricks in the semidarkness.

Klara inspected the bath, dipping her hand in the water.

"It's dirtier than usual," she complained.

"Dominika has been helping me in the yard," my dad told her.

"I cleaned a pile of bricks," I announced to her. "I've become very good at hitting them with a hammer."

"Great," my sister said. "And now the water looks like coffee."

"At least it's warm coffee," my father growled. "It's cold and black by the time I get to it."

Klara sighed and climbed in, while I put on my slippers and trotted down to the kitchen. My mother had just finished cooking *kulajda,* a traditional Czech meal of potatoes and hard-boiled eggs in white sauce. She had recently started serving our dinners on small plates to make them look bigger, and the delicious smell of the neighbors' sausages was often quite distracting. I loved my mother's cooking, though. She could make the tastiest of meals out of the plainest of ingredients.

We ate dinner together, and then my father attached the TAXI sign to his car and drove away to work the night shift in Prague. Every so often, Dad's schedule would become very frantic, and I would later learn that this was due to a small group of West Germans personally requesting him whenever they came to town. My father spoke fluent German and had dealt with many Germans during his government years, so whenever a visitor with dissident connections would come to Czechoslovakia, the network put him in touch with my dad and he would become their personal chauffeur. They paid in deutsche marks, which he could exchange on the black market, and often required him to shake off state secret security cars that were tailing them. Westerners were automatically tailed during communism. The secret police liked to lure them to hotels and photograph them in compromising situations. Dad was very familiar with the secret police, and was able to keep his German clients out of trouble.

After he had driven away, my mother led me upstairs to my cot in the living room, the only room in the house that wasn't under construction. It was crowded with furniture and all my mother's books, and there was so little space, my mother and father had to sleep underneath the piano. My cot was in the middle of the room, and I would fall asleep listening to my mum and Klara turn the pages of their books on either side of me. Around sunrise, I would hear my dad return home and crawl under the piano. The strings reverberated as he slumped beside the pedal stand, and the warm hum of the piano always made me feel safe. We had a great piano. It was the Red Countess's German Steinway grand, and was very rare, as most of the German Steinways had been destroyed during the war. After the court case, my mother expected the Red Countess to reclaim it, but moving the piano was too much trouble for her. So she left it in our villa, and it was the one expensive thing we owned. We were very poor when I was growing up, and selling the piano would have solved a lot of problems, but my mother wouldn't hear of it. It was the piano she had practiced on as a child, and was the one remaining link between her and her parents. She played it beautifully and sadly.

I HAD SUCH A GOOD TIME cleaning bricks with my hammer, I didn't want to stop. I worked at the pile every day for a week, and was so determined to clean every brick that my mother eventually had to send me out to play.

"I was just talking to Mrs. Liskova," she said one morning. "And she tells me that the ladies have baked you a cake. But they're worried that you might not want to come around and eat it. They're afraid that you might be too busy to see them."

"They baked me a cake?"

"Yes. They miss you," my mother smiled. "They also said they would be happy to read you a story, but they're afraid that you might be too old for them to read to."

"I'm not too old," I exclaimed. "I'd love to go!"

"Well, you can," she said. "I've told your father you're taking the day off, and Mrs. Liskova's expecting you."

I collected my big book of fairy tales and walked down the street. It was a windy day and the trees were changing color. Summer was coming to an end.

I trotted past Mr. Hasek's garden, said hello to his dog Alf, and was about to cross the street to Mrs. Liskova's gate, when a head popped up from behind Mr. Acorn's fence. The head belonged to a little boy who couldn't have been much older than me.

"Hello," I said. "Who are you?"

"I'm Petr Acorn," the boy replied. "Are you the girl who ran away from home?"

"I didn't run away from home," I told him. "I went for a walk in the forest. My name is Dominika Furmanova."

The boy ducked behind the fence. A moment later, he reappeared with a little girl beside him. The girl had a round face and frizzy hair, and she giggled when she saw me.

"My name is Mary Hairy. Petr and I have been watching you for ages!"

"You've been watching me?" I was surprised. "How come I haven't seen you?"

"We were inside the house," Petr said. "Whenever we saw you, you were with the old lady with the stick and we were too frightened to come out and say hello."

"Is she your grandmother?" Mary asked.

"She used to be, but now she isn't," I explained. "She became too tired and had to have a rest. But now I have three grandmothers! They've baked me a cake and I'm on my way to eat it."

"They baked you a cake!" Petr exclaimed. "What kind of cake is it? Do you know?"

"I'm not sure," I said. "Maybe you could come and have a look. I bet Mrs. Sokolova would let you have a piece."

"Mrs. Sokolova can't be your real grandmother," Mary pointed out. "If she was, she would live in your house."

"I would like her to live in my house, but we don't have a roof at the moment," I told her. "So I go and visit her in her apartment instead. Would you like to come with me?"

Petr looked at Mary. "What do you think?"

"We should ask our parents. Can you wait for us?"

"Okay," I said.

The two children ducked back behind the fence. A few minutes later, they reappeared at the gate.

"We can't come," Petr said sadly. "We're not allowed to play with you."

"Why not?" I asked.

"Petr's mother said so," Mary shrugged. "We're just not allowed."

"Oh," I said, disappointed. "Well, maybe we can play together another time. What do you think?"

"Maybe," Petr said doubtfully.

"Okay, then. It was very nice to meet you. *Ahoj!*"

And then I crossed the street and climbed the stairs to Mrs. Liskova's front yard.

The ladies were sitting at a small table in the garden, chatting and catching what little sun they could. They were happy to see me, and it turned out that they knew Petr Acorn and Mary Hairy's parents. Mrs. Sokolova's cake was delicious as usual and, after lunch, Mrs. Liskova read me a long story from my book. Then Mrs. Noskova gave me a jar of her son's homemade honey and took me around back to see his beehives. Each hive was made of a log that had been carved into the shape of a face. The entrance was an open mouth that was either smiling or frowning. The bees took off and landed like airplanes at a busy airport, and Mrs. Noskova frowned as she listened to their drone. She looked up at the sky and studied the clouds, and then we walked back to Mrs. Liskova's house. By the time we joined the other ladies in the garden, the sun had disappeared.

"It's going to rain," Mrs. Liskova announced. "My joints are aching in all the old places."

"The bees are sounding anxious," Mrs. Noskova agreed. "And the swallows are flying low to the ground."

"I think we might be looking at a storm," Mrs. Sokolova sighed. "The air pressure is low and my ankles are swelling, and I'm really not liking the look of those clouds."

As soon as she said this, a loud clap of thunder resounded in the distance, and a fat raindrop fell onto my book.

"Quick, Dominika. You had better get home while you can," Mrs. Noskova told me.

She gave me my jar of honey and sent me out of Mrs. Liskova's gate, and as I ran up the street, I saw my father on the roof, nailing a thick sheet of plastic to the truss. The wind was howling in the forest, and then the heavens opened and it started to pour. I was completely drenched by the time I reached the house. I had never seen a storm like this before and I was terribly afraid. I huddled in the stairwell with Klara and listened to the thunder, and suddenly all the lights went out.

"Dad!" I cried. "Dad! Where are you?"

My father came down from the roof and herded us to the kitchen. We lit all the candles we could find and waited for the storm to go away.

"I hope we're not looking at a week of rain," my mother said nervously.

"This is nothing," my father growled. "Just a typical end-of-summer storm. It'll go away as quickly as it came."

But my father was wrong. It continued to pour for the rest of the day, and we fell asleep listening to the rain drumming against the plastic sheet on the roof. It was coming down in buckets the following morning, and the plastic sheet started to leak. A yellow stain appeared on the ceiling, and my mother's face was very grim.

"When clouds get trapped between the hills, it often rains until they're empty," she observed.

"That's the last thing we need," my father groaned. "This house is built on clay and I have an open foundation beneath the garage. What bad timing!"

"We had a storm like this when I was sixteen," my mother remembered. "The whole valley flooded. The river became a lake and a lot of people had to be rescued in boats."

"We don't have to worry about a flood, do we?" my sister asked. "We're right at the top of the hill."

"Exactly," my father said. "You worry too much, Jana! I can fix the ceiling when the rain stops. The furniture is safe, so the main thing is to stop the water from ruining the carpet and the floorboards. Let's get to work."

We used cooking pots to catch the drips, and I spent the day running around the house and emptying them while my parents and sister worked in the rain. My dad decided that the best thing to do would be to finish the upstairs walls, so my mother and Klara carried buckets of mortar up to him while he frantically laid the bricks I had cleaned. I went up to the roof and looked out across the valley, and it was really like we were sailing the stormy seas. The plastic sheet rippled violently, like a sail, and the tree-tops buckled and thrashed in the wind. After two days, the river burst its banks and flooded into the neighboring fields, and a few of the houses at the bottom of the hill had to be evacuated.

By the end of the third day, my father finished the walls. He had worked more or less without a break, using a hurricane lamp throughout the night, and while the rain may have pounded the plastic sheet into submission and our garden may have turned into a swamp, it started to look like we might survive the storm. We had saved the floorboards and most of the carpet, and the ceiling plaster had miraculously held. My mother cooked the first hot meal of the week and we gathered in the kitchen to eat it. We were incredibly exhausted, and my father's hands shook as he lifted his fork. He didn't say a word, but I could tell he was proud that his family had faced adversity so well. In his yellow raincoat and hat, he looked like an old sea captain who had somehow managed to save his boat from sinking.

"I was listening to the weather forecast on the radio," he said finally. "The storm should be over tomorrow afternoon."

"Thank God!" my mother said. "I really thought the ceilings were going to collapse!"

"That's because you always anticipate the worst," my father scolded. "Things are never as bad as you expect them to be. In a funny kind of way, the storm has been beneficial. It forced us to get the walls up quickly. Now all we have to do is tile the roof!"

This was a classic example of my father's crazy optimism. My dad, by all accounts, had lived a terrible life. Not only had he grown up in the most abject poverty, but he had been forced to work in the coal mines as a teenager and had been buried alive on two occasions. He had struggled through university and was just beginning to settle into his government job as an engineer when the Russian invasion dashed his hopes and dreams. In spite of this, he was bewilderingly positive. Many people would have resented driving taxis for a living, but my father convinced himself that he really loved the work. He paid a friendly policeman to issue him false papers and cheerfully drove around Prague under the full scrutiny of the STB. He was pulled over and interrogated many times, but the secret police never thought to question his license. Despite the obvious danger, he enjoyed the challenge of making a living on his own terms.

"Nothing like hard work to make you sleep well at night!" he would declare. "When I go to bed, I sleep the sleep of the righteous!"

WE ATE OUR HOT DINNER and went upstairs to the living room. It was still raining heavily, and I watched my father crawl under the piano. He got down on all fours and inched his way toward the mattress, and my mother had to massage his back and shoulders before he was able to relax enough to lie down properly.

I fell asleep the moment I lay down in my cot, and was awakened later by the sound of my father running up the stairs. He was shining a flashlight around the room, his voice unusually urgent. I immediately knew that something terrible had happened.

"Get up, Jana!" I heard him whisper. "Quickly! The kitchen is ankle deep in water!"

"What?" my mother said sleepily, sitting up and banging her head against the underside of the keyboard.

"We're flooded!" my dad said hoarsely. "Don't ask me how, we just are!"

We ran downstairs to survey the damage, and it was worse than any scenario my mother could have dreamed up. It turned out that an underground creek ran the whole way down the hill, and the flood had made it swell up and burst through the foundation trench my father had dug between the house and the garage. Water poured from the trench, and it was like we had a mountain stream gushing from one end of the house to the other. The force of the water had stripped all the topsoil off the garden, and the kitchen and Mr. Kozel's old apartment were flooded.

A thick layer of clay covered everything in sight, and our backyard was starting to slide down the hill.

"It's washing away the foundations of the house!" my father cried. "We're going to have to dig drains or else the house will collapse!"

"Ježis Marja!" My mother turned pale.

My father sprang into action. He gave my mother a hoe and sent her to dig a drainage ditch in the garden. Then he took Klara and me into the kitchen, gave us each a bucket, and told us to bail as much water as we could out of the window. Finally, he threw off his shirt and leaped into the foundation trench. Wielding a mattock and a spade, he attacked the muddy clay with all his might, attempting to block the creek. It was such a futile task. The water was too strong, and he quickly realized that the only thing he could do was try and save the foundations of the house by diverting the water around them. He dug a network of drains, but for every two spadefuls of clay he threw out, one would immediately slide back. He wedged pieces of wood to stop the drain walls from collapsing, and shoveled clay without a break well into the morning.

Klara and I bailed frantically in the kitchen. I was too small to lift the buckets, so we had a system where I would fill the empty one with a saucepan while my sister tipped the full one out the window. We worked as quickly as we could, but the water kept rising. After four or five hours of filling and lifting, we were dizzy with fatigue. The rain showed no sign of letting up, and my sister and I were crying as we worked. Eventually, my father burst into the room.

"Klara! We're not going to make it on our own!" he said. "You're going to have to run and ask the neighbors for help!"

Asking for help was not something my father did easily, but there was no mistaking the desperation in his voice. My sister abandoned the buckets and ran out into the rain, while my dad went back to digging drains. I was left alone in the kitchen with my little saucepan. I stood on a chair to empty the saucepan out the window, but the water had risen past my knees, and when I accidentally stood on the floor, it completely filled my rubber boots. I became very frightened and went outside to find my mother.

"Mum!" I cried. "The water's too high!"

My mother looked up from the drain she had been digging. Her face was splattered with mud and it looked like she had been crying, too. Her ditch had closed up behind her, and she looked defeated.

"Come here, sweetie," she said.

I sloshed my way through the muddy backyard, and was halfway to my mother when my rubber boots were sucked into the clay. Unable to move, I cried out in terror. My mother dropped her hoe and waded through the mud to liberate me. She grabbed me under the arms and pulled so hard, my feet popped out of my boots. The mud made a greedy slurping noise and the boots disappeared beneath the ground forever. We never saw them or my father's hoe again.

My mother carried me to the back doorstep as Klara returned from the neighborhood in tears.

"I knocked at every door in our street but nobody answered," she sobbed. "No one came to the door."

"Maybe they weren't home," my mother said.

"Of course they were!" my sister said angrily. "The lights were on in all of their houses!"

My dad climbed out of the ditch and staggered over. He was covered in mud from head to toe.

"Well?" he said expectantly.

"I went to every single one of the neighbors, Dad. Nobody answered. The only people who came to the door were the old ladies, but their sons are all in Prague. No one wants to help us."

"You went to the Acorns and the Haseks?" my father said incredulously.

"Yes. Their lights were on, but they didn't answer the door," my sister said.

My father's eyes were bright yellow. He wiped his forehead with the back of his hand.

"I see," he said quietly.

"So we're on our own, then," my mother sniffed.

"That's right. We're on our own," my father growled.

He threw a muddy arm around my mother's waist and pressed her tightly against his chest, and without saying another word, he turned on his heel and went back to his drains.

THE DAYS RUSHED BY IN A BLUR. My sister and I must have bailed several swimming pools' worth of water out of the kitchen, and my mother dug ditch after ditch until the mud eventually stopped closing up behind her. My father worked like a madman, shoveling clay until the sky finally cleared. Drawing on a startling reserve of energy, he single-handedly battled the forces of nature to stop our house from collapsing, and in the end the flood abated and the underground creek soaked back into the ground. Our house stayed firm on its foundations, which was more than we could say for the backyard. Every single flower bed and shrub had been carried away by the mudslide, and the fence at the bottom of the yard was ruined. Stones from my mother's rock garden jutted out at all angles from a thick crust of mud, and the sand and cement powder had fused together into a solid block of concrete. Our initial joy at overcoming the flood was replaced by numb disbelief at the sheer size of the loss. It would take weeks of digging and cleaning and salvaging before we would be in a position to continue building, and there was no way we would finish the roof before winter.

We spent the next couple of days recovering. My father lay under the piano for a very long time, until the smell of the mud drove him back into action. The kitchen and Mr. Kozel's apartment were covered in a rich layer of clay and dirt, and a thick organic stench permeated the whole house. My mother and Klara washed and scrubbed the downstairs walls, but the real problem was the backyard. It looked and smelled terrible.

My father came outside and lit himself a cigarette.

"You know," he said thoughtfully, "one of the things I've always wanted to do is make the backyard flat. I never liked the way it sloped down the hill. The way it is now, we could probably level it out without too much trouble. What do you think?"

My mother looked at him as though he was insane.

"My rose garden!" she spluttered. "My peach and lemon trees!"

"We'll plant new ones," he said decisively. "If we could get a spade truck down here before the clay hardens, we could dig the yard out further, make the whole thing nice and level, and then plant a layer of topsoil above it."

"Would that be difficult?" my sister asked him.

"Not really. The main thing is to get on top of it quickly. I'll nip down to the pub and try to find a few workers, and then I'll see if I can borrow a spade truck from one of the cooperatives in Radotin."

"Do you think they'll lend you one?" my mother frowned. "After the floods, I'm sure all the cooperative trucks will have been spoken for. You'll be lucky if you can find one, let alone get one for free."

"I have a couple of leads," my dad said cheerfully. "There's one old farmer in particular who owes me a favor. Now might be a good time to collect." He reached down and ruffled my hair. "Would you like to come to the pub with me?"

"Which one?" I said nervously.

"The Hotel Kazin," my father smiled.

There were three pubs in Cernosice: the Hotel Slanka, the Under the Forest Pub, and the Hotel Kazin, which literally translates as the "Rotten" pub.

In Czech, *kazit* means "to rot," so *kazin* is technically a place where rotten things are kept. Appropriately enough, the Rotten pub was where the town's National Committee staged its Communist events. It was a large and popular hotel, featuring two bars, a restaurant, and a small ballroom at the back. On Friday and Saturday nights there was a disco for young people, but the social core of the Rotten Pub largely consisted of the correct-line Communist families who had been running the town since the 1948 putsch.

I understood, from a very early age, that my family wasn't welcome at the Hotel Kazin. It had to do with my parents' expulsion from the party. After the Czech cabinet signed the normalization agreement endorsing the Red Army's invasion in 1968, my father resigned from the Ministry of Foreign Affairs in protest and disgust. He joined my mother at the Economic Institute and worked there for six months, until the institute's normalization committee called him in for an interview and presented him with a document similar to the one the Russians had forced our government to sign in Moscow. The document required him to agree that the progressive politics of the Prague Spring were counterrevolutionary and that a return to Soviet-style communism was in the country's best interests. My dad was interviewed by a seven-person committee that quietly and patiently laid out the terms of the document, read him a long list of all the people he knew who had already signed it, and told him, in no uncertain terms, exactly to which level of hell he would descend if he refused to sign.

My father had known that the committee would call him, and had plenty of time to consider his response. He had a wife and child to protect, and, more important, he had an insider's knowledge of the system. The committee didn't need to threaten him. He knew the dangers all too well. In spite of this, when the time came, he said simply, "No. I cannot possibly sign an agreement I don't agree with," and from that day, April 13, 1970, he went directly to the underclass. He was expelled from the party, fired from the Economic Institute, and demoted from his rank of captain in the army. My mother also declined to sign and was expelled from the party shortly after my dad, but she kept her job at the institute because her bosses weren't sure how much influence she had with the Red Countess. She was tolerated at work, but she made her coworkers nervous. In the strange psychology of the times, the small minority of dissidents who refused to sign the normalization agreement were really hated by the majority who signed. The Russians obviously had no business in our country, but the anger we felt at having to agree with their presence was quickly channeled politically and directed at easy targets. My dad had been an important man in Cernosice, but the second he was expelled from the party, the town wasted no time in aligning itself with the Red Countess. Even after we won our court case and Kveta had left town for good (to the town's great relief, it should be noted), the Communist families of Cernosice continued to shun my parents.

Nowhere was this more evident than at the Hotel Kazin. It was just around the corner from the National Committee Headquarters, and its front bar was the watering hole of the local Politburo. If you were part of the system, you could make your bureaucratic problems disappear at the pub. Failing that, you had to wait in line for hours at the National Committee, and if you were an enemy of the state, the hours could turn into days. There was nothing the town bureaucrats loved more than trying to bury my dad in paperwork, but he was very good at working around them. He was also very intimidating. A well-known fact about my father was that you could only push him so far. If things came to a serious head, he would win at all costs, and very few people had the courage to confront him directly. He was denounced anonymously instead, and on the occasions where he knew who had informed on him, he would go to the Rotten pub for a beer and take his time drinking it. The front bar would become extremely quiet until he left.

We may have been unwelcome at the Hotel Kazin, but it was the one place where workers could be found at any given hour, so we drove down the hill and parked outside. My dad often took me along when he cut deals in town, because a man with a little girl beside him was a lot harder to refuse than a man without one. I had learned to sit still and not interrupt him as he talked. He had what we call in Czech a "sweet voice," which was particularly deadly where women were concerned.

The front bar fell silent as we walked in. A small group of men from the neighborhood sat at a long table near the doorway, and they nodded apprehensively as my father growled hello. He walked over to the bar, ordered a beer for himself and a glass of lemonade for me, and then he made the extraordinary (but calculated) move of sitting down at the same table as the men. There was an embarrassed silence. The men studied their beer glasses and cleared their throats nervously.

"Heard you had some trouble with the rain," one of the men ventured after the suspense became too great.

"That's right," my father growled. "The house nearly slid down the hill. I was lucky to save it. And now I'm looking for a few men to help me save the backyard."

The men squirmed in their seats. Almost in unison, they reached for their cigarettes and lit them, continuing to stare at their glasses while they smoked.

"I wouldn't expect you to do it for free," my dad continued. "I can pay up to twenty crowns an hour."

The men's eyes widened imperceptibly. A few of them appeared to consider the offer. But the word of our damaged garden had obviously spread. No one was in any hurry to volunteer for such a labor-intensive job.

My father watched the men impassively.

"Okay." He put his beer glass on the table. "Thirty an hour. That's my final offer."

His face betrayed nothing, but he was offering more money than we really could afford. The going price for labor was fifteen crowns a hour, so my father was being uncommonly generous. If the men were to accept, my mother would have to start serving our meals on saucers.

"We'd like to help you, Jarda," the man who spoke first said cautiously. "But we have our own work to do. The rain has damaged our houses as well, and we're really very busy."

"Terribly busy," the other men muttered.

"No offense or anything," the first man said hastily. "It's just, you know, there's lots of work to be done."

"Lots and lots of work," the other men agreed.

My father looked at the row of empty beer glasses in front of them, and snorted mirthlessly. "I see," he growled. "Well, I guess I'd better let you get on with it then."

We returned to the car and drove back up the hill, and my dad went out into the backyard and stared at the trees. The forest side of our garden was lined by a thick row of trees inside the fence. The fence had a side gate that we hardly ever used, and my dad lit a cigarette and squinted thoughtfully at the gate and the trees. After a few minutes of smoking and squinting, he went up to the garage and came back with a tape measure. He got me to hold the end of the tape for him and we walked from one tree to the next, measuring the space between them.

"What are you doing, Dad?"

"I'm deciding which tree to cut down," he explained. "If no one wants to help us, I'll do the work myself. All I have to do is find someone willing to lend me a spade truck, and then I can ask Tomas Glatz if I can borrow his chain saw. After that, it's simply a matter of cutting down this tree so we can drive the truck into our yard."

He slapped the trunk of a big silver yew that was actually the nicest tree in our garden. A woodpecker had made its nest inside the trunk, and I loved to listen to the hollow rat-a-tat-tat of its beak every morning. The flood had driven the bird away, but I hoped it might come back soon, and I spent the rest of the afternoon wondering what would happen if the woodpecker came back and found his nest missing.

I voiced my concern at the kitchen table that evening.

"I wish you didn't have to cut down that tree, Dad. If the woodpecker comes back, he won't have anywhere to live."

"You want to cut down a tree?" my mother asked.

"I don't have a choice," my father shrugged. "The garden is completely fenced in. The only way I can get a spade truck into the yard is by chopping down the silver yew near the gate."

My mother's eyes widened in horror. "The silver yew?" she cried. "That's my birth tree! My father planted it on the day I was born!"

"The firs and pines are too big to cut down," my dad told her. "The yew is younger and it has a thinner trunk. It's the only tree near the gate that I can handle by myself."

"The yew is younger because it was planted on my birthday!" my mother roared. "I would rather have a foul-smelling mud pile in the backyard than see you cut down that tree! You had better come up with another solution, Jarda Furman, because I'll divorce you if you so much as touch that silver yew! I'm serious! You leave that tree alone!"

None of us doubted that my mother was serious. She was gentle and sweet, but she was also very stubborn. Whenever she had her mind set on something, she would fight to the death before she compromised, and my father knew better than to argue with her at the table. It would have been easier to level the yard by hand than to talk my mother into changing her mind, so my father did what he always did, which was change the subject.

"The truck is the least of our worries," he said. "The real problem is that no one wants to work. I think the word has got around that our backyard's a mess. The men at the pub were even shiftier than usual. They said no to thirty crowns an hour."

"Can we afford thirty crowns?" my mother frowned.

"Probably not. Although I do have some deutsche marks to exchange. If I can get a good rate, we might be okay, but I think it's more a matter of whether we can find someone who wants to work in the mud."

"It smells horrible," my sister grimaced.

"That's because it's still wet," my dad told her. "Once it dries, the smell will improve, but the mud will be ten times harder to dig. I'll get up early and look for workers tomorrow, otherwise we might have to leave the whole yard until spring."

We woke up early the following morning and were down in the kitchen eating breakfast when the front doorbell rang. My parents looked at each other. The doorbell had pretty much stopped ringing since April 1970, and the few remaining friends who did come to visit tended to call first. These days, the only people who turned up at the front door unannounced were local bureaucrats or the secret police, and as a consequence we all went up to the front door together.

"Who is it?" my father called out.

"Workers!" a muffled voice replied. "We heard you're looking for people to work in your yard!"

My dad cautiously opened the door, and there, on our doorstep, were three smiling men.

"*Dobry den,* Mr. Engineer!" one of the men said cheerily. "Allow me to introduce myself. I'm Mr. Pinos and these are my friends Mr. Schlosarek and Mr. Moucha. We're qualified laborers looking to do a bit of work on the side, and word has it you've suffered some water damage as a result of these floods."

"More than a bit," my father said gruffly. "Half the backyard slid down the hill."

"Mind if we take a look?" Mr. Pinos suggested.

A bemused smile appeared on my father's face. "Sure," he said. "Let me put on my boots."

He winked at my mother, put on his boots, and led the workers around the side of the house. I followed my mother and Klara downstairs to the kitchen. They both seemed oddly subdued in spite of the miraculous appearance of Mr. Pinos and his friends.

"What do you think, Mum?" my sister asked doubtfully.

"I'm not sure," my mother replied. "Let's wait and see what your father has to say."

After we had finished our breakfast, Klara took a bucket of hot water and a sponge and disappeared into Mr. Kozel's old apartment, while my mother and I went to see what my dad and the workers were up to. We found the three men standing in the mud, listening attentively as my father explained what needed to be done. Mr. Pinos and his friends seemed eager to get started. They had brand-new tools and tool belts and boots, and behaved in a more professional way than any of the *melouch* workers we had hired in the past. The smell of the mud didn't seem to bother them, and they looked very cheerful and competent. When my dad told them that he wanted to spend the next three days loosening the mud with pickaxes before the spade truck arrived, they didn't seem the slightest bit bothered by the amount of work. They shook hands with my dad and went to retrieve their tools from the tiny flatbed truck they had parked in the street. As soon as they had disappeared, my mother and father had a quick conference.

"Are these people who I think they are?" my mother asked.

"Oh, yes," my dad said calmly. "You only need to look at their hands to see they're not laborers. And didn't you just love the way they called me 'mister' instead of 'comrade'? They're definitely on the STB payroll. They might even be agents."

"But why? Why are they bothering us?"

"It probably has something to do with the Germans I drove around the week before the flood," my father shrugged. "I had a new guy in the cab who seemed to know an awful lot about the way things work in Prague. The cops had two cars outside his hotel."

"*Ježis Marja!*" my mother cried. "That's the last thing we need. As if we don't have enough problems already."

"You're putting the cart before the horse, Jana," my dad said mischievously. "We have plenty of problems, and our laborer friends might very well help us solve them."

"How?" my mother asked. "What do you intend to do?"

My father pulled out his cigarettes and lit one with an aggressive flourish.

"I intend to put them to work," he grinned.

BY THE END OF THE FIRST DAY, Mr. Pinos and his friends were already regretting the hazardous nature of their mission. They had been deliberately vague on the subject of how they found out we were looking for workers, so my dad was able to haggle them down to fifteen crowns an hour by simply pretending that his offer in the Rotten pub had never taken place. The three men looked at each other and were about to contradict him, when they realized that this would require them to name the person who had referred them. Instead, they took a deep breath, accepted my dad's terms, and spent the rest of the day loosening mud under his close supervision.

While this was going on, my mother called Klara and me up to the living room and briefed us on the situation. We were to be friendly to the laborers, but the minute they started asking questions about anything other than the work, we were to politely excuse ourselves and leave as quickly as possible. It would only be a matter of time before the men realized that their cover had been blown, and when they did, they would stop helping us in the garden. So the object of the exercise was to make Mr. Pinos and his friends believe that they were gathering useful information as they dug out our backyard. To this end, my father would send Klara down to the Under the Forest pub for beer in the late afternoons, and he would get the laborers drunk and tell them stories. Apart from that, he worked them tirelessly. My mother served them their lunches on little plates, and they spent their days loosening and shoveling mud while my dad tracked down the farmer who owed him a favor, and arranged to hire his tractor for a week.

The STB must have been very interested in my dad's German passengers, because the smiling Mr. Pinos appeared on our doorstep every morning for the next week and a half. Mr. Schlosarek and Mr. Moucha tried to match his enthusiasm, but my father's merciless treatment quickly wiped the smiles off their faces. In the course of drinking with them, he had learned that Mr. Pinos had recently been in a car accident and was very nervous behind the wheel; Mr. Schlosarek suffered from a weak stomach and was prone to severe bouts of nausea; and Mr. Moucha was terrified of heights. My father tailored the work to suit their various phobias. After the backyard had been prepared for the tractor, Mr. Schlosarek was delegated the responsibility of salvaging roof tiles from the foul-smelling mud, while Mr. Moucha was sent up to the truss to prepare the roof for tiling. While they did this, my dad would take Mr. Pinos for a drive. They would roar down the hill and return with construction materials around the same time Klara would be carrying her beer pitcher up from the Under the Forest pub, and the combination of the bad roads and my father's driving made poor Mr. Pinos even more miserable than his colleagues. The three men would stagger up to their truck and compare notes, then grimly return to our yard and spend the next couple of hours drinking toasts to the Czechoslovakian working class.

"Excellent work as usual, comrades!" My dad would raise his glass. "You men are a credit to your profession."

The three laborers stuck at their jobs long enough for my father to not only salvage the yard but to prepare all the materials he needed to tile and insulate the roof before the winter. We had a quiet weekend, and then Mr. Pinos and his friends reappeared on Monday, determined to wage a week-long assault on my father's taxi-driving secrets. My mother was back at the Economic Institute, and the local school had reopened after the flood (to Klara's great relief), so it was just my dad, Barry, and me supervising. Mr. Pinos, Mr. Moucha, and my father worked on the roof, while I helped Mr. Schlosarek in the backyard. Mr. Schlosarek would dig tiles out of the mud and I would wash them and stack them by the side of the house. I quite enjoyed it in spite of the smell and Mr. Schlosarek's bad temper.

Mr. Schlosarek was actually quite nice. He and Mr. Moucha were genuine laborers who worked as informers on the side. Mr. Pinos was a professional informer who had been given an apartment in Prague by the STB (we found this out after the revolution) and had coerced the other two into helping him on his intelligence-gathering missions. Mr. Schlosarek was a roof tiler by trade, and every day he and Mr. Moucha would practically beg my father to let them change positions, but my dad would move too fast and make too much noise to hear them, and poor Mr. Schlosarek would end up in the mud. He poured aftershave onto a handkerchief and tied it around his face like a bank robber, and then he ventured out into the yard to dig tiles out of the clay with a pitchfork. There were a surprising number of tiles scattered throughout the garden, and we were able to salvage most of them in the course of the week, but the work took its toll on Mr. Schlosarek's stomach. His face had taken on a greenish hue and by Wednesday afternoon he was too sick to drink beer.

"I don't think I'll be coming in tomorrow," he told my dad and Mr. Pinos. "I feel really sick."

"That's what you said yesterday," my father said cheerfully. "Have a beer! The vitamin B will do you good."

"I can't," Mr. Schlosarek moaned. "You should have put me on the roof! This mud has completely turned my stomach. I haven't been able to eat in three days!"

"We'll put you on the roof tomorrow," my dad assured him. "We have to attach the gutters, which is going to be a difficult and dangerous job."

"It is?" Mr. Moucha said nervously.

"Oh, yes. We don't have enough scaffolding to go the whole way around the house, so we're going to have to use a ladder. We might have to wedge it into the space between the cab and the bed of your truck."

Mr. Pinos frowned. "Why is that?"

"I've measured all the ladders and they're a couple of feet too short. What I'm thinking is, we can drive your truck down into the yard, wedge a ladder behind the cab, and drive around the house with one man on the ladder and the others on the roof handing the gutter down to him."

"That sounds completely insane," Mr. Moucha gasped.

"You want to drive the truck into the yard?" Mr. Pinos said incredulously. "Do you think it will fit through those trees?"

"Of course," my father snorted. "I've measured it already."

Mr. Schlosarek shook his head. "I'm staying in bed tomorrow. I can't believe I worked in that mud for three days with my condition. I'm finished!"

After the three men had left for the day, my father surveyed the backyard and pronounced it ready for the tractor. The truss was prepared for the roof tiles, and once the gutter had been attached, he was confident that he would be able to finish the house and yard by himself if the laborers abandoned their mission. He still hadn't solved the problem of how to drive the tractor through the row of trees, but he intended to stage an experimental run with Mr. Pinos's truck the following morning.

"What if it doesn't fit, Dad?" I asked him.

"We'll cross that bridge when we get to it," he smiled. "In situations like this, I've always found that brute force and ignorance can work wonders."

"Do you think Mr. Schlosarek will come tomorrow?"

"No," my dad replied. "Do you?"

"No," I agreed.

When Mr. Pinos and Mr. Moucha arrived at work the following morning, Mr. Schlosarek was unsurprisingly absent, and Mr. Moucha seemed determined not to climb any ladders, especially ladders attached to moving vehicles. Barry and I watched from a distance as the two men attempted to reason with my dad, but it was only a matter of time before Mr. Pinos was maneuvering his truck up the walking path and preparing to drive it down through the forest and into our backyard.

Mr. Pinos's truck was extremely tiny, with a two-seat cab and a bed the size of a small desktop. It was ideal for Communist-style transportation, as it gave an excuse to its driver to make lots and lots of trips between factory and work site. My dad's experimental run was a success, and the truck miraculously managed to squeeze between an overgrown fir tree and my mother's silver yew. But it was obvious he would have to find another way of getting the tractor into the yard.

"That went well," my dad told the two men when the truck was safely in the yard. "Why don't you take a break while I bring my ladder down from the garage?"

"I draw the line at working in unsafe conditions," Mr. Moucha said firmly. "Attaching the ladder to the truck is madness. I simply won't do it!"

"Mr. Moucha," my father said in his "sweet voice." "If you and Mr. Pinos had a bigger ladder, none of this would be a problem. We're working with limited resources here, and I have to say, for a couple of experienced laborers like yourselves, you do strike me as being ill equipped for the job."

"What are you trying to suggest?" Mr. Pinos blustered.

"Not a thing," my father said innocently. "Just let me get my ladder, and let's see if we can improvise a solution."

Unfortunately for the two men, my dad had measured the ladder and the truck very carefully, and he had indeed devised a clever way of wedging the ladder between the cab and the bed. While Mr. Pinos and Mr.

Moucha looked on with sinking hearts, my father tied the ladder firmly to the cab and then got Mr. Pinos to drive the truck to the side of the house.

This was, of course, a ridiculous way to work. And my father did actually have scaffolding materials, but he knew that the time it would take to erect and pull down a scaffold was more time than he could reasonably expect Mr. Pinos and his colleague to stay on the job. The ladder was quicker and easier. But it was also much more dangerous, and despite his loud protestations, poor Mr. Moucha eventually found himself at the top of the ladder, bolting six-foot lengths of gutter to the bottom of the truss. As a concession to his fear of heights, my dad climbed up behind him and tied his legs to the ladder, and for the rest of the morning, Mr. Moucha's screams could be heard throughout the valley as he completed a slow revolution of our house.

In the meantime, I helped my mother prepare lunch for the men. We set up a table in what had once been Mr. Kozel's living room, where the men could eat and drink beer with my dad. I carefully carried the small plates of sandwiches to the table and then I set the knives and forks, which was something I had recently learned to do. I had to stand on a chair to do it and was admiring my handiwork when I heard Mr. Moucha coming down from the roof. It sounded like he was shouting. When he was safely on the ground, I watched him remove his brand-new tool belt and throw it in the mud.

"I don't know which of you is worse!" he roared. "You"—he pointed at my dad—"for coming up with such an idiotic plan, or you"—he pointed at Mr. Pinos—"for going along with it! You guys are stark raving mad! I'm catching the train home, and don't bother coming to pick me up in the morning!"

Mr. Pinos tried to calm his comrade down, but it was obvious that Mr. Moucha had passed the point of no return. We went up to the garage and watched him storm off down the street. He really did seem very upset.

"Well, that's a shame," my father said. "I quite liked Mr. Moucha. I liked both your colleagues, as a matter of fact. I do hope you'll be able to work with them again."

"I hope so, too," Mr. Pinos said grimly.

When Mr. Pinos knocked on our door the next morning, he made no pretense at smiling. He and my dad had spent a very tense couple of hours getting his truck out of the yard, and its doors had been badly scratched in the process. He had lost his coworkers and had made absolutely no progress ferreting out information for the STB, so my father decided to go easy on him. When I came out into the garden, I found them drinking beer and staring thoughtfully at the trees. It was ten o'clock in the morning.

"Hello, Mr. Pinos!" I said. "You're all by yourself today."

"That's right, young lady." Mr. Pinos sighed. "Never send a couple of boys to do a man's job."

"Mr. Schlosarek and Mr. Moucha weren't boys," I pointed out. "They were grown-ups like you."

"Yes, but when the going got tough, they ran for their beds," Mr. Pinos snorted. "At the end of the day, when you sign on for a job, delivering the goods is the only measure of how seriously you and your work can be taken."

"Another beer?" my dad interrupted.

"Please," Mr. Pinos said. "So you see, the reason my colleagues work for me instead of the other way around is simply because I see things through to the end. My reputation depends on it."

He watched my father disappear into the kitchen.

"Your dad tells me he's been doing a lot of taxi driving lately," he said casually. "I guess he sometimes brings people home with him late in the night, right?"

"Oooh! I have to go now!" I exclaimed, and ran inside the house.

For the rest of the day, my father and Mr. Pinos walked up and down the row of trees, drinking beer and discussing various strategies for getting the tractor in the yard. At one point, my dad went up to the garage and returned with Mr. Glatz's chain saw, and a lot of time was spent studying tree trunks and ferrying beer from the kitchen. By the early after-noon, Mr. Pinos's good humor appeared to have returned, and he and my father were in high spirits as they ate my mother's sandwiches. Empty beer bottles littered the garden, and while my dad hadn't made much progress solving the problem of the tractor, I did notice that he and Mr. Pinos kept coming back to my mother's silver yew. It was a pretty, slen-der tree that could be cut down very easily, and it was perfectly positioned in front of the side gate. The rest of the trees were much too big to con-trol, and if they fell the wrong way, they could damage the house, whereas the yew could be cut in such a way that it would fall into the forest through the open gate. Mr. Pinos was very much of the opinion that this was the only way to solve my father's problem.

"I keep thinking I should take down the fence," my dad muttered for the hundredth time.

"You're crazy!" Mr. Pinos told him. "Taking down the fence is a seri-ous job, not to mention even trying to cut down one of those firs or pines. You'll wreck your house!"

"Or I'll wreck my marriage," my father said ruefully. "I can't believe there's no other way around this."

The two men continued to stare at the trees until the blare of a horn announced the tractor's arrival. We went up to the garage and found a massive flatbed truck reversing slowly up our street. Sitting on the bed was an extremely old tractor that looked like it hadn't been driven in years. My father had made two very long phone calls arranging to hire this semiderelict vehicle, and judging by the way the farmer had haggled, my dad had assumed he was dealing with a first-rate piece of machinery. He gaped at the tractor in astonishment.

"You've got to be joking," he growled.

An old man and a teenage boy climbed out of the truck, and as the man wandered over to talk to my dad, the boy busied himself at the back of the flatbed, arranging a ramp for the tractor to drive down. As Barry and I watched, taking care to keep away from what was quickly shaping up to be a heated argument, the boy lowered the ramp and backed the tractor down to the start of the walking path.

My dad, the old man, and Mr. Pinos walked over to the tractor.

"*Ježis Marja,* it's ancient!" my father groaned.

"It's old, yes, but it works just fine," the old farmer reassured him again. "I've plowed many a field with this tractor, let me tell you."

The farmer was obviously the boy's grandfather, and he reminded me of Mr. Doskar, my grandmother's fiancé. His hands trembled, too. It would have been many years since either he or the tractor had been anywhere near a field that needed plowing.

"The question is," the old man wheezed, "how are you going to get the tractor into your yard?"

My father squared his shoulders to take the weight and responsibility of a tough decision, and pointed his chain saw in the direction of the trees.

"Okay, I'll cut the silver yew and you help me move it," he told Mr. Pinos. Then he turned to the farmer. "When we're done, you can drive the tractor through the gate."

A look of alarm appeared on the farmer's face.

"Drive it?" he said. "Oh, I couldn't. I'm too old. I couldn't possibly drive it through the forest."

"Fine," my dad shrugged impatiently. "Get your grandson to do it."

"He doesn't have a license," the old man said quickly. "He's not yet sixteen."

"So?" my father asked. "He drove the tractor off the truck without any difficulty."

"He wasn't supposed to," the farmer told him. "He's really not allowed to drive. Are you?"

"Not really," the boy admitted.

My father glared at the hapless collection of men standing around him.

"Get the tractor ready," he snapped at Mr. Pinos. "And you come with me," he told the boy.

Mr. Pinos opened his mouth to protest, but the look on my father's face made him close it. He climbed behind the wheel of the tractor and asked the farmer to explain the gears and levers, while the boy, Barry, and I followed my dad to the gate and watched him apply brute force and ignorance to my mother's silver yew. With a slow and terribly sad creaking of timber, my mother's birth tree fell into the forest without touching the gate, and our garden was suddenly a lot less attractive. My father trimmed the stump with his chain saw, and then he and the boy moved the fallen trunk so that Mr. Pinos and the tractor had a clear shot at the yard. The tree had been growing for over thirty years, and we had cut it down in less than thirty minutes.

"I'm very sorry, Mr. Woodpecker," I said under my breath. "I hope you find another place to live in."

I led Barry away from the gate as my dad cupped his hands and called out to Mr. Pinos. "Okay. Come on down," he ordered. "Take it nice and slowly. You should be able to drive over the stump without too much trouble."

We looked up at the path and listened to Mr. Pinos as he reluctantly revved the tractor's engine. He had been very nervous driving his own truck down this incline, but the tractor was ten times more frightening. It was bigger and heavier and Soviet-made, and, as Mr. Pinos quickly discovered, completely without brakes. A small detail the farmer had neglected to share.

I held Barry's collar and watched. Mr. Pinos started quite slowly but quickly gathered speed, and by the time he was halfway to the gate, the tractor was literally bouncing through the forest. It made a tremendous amount of noise, and as it crashed and rattled toward the house, I could see Mr. Pinos in the cab. His eyes were very wide and his mouth was open. He held the wheel at arm's length and screamed the whole way down the hill, and I leaped back in amazement as the tractor shot through the gate, jolted over the top of the tree stump, and hurtled toward the stone fence on the opposite side of the garden. It looked for all the world like Mr. Pinos would crash, but as he slewed across the mud pile, he did a remarkable thing. Somehow, he managed to activate the primitive digging arm, and as my dad, Barry, and I held our collective breath, he brought the arm over the top of the cabin and planted the spade in the mud directly in front of the front wheels. The tractor jerked violently. For an electrifying couple of seconds, it looked like it was going to somersault over the arm and keep going, but it didn't. The rear wheels flew up in the air and the entire machine stood on end, and then it slowly crashed back down to earth. We hurried over and found Mr. Pinos spread-eagled across the hood, his hands firmly grasping the steering wheel behind him. His mouth was still open and all the blood had drained from his face.

"That was incredible!" My father whistled. "Are you all right?"

"No brakes!" Mr. Pinos whispered. "The goddamn tractor didn't have any brakes!"

My dad had to pry his hands loose from the wheel and help him into Mr. Kozel's apartment. He told me to fetch some beer and pickles from the kitchen, and set about calming Mr. Pinos down.

I fetched two beers and a jar of pickles and then walked out into the yard, where I found the farmer and his grandson checking the tractor for damage. Once they had satisfied themselves that the digging arm still worked, they disappeared through the side gate and hastily climbed the hill to their truck, and I heard them start it a few minutes later, around the same time Mr. Pinos staggered out into the yard. Despite his remarks about seeing a job through to the end, it was obvious that his covert mission was over. Whatever the STB was paying him, it wasn't enough to compensate him for the life-threatening experience of working with my dad. He collected his tools and we helped him load his ladder into his truck, and he looked truly miserable as he drove off down the street. I could tell that he bitterly regretted the day he had knocked on our door.

I looked at my dad, who had a wistful smile on his face.

"Those three men just might have saved our house," he said thoughtfully. "I think the worst might be over."

There was a distant squeal of brakes from the bottom of the valley, and the smile disappeared from my father's face. My mother's train had just pulled into the station.

"Mum is going to be very upset that you cut down her tree," I said.

"You're right," my dad agreed. "The worst isn't over by any stretch of the imagination."

He grabbed Mr. Glatz's chain saw and tidied up the tree stump. Then we nervously awaited my mother's arrival. I had never seen my mother really angry before, but I somehow knew that it would be terrible. My father seemed to understand this as well. We stood beside the fallen tree like criminals, and Barry came over and sat down beside us. With his sad, bloodshot eyes, he looked even more guilty than my dad.

"We're going to get in a lot of trouble," I told him.

The words had scarcely left my mouth when a high-pitched howl floated down from the balcony. We looked up to see my mother disappearing into the living room. A few moments later, she burst out into the yard, her anguished cries increasing in pitch and volume. She ran furiously through the mud toward us, wobbling unsteadily in her high heels.

"How could you?" she shrieked. She raced over to my father and started to beat her fists against his chest. "You promised me you wouldn't touch it! You promised!"

"Janitchka," my dad said, using the diminutive of my mother's name. "I feel terrible about cutting down the tree, believe me, but I had to do it to save the garden. I'll take the wood to a sawmill and make you a nice bed out of the timber, okay?"

"Don't you 'Janitchka' me!" my mother roared. "A bed? You can take the wood and make me a coffin! Do you hear me? A coffin!"

She continued to scream and hit my father's chest, and then she whirled around and stalked back to the house. To my great surprise, my dad didn't follow her. He just sat down on the tree stump and lit himself a cigarette. I wasn't sure what to do, so I ran inside and found my mother throwing clothes into a suitcase. Her lips were tightly compressed and her face was very white, and there was a look in her eyes that I hadn't seen before. She packed her suitcase, and then she sat on the piano stool and cried for a very long time. I tiptoed over and put my arms around her knees.

"Please don't be angry, Mummy."

My mother didn't answer. When she had finished crying, she stood up and carried her suitcase to the door. If she had had somewhere to go, I'm pretty sure she would have left. But the sad truth was that she had no family or friends to turn to. She had made her bed and had no choice but to lie in it with her husband and children. While the adversity of being a dissident was often unbearable, it kept my parents together in many situations where they might have otherwise divorced. My mother stood at the door for a while with the suitcase in her hand, and then she looked at me and sighed.

"I should probably make you and Klara some dinner," she said. "If you go to the kitchen and get some onions from the pantry, I'll come down and join you in a few minutes."

We had a very tense dinner. My father tried to make cheerful conversation while my mother subjected him to the most withering of silences, and the second we had finished, she left the table and stormed upstairs. Klara, Dad, and I huddled together in the kitchen until we ran out of things to wash and dry, and then we summoned our courage and went up to the living room.

We found my mother reading a book under the piano. She had carried a single mattress down from the garage and positioned it on the opposite side of the pedal stand from the mattress she usually shared with my dad. My father crawled beneath the piano and attempted to reason with her, but she made it very clear that she would have nothing to do with him. In the end, he sent Klara and me up to the bathroom. We shared a bath and changed into our pajamas, and then my father came up in a very bleak mood. Without saying a word, he pulled himself up through the beams of the truss, and then he sat on the exposed roof, smoking cigarettes and looking out across the valley.

"*Dobrou noc,* Dad," I sniffed. "Night, night."

"*Dobrou noc,* Little Trumpet," he said gently. "Don't worry. Tomorrow is a new day. We'll wake up in the morning and everything will be back to normal, I promise."

"I hope so," I said tearfully.

I followed Klara downstairs and crawled into my cot. I felt terribly afraid. I understood that things were hard for my parents, but as long as they loved each other, the outside world didn't matter very much. When they fought, it was worse than an army of secret policemen sniffing around our house, and the image of my mother's suitcase beside the front door was so haunting I found it hard to fall asleep. After what seemed like hours, I heard my father come down from the roof and run himself a fresh bath. Some time after that, he crept into the living room and crawled beneath the piano, and then the whole room became very quiet and still.

I awoke to the familiar sound of birds chirping in the forest, and the warm, safe hum of my grandmother's piano. I opened my eyes and listened. There was no mistaking the sound of my dad moving around to the other side of the pedal stand. The piano sang as he bumped the frame with his shoulders, and I could hear him whispering to my mother in the same way he did every morning when he came home from work. After a moment's pause, I heard my mother whisper back, and I snuggled happily in my blankets as the predawn light seeped into the room.

It was indeed a new morning, and my dad had kept his promise.

We would wake up and face the day together as a family.

f o u r

THE SWAN

MY DAD WORKED TIRELESSLY on the roof for the next three months, padding the space between the rafters with big pillows of asbestos and laying all the tiles before the snow started to fall. Despite his efforts, we had a cold and austere winter. Our boiler and central heating remained broken, and the topsoil my father laid in the yard didn't mix well with the clay. Whenever it rained, the garden turned to mud, and countless pairs of shoes and boots were ruined. We had a nice, level yard that was impossible to walk on. Even when it was covered with snow, it was so sludgy and horrible that no one except my father was prepared to brave it.

Barry spent most of his time on Mr. Kozel's doorstep, howling indignantly until we let him in downstairs.

We spent our winter nights in the kitchen, watching television and drinking tea and hot soup, and I was delighted to see Barry on TV at Christmas once again. There was a carp in the bath and the Baby Jesus sneaked another tree into the house without my catching him. The highlight of

Christmas, though, was the morning my father took Klara and me up-stairs to see the bedroom he had built us. The walls were roughly plas-tered and would require a few coats of paint, but the room had a big window that looked out across the valley and there was plenty of space for both of us. My sister was particularly happy. She was fourteen years old and this was her first bedroom. She immediately claimed the space be-side the window and announced that she wanted to paint the walls yellow.

"When I catch my breath, I'll build you a room next door," my father told me.

"I like this bedroom!" I assured him. "And I like sharing with Klara. It's nice to have someone in the room with me at nighttime!"

"Nice for you," Klara said. "Some of us like to read or sleep when we're in bed. You just like to talk."

"I like to read and sleep, too, but I like to have someone there in case I get scared," I admitted.

A few weeks after Klara and I had settled into our new room, my mother woke up earlier than usual one morning and left the house while it was still dark. She returned home that evening with a mysterious smile on her face, and we later discovered that she had spent the morning stand-ing in the freezing cold, waiting to buy tickets for the National Theater Ballet Company's production of *Swan Lake*. Tickets for the performing arts were very cheap, but the price was offset by the long time you had to stand in line to buy them. Working-class families were usually too busy to wait, so the tickets that weren't automatically sent to high-ranking party officials tended to be snapped up by housewives and pensioners who would bring sleeping bags to the box office and camp out. On this oc-casion, my mother had managed to outwait the waiters, and she was re-warded with four excellent box seats, which was the family's present to me for my fourth birthday.

I was very excited about turning four. My dad had removed the bars of my cot so that I could sleep in a proper bed, like my sister, and when-ever he and I went driving, I would sit on the passenger seat instead of climbing into the space behind the gearbox. I was growing up quickly, even though I was still small for my age. The night of my birthday, my mother cooked a delicious dinner and then we took a bath and put on our best clothes. My father sucked in his tummy and squeezed into his old tuxedo, while my mother put on a lovely red silk dress and one of her exquisite hats. Despite the fact that we didn't have much money, my mother always looked great whenever she went out in Prague. She knew a good tailor who was able to work magic on the expensive clothes she had worn as a teenager. My mother still had the figure of a seventeen-year-old, so most of those clothes still fit. With a bit of clever tailoring, they could be altered to look like the most recent fashions. The material was of the highest quality, as the Red Countess had used her party connections to buy her daughters clothes made in Paris and Milan. All of my mother's dresses were at least fifteen years old, but she took such good care of them that she really was one of the best-dressed women in Prague. She knew how to match colors and accessories, and could throw on the most flamboyant of hats with an aristocratic carelessness. Hats were a big part of who my mother was. She wore them defiantly, knowing that they were symbolic of the capitalist values the party elite pretended to despise (while secretly raising their children to embrace them), and she would be damned if she was going to dress badly to keep a bunch of hypocrites in the Politburo happy.

When we were all ready, my father picked my mother up and carried her to the garage to save her shoes from the mud, and then we drove to Prague. The Smetana Theater was a small but elegant neoclassical building at the top of Wenceslaus Square. We walked through the lobby and up a wide marble staircase to the first floor, where we were intercepted by an old lady who inspected our tickets and led us to our box. Inside, I crawled into my mother's lap and pressed my chin against the velvet upholstering of the balustrade, looking out through the opera glasses my father had rented for ten crowns. Then the orchestra walked out into the pit and started to tune their instruments. Ripples ran across the curtain, and the enormous chandelier was slowly pulled up through a reverse trap-door. The lights dimmed, and I held my breath as the conductor appeared and tapped his baton on the stand. For a few moments nothing happened, and then the curtains drew open as a sad and beautiful overture surged up from the pit. Blue and white spotlights transformed the stage into a lake, and a flock of swans fluttered around the swan princess, Odette. As the music dipped and swelled, she began to dance on the silver surface of the lake, barely touching the stage with the points of her slippers. She was incredibly graceful, and it was just like watching a real swan gliding across the water. Then the kettledrums sounded, and the swans and Odette looked up in alarm. A moment later, a muscular prince bounded out onto the stage, and I almost dropped my opera glasses in astonishment. The prince was blond and handsome, and was exactly how I imagined a prince should be. I watched as he swept Odette off the ground and twirled her majestically above his head, and when he gently swung her back down to the stage, she seemed to be as much in love with him as I was. It was as though he had captured her heart with the grace and precision of his dancing, and now she couldn't take a step without swooning into his arms.

"I like the prince," I told my mother during intermission. "He's strong and handsome, like Prince Bajaja!"

"His name is Jaroslav Slavicky," my mother said, reading from the program. "He's the son of a famous composer."

"I would like to marry him," I announced. "If I married him, that would make me a princess, wouldn't it?"

"Maybe it would," my mother laughed. "But don't you think he'll be too old for you by the time you're ready to marry?"

"I hope not." That worried me. "How old is he now?"

"Shh," my mother whispered. The golden chandelier had disappeared again and the house lights were starting to dim.

I spent the next hour imagining that I was Odette up there dancing with Mr. Slavicky. My childhood (and my imagination) was greatly influenced by Czech fairy tales, but as I watched *Swan Lake*, it occurred to me that Mr. Slavicky was a real prince, even if he didn't come from a royal family and live in a castle. For the two and a half hours that he danced, his kingdom was the stage and the lake, and everyone in the Smetana Theater was transfixed by his performance. When the curtains finally closed and opened and the dancers moved forward to take their bows, I applauded as loudly as I could and continued clapping long after everybody else had finished. From that moment on, I knew that what I wanted most in the world was to become a ballet dancer. When we arrived home, I leaped out of the car and danced all the way from the garage to the front door, humming part of *Swan Lake* as I kicked off my muddy sandals. My parents watched with amusement, but Klara frowned and tapped the side of her head as though she thought I was crazy.

"I hope she's not going to start dancing all the time," she told my mother. "Talking I can put up with, but if it's going to be talking and dancing, our bedroom isn't big enough for both of us."

"I wouldn't worry," my mother replied. "I'm sure she'll wake up in the morning and find something else to do."

But my mother was wrong. The first thing I did when I climbed out of bed was try to stand on the tips of my toes. Then I began to dance. I danced to the sound of Radio Free Europe; to the marching band music that echoed out of the speakers mounted on every telegraph pole in the village; even to the squeal of my dad's circular saw. If it was quiet, I would dance to the melodies I invented in my head. I performed for Barry at least three times a day. He wasn't a very receptive audience, though. He would fall asleep before my performances ended, so I took to dancing for the old ladies instead. The cold weather had confined them to their apartments, so they were always happy to see me, and I would perform in their kitchens and living rooms while they sat in their armchairs doing their best to encourage me.

One day in early spring, I went down the street to show Mrs. Noskova my latest choreography, but when I came to her door, I was surprised to discover that it was locked. It had never been locked before, because Mrs.

Noskova couldn't open it and use her crutches at the same time. When I went next door to ask Mrs. Sokolova about her neighbor, she looked very sad and told me that Mrs. Noskova had gone away. Mrs. Sokolova and Mrs. Liskova said they would be happy to watch my new performance, so I danced for them in Mrs. Sokolova's apartment. Both ladies seemed terribly distraught. I tried my hardest to cheer them up, but on this occasion there was nothing I could do.

"I hope Mrs. Noskova comes back soon," I told them. "It doesn't seem right just seeing the two of you. It's much better when you're all together in the garden."

"We know, sweetie," Mrs. Liskova said tearfully.

A few weeks later, my mother took me into Prague with her to buy tickets for *Romeo and Juliet*. The box office opened at ten o'clock, but there was a crowd of people already waiting when we arrived at seven-thirty. I was very excited, and I couldn't wait to see Mr. Slavicky again. As we waited, I danced on the sidewalk and did my best to imitate a swan. The pensioners in line watched with amusement, and one of the women even asked my name.

"My name is Dominika," I told her. "And I'm going to be a dancer when I grow up!"

"Really?" she smiled. "Are you studying at one of the ballet schools?"

"No," I said. "I would like to, though. Do you know any ballet schools I could go to?"

"I'm afraid I don't," the lady replied. "But the woman in the box office might. Why don't you ask her?"

"That's a good idea! Mum, can we ask the ticket lady if there's a dancing school I can go to?"

"We'll see," my mother said patiently.

I danced until the theater doors finally opened and the long line snaked into the lobby. It took another hour before my mother and I reached the box office window.

"Are there any good tickets left for the *Romeo and Juliet*?" my mother asked the lady in the booth.

"I have a few tickets at the front," the lady shrugged. "How many do you want?"

She was a stern-looking woman with the indifferent manner of a typical Communist salesperson. As my mother bought two tickets, I stood up on my tiptoes and peeped over the wooden ledge.

"Excuse me," I said. "Do you know any ballet schools I could go to?"

The ticket lady had to lean forward to see me standing there.

"Ballet schools?" she repeated. "The National Preparatory School is right next door. Why? Do you want to be a dancer?"

"Yes!" I told her. "I want to marry Mr. Slavicky and dance with him in *Swan Lake*!"

A bemused smile appeared on her face.

"Do you now?"

My mother was blushing with embarrassment. The ticket buyers behind us were already starting to grumble.

"Usually it's the parents who make this decision," the ticket lady told me. "Are you sure you want to be a dancer?"

"I'm very sure," I declared. "What do you think, Mum?"

"We'll see," my mother said.

The ticket lady wrote an address on the back of our ticket envelope, along with the name of the woman who was the head of the children's section. She took her time and glared at all the people who cleared their throat while she kept them waiting. (She would keep an eye out for me in the future. Whenever there was a good ballet, she would put tickets aside for my mother and me, and we never had to wait in line again.)

"Good luck." She handed me the envelope. "I look forward to seeing you in *Swan Lake* someday."

"Me, too!" I waved. "Thank you very much!"

My mother grabbed my hand and led me out the side door of the theater, and we found ourselves next to the Federal Parliament building. It was a huge structure of granite, aluminum, and glass, decorated with Czech and Soviet flags and a sculpture of men in overalls, wielding rifles. Every so often, a small fleet of limousines would pull up in front, but for the most part the place seemed deserted. Only the back door appeared to serve any purpose. It was an enormous glass revolving door and people came and went in a continuous stream. My mother studied the National Theater emblem and directory that was mounted on the wall beside it.

"The Preparatory School for the National Ballet," she read. "Well, I guess this is it."

"Can we go inside?" I begged.

"I don't know, little one," my mother said. "Are you really serious about becoming a dancer?"

"I'm very serious," I told her. "I want to dance Odette. I really do!"

"Well then," my mother sighed. "Let's go and see what the teachers have to say."

She pushed through the revolving door and we walked inside, climbing the stairs to the first floor. At the end of a long corridor, we found a group of dancers in sweatshirts and legwarmers standing around a water fountain.

"Excuse me," my mother said. "I'm trying to find Mrs. Saturday? I think she's the head of the Preparatory School."

"Second door on the left," one of the dancers told her.

We walked back up the corridor, listening to the music and the muffled pounding of feet, and sometimes even the cursing of the instructors. Eventually, we came to Mrs. Saturday's door. My mother took a deep breath and knocked twice.

"*Entrez!*" a voice barked from inside.

We entered a large, bare studio with mirrored walls and a battered grand piano in the corner. A wooden bar ran along three sides of the room, surrounded by little girls dressed in white leotards and pink stockings. A fat lady with thick glasses and a grim expression sat behind the piano, playing a cheerful waltz, while a short and sinewy woman clapped her hands in time with the music. The woman wore an orange dress that looked like an apron, and her calf muscles were enormous. I watched as she strode around the room, correcting the postures of her students. She slapped their arms and legs and sometimes even pinched their bums to make them kick their legs higher.

"Un, deux, trois, piqué!" she snapped. *"Un, deux, trois, piqué!"*

The girls hung onto the bar and tapped the floor with their toes as if their lives depended on it. Then the music stopped abruptly and the teacher whirled around. "Yes?" she asked irritably.

"Excuse me, are you Mrs. Saturday?" my mother inquired.

"I am," the woman said. "What can I do for you?"

"My daughter would like to study ballet," my mother told her. "And I was told to come and ask about your school."

Mrs. Saturday looked at me with her watery, blue eyes.

"How old are you?" she asked.

"Four," I replied.

"Well, then, you're two years too young," she said. "Come back for an audition when you're six."

She turned and nodded to the pianist, and the waltz started up again. My mother's cheeks were bright red. She took my hand and started to walk back to the door.

"But I don't want to wait until I'm six," I blurted. "I want to start now. I want to dance with Mr. Slavicky before he's too old!"

Mrs. Saturday silenced the piano player with a wave of her hand.

"You want to dance with Mr. Slavicky?" she asked me.

"Yes, I think he's wonderful," I explained. "I want to learn to dance so that I can be his princess and dance Odette with him in *Swan Lake.*"

Mrs. Saturday and the pianist looked at each other and laughed.

"Does Mr. Slavicky know this?"

"No." I blushed. "I don't think so."

"I see," she said. She turned to her students and clapped loudly.

"That's it for today," she told them. "See you on Wednesday, and please try not to be later than usual."

She walked past my mother, flung the door open, and indicated that we should follow her.

"Quickly," she said. "I haven't got all day."

We followed Mrs. Saturday through a series of passages to the studio where the National Theater Ballet Company was rehearsing. A dozen men and women were warming up in front of the mirrors. Sweat poured down their faces and it was very stuffy in the room, but they wore many layers of clothes, like homeless people in winter. They exercised without any music, and I could hear the cracking of joints as they contorted their limbs.

"Excuse me, Marta?" Mrs. Saturday called out to one young dancer. "Is Jaroslav around today? There's someone I want him to meet."

"He should be here any minute," the young dancer replied.

"This is Marta Drotnerova," Mrs. Saturday said. "She played Odette in our most recent production of *Swan Lake*."

"Hello!" I was dumbstruck.

The young dancer looked nothing like the beautiful swan I had seen at the Smetana Theater. She had big, sad eyes and a prematurely old face, and her ribs jutted through her costume like the skeleton of a chicken.

"How do you do?" she said politely. "What's your name?"

"My name is Dominika," I said. "I would like to dance Odette as well."

"Dominika is in love with Jaroslav," Mrs. Saturday explained. "She wants to dance with him before he becomes too old for her."

"Really?" Marta Drotnerova smiled. "I'm sure he'll be delighted to know he's captured the heart of a lady."

The other dancers laughed knowingly.

"Ah, here he comes now," Mrs. Saturday said.

We turned to see a blond man stroll through the door. He wore a tracksuit and a scarf, as well as thick woolen socks and a pair of checkered slippers. His face was pale and handsome, and he moved lightly and elegantly as he crossed the room.

"Good morning, ladies!" he boomed in a deep and cultivated voice.

Mrs. Saturday presented me to him and explained why I had come to see her. When she told him that I wanted to be his princess, he looked very pleased and gave me the nicest smile.

"I'm very honored that you would like to become a dancer because of me," he said earnestly. "You will have to work extremely hard to dance Odette, because it's one of the toughest roles, but if I'm still around when you grow up, I would be delighted to dance with you."

Ballet enthusiasts might know that Jaroslav Slavicky was our country's Mikhail Baryshnikov. He was a tremendous dancer, and the fact that he was kind enough to encourage an undersized, overconfident little girl shows that he was not only a wonderful dancer but a great gentleman as well.

I felt my cheeks burning with embarrassment and pleasure.

"I would like that very much," I whispered.

"Where are you studying?" Mr. Slavicky asked.

"I'm thinking of sending her to Mrs. Sprislova," Mrs. Saturday told him. "She can learn the basics before she comes to me."

"That sounds like an excellent idea," Mr. Slavicky said pleasantly. "Well, the very best of luck to you, young lady, and I do hope to see you in one of these rooms someday."

He joined the dancers, and Mrs. Saturday ushered us out into the hall.

"Come up to my office," she told my mother. "There's a school in North Prague that might take your daughter. I'll give you the address and make a call on your behalf."

This turned out to be an incredible stroke of luck, because the national theater, opera, and ballet companies were the domain of the party elite. In the selection process for the various schools that prepared children for the State Conservatory, party connections outweighed talent every time. An unconnected kid like me wouldn't have even heard about Mrs. Sprislova's school. But by charming the lady at the ticket office, and then warming the hearts of Mrs. Saturday and Mr. Slavicky, I somehow managed to walk through a door that hardly anyone walked through of their own free will.

When my mother and I eventually arrived at Mrs. Sprislova's school, we discovered that Mrs. Saturday had indeed made a phone call on my behalf, and I was signed up for the beginners' class without so much as taking off my sandals. Mrs. Sprislova seemed much more easygoing than Mrs. Saturday, and I liked her immediately. She was a tall woman with a kind face and blond hair tied back in a ponytail. When I told her that I wanted to dance Odette in *Swan Lake*, she smiled with pleasure, revealing a gap between her front teeth.

"I danced Odette, when I was young," she told me.

"Really?" I cried. "So you can teach me all the steps!"

Mrs. Sprislova chuckled. "I would be delighted to teach you, but you'll have to learn the basics first."

"Okay! When can I start?" I asked eagerly.

"The school year starts in September, but Mrs. Saturday tells me that you're in a hurry, so I'm willing to make an exception," Mrs. Sprislova said. "I can put you in the second semester class, but you must promise to work very hard and catch up with the other girls as quickly as you can."

"I will!" I told her. "I'll work very hard, I promise."

Mrs. Sprislova took my word and told my mother to bring me to the school the following Monday afternoon. Classes were held on Mondays, Wednesdays, and Fridays, and I would need a white leotard, pink stockings, and soft white slippers with leather soles, which ballet dancers called *piskoty* slippers after a popular brand of sponge biscuits. The hard slippers, the pointes, were pink and had wooden soles, but I wouldn't be wearing them until the following year. Mrs. Sprislova told my mother where she could buy all the dancing gear, and the next thing I knew we were sitting on a tram, heading back into the center of Prague.

The tram rattled along the left bank of the river, passing Stvanice Island and the Albatross Boatel, which floated near the quay like a big wedding cake. As we approached the Letna Gardens where the statue of Stalin had once stood, my mother pointed across the water to a majestic yellow building with large windows.

"That's the Frantisek Hospital," she told me. "See that window with the blue light in it? It's an operating theater. Your grandfather might be performing surgery in there."

"Really?" I said. "I'm sad that Grandma and Granddad don't want to be our friends."

"It is a shame," my mother agreed.

"Tell me about Grandfather," I asked. "What's he like?"

"His name is Wenceslaus Cermak," she replied. "He's the chief surgeon of the hospital and has saved the lives of many people, but his real passion is music. He always wanted to be a musician, but his parents made him study medicine instead. When I was a girl, he and I would go to the ballet and the opera, because my mother wasn't interested. And I would accompany him on the piano while he played his violin."

I pressed my face to the window of the tram, watching the blue light and trying to imagine what my grandfather looked like.

"It's been fifteen years since we played together," my mother said quietly. "I'm sure he'd be delighted to know that his granddaughter has inherited his love of music and dance."

"Would he?" I exclaimed. "Well, why don't we tell him? He might become friends with us again!"

"I'm afraid it's not that easy, Trumpet," my mother sighed.

I kept my eyes on my grandfather's window as we curved around the river beneath the Prague Castle and clattered past the narrow streets of Mala Strana, until the blue light disappeared from view.

The following Monday, I began my new ballet routine. I would get up very early and accompany my mother to work. She, Klara, and I would eat a hasty breakfast, tiptoe across our muddy front yard, and dash down the hill to catch the 7:15 train. More often than not, we would arrive at the station just after the rickety wooden road gates had fallen, but with just enough time to cross the rails to the opposite platform. A few seconds later, a train would thunder past without stopping, and everyone on the platform would groan. Trains always ran late under communism, but you could never actually rely on their lateness. Whenever you tried to anticipate the delay, the trains would miraculously arrive on time, or even half an hour early. The unpredictability of public transport added tremendous latitude to the Czech working week. Commuters could arrive at their offices anywhere from late morning to the mid-afternoon, raise their hands in defeat and say "Trains," and all their colleagues would shake their heads knowingly. My mother, who prided herself on being very punctual, would insist upon us being at the station at 7:10 sharp. I would stand beside her and Klara, hugging the little backpack that contained my leotard, legwarmers, and *piskoty* slippers. They were the smallest slippers we could find, but my feet were so tiny I had to wear three pairs of socks to keep them on. My leotard was also too big, and my mother had tried to take it in by hand. She had spent a whole day working on it, but she wasn't very good at sewing. In spite of her efforts, the leotard hung raggedly on my body, making me look more like a wet chicken than a swan.

Usually at about quarter to eight, the 7:15 train would shudder into the station, and everyone would fight for seats. My mother, Klara, and I would invariably end up standing in the aisle, and the train rattled so violently I would have to hang on to my mother's legs to keep from falling. After about twenty minutes, the screech of rusty brakes would announce our arrival at the Central Railway Station, and the disembarking crowd would push us out onto the platform and all the way down the steps to the tram stop. Klara's school was right in the center of town, so she would run for the number 9 tram, while my mother and I would squeeze inside the number 18, which went to the Prague Castle and the Embassy District, where my mother worked. The Embassy District was where all the foreign diplomats and high-ranking Soviet officials lived. The streets were lined with chestnut trees and the embassies were surrounded by a large, floating population of cigarette-smoking, newspaper-reading STB agents propped up casually against lampposts and road signs. I was quickly able to recognize their faces in spite of the position rotations they half-heartedly undertook. The Czech secret police agents took their jobs about as seriously as everyone else in the country. Many an arrest was botched as a result of bad public transport; many an interrogation was suspended because the interrogating officer was too hungover. Whenever we walked past, they would pretend not to see us, but I often caught them staring at my mother's legs from behind their newspapers.

On Mondays, Wednesdays, and Fridays, Mother and I would climb the steps of the Economic Institute, which had a crumbling facade and a yard filled with stinging nettles. Her office was on the ground floor and was furnished with a battered desk and a single filing cabinet. She would make me sit on the floor and draw pictures while she worked. When I got bored, I would get up and walk through the building in search of someone to play with. Fortunately, there was usually some kind of party going on. Of the fifty economists who worked at the institute, my mother was the only one who appeared to take her job seriously. Everyone else, including the two men whose names appeared on her books, seemed to spend their afternoons celebrating their colleagues' birthdays and name days.

By lunchtime, a crowd would gather in one of the larger offices to drink wine and sing "Happy Birthday" to a colleague, and by mid-afternoon, the damp corridors would be echoing with laughter. I was always welcome at these parties, and had lots of fun drinking lemonade and eating little cakes with the people who would end up running the country after the revolution. I spent many a happy afternoon watching the future leaders of Czechoslovakia drink themselves under the table, until my mother finished work and came to collect me. Then we would walk down the hill from the castle and cross the Charles Bridge to the Old Town and take the tram to Mrs. Sprislova's school.

I loved these walks with my mother. We would explore the ancient streets of Mala Strana, looking at the houses with painted or sculpted signs above their doorways. My mother told me the stories of these buildings—wonderful tales of ghosts, mysterious deaths, and intriguing historical events. Mala Strana after dark was the haunt of headless knights, black dogs, and howling women, according to local folklore. We would buy cheese rolls at our favorite little bakery and carry them over the Charles Bridge, looking out across the Vltava River and up at the blackened statues of the saints. Then we would make our way around the Klementinum Library until we came out into the Old Town Square, which has always been my favorite place in Prague. I always nagged my mother to let me watch the striking of the hour on the Astronomical Clock. The clock was mounted on the tower of the Town Hall. Whenever it chimed, the twelve apostles would appear in little windows, and a tiny figure of Death would ring his bell. It was over almost as quickly as it had started, but I would always watch it with great anticipation.

"I wish the apostles would hurry up," I would complain as we waited. "Do you think the clock might be broken?"

"No, but it's been damaged a number of times," she told me. "The eastern wing of the Town Hall was blown up by the Nazis on the very last day of the war. And when the Red Army came to liberate Prague in 1945, one of the first things Marshal Konev tried to do was have the clock dismantled and sent back to Russia. Fortunately, it was too big for their transport vehicles, so they had to leave it here."

"Why would the Russians want it?"

"Good question," my mother smiled. "For some reason, the Russians have always been obsessed with clocks and watches. Whenever their armies came to Prague, the first thing their soldiers would do was steal every wristwatch and clock they could find."

"Well, I'm glad they didn't take this one," I said.

"So am I," my mother laughed. "Ah, here come the apostles now."

After the striking of the hour, we would walk along the side of the Town Hall, with white crosses embedded in the cobblestones. They represented the twenty-seven Czech aristocrats beheaded in 1621 for trying to lead an uprising against the Hapsburgs. Then we would cross the square and eat our cheese rolls on the steps of an enormous statue of Jan Hus surrounded by a group of defeated men and women groveling at his feet.

"He was a Catholic priest who was killed in 1415 for preaching against the Church," my mother told me.

"Why did he want to preach against the Church?" I asked.

"Well, back in those days, the Church was selling pardons, which were like tickets to Heaven, to anyone who was rich enough to pay for them. Jan Hus didn't think that Jesus would have approved of this, so he accused the Church of making an enterprise out of the Christian faith."

"But why did they kill him?" I asked. "Couldn't they have just told him to stop?"

"They did, but he refused. The Church was very angry, because people were listening to him and not buying their pardons, so they called him a heretic and had him burned at the stake. He had many chances to back down, but he ended up dying for what he believed in. After he died, he became a symbol and a hero of the Czech nation in much the same way that Joan of Arc became a French one after leading an army against the English."

She took a bite of her cheese roll and smiled at me.

"We're not a particularly religious or righteous country, but in times of war or occupation, many Czech parents will name their children 'Jan' or 'Jana' as a form of protest," she said. "You can always tell when we've been invaded by the number of little Johns and Janes running around."

"Your name is Jana," I pointed out. "So you must have been named after Jan Hus as well!"

"I was," my mother said. "I was born during the German occupation. My father was hoping for a son and he had the name Jan already picked out, but when I turned out to be a girl, he named me Jana instead. But he would often call me 'Jan' or 'Honza' as a joke. He wanted a son so that he could teach him medicine, but he ended up teaching my sister instead."

Whenever my grandfather came up in conversation, my mother would always become sad and reflective. We sat underneath the Jan Hus statue for a while, and as the Astronomical Clock began to chime the next hour, we got up and walked through the Jewish Quarter to the number 12 tram that took us across the river to Mrs. Sprislova's school.

The North Prague School for Junior Dancers was located in the basement of the Prague Transport Office; an ugly tower block covered in dirty white tiles. It was a strange place to study dancing, as the upper floors were teeming with disillusioned public servants who would roll their eyes at the young ballerinas who gathered in the lobby. My mother and I would take the ancient paternoster elevator down to the basement, where we would find the changing rooms overflowing with half-naked girls and their well-dressed mothers, and I would change into my leotard and slippers while my mother tied my hair up in pigtails. Then Mrs. Sprislova would appear in the room and clap her hands.

"Hurry up, and try to keep the noise down!" she would cry. "This is a ballet school, not a farm!"

We would trot out onto the floor of the studio, which was a shabbier version of those at the preparatory school. There was a battered grand piano in the corner, and as I self-consciously stood with the other girls, an elegant lady on crutches hobbled over to the piano, sat down, and started to thumb through the scores. The woman's name was Miluska, and she had contracted polio as a child. She was an excellent pianist, and after she had put her crutches on the floor, she would run her fingers effortlessly over the keyboard while Mrs. Sprislova took us through the basics. We would start with a warm-up and some stretching, and then we would exercise at the bar.

I was quiet and shy my first day, and looked at the other girls with envy. They were all at least a head taller than I was, and not only did their leotards and slippers fit properly, but they wore elegant cotton socks instead of three pairs of woolen ones. Mrs. Sprislova called out her instructions in French, and they executed them with confidence. I began to worry

I might never catch up. I desperately tried to copy what the other girls were doing, which was particularly hard, as the bar was too high for me to reach, but to judge from Mrs. Sprislova's smile, I wasn't doing too badly. She didn't scream like Mrs. Saturday, and, if someone made a mistake, she would silence Miluska with a regal wave and patiently explain how to do the exercise properly. On my first day, she showed us how to make halos above our heads with our arms and how to keep our balance on the points of our toes. I followed her instructions until my whole body ached, and at the end of the lesson, she complimented me in front of the class.

"Good work, Dominika," she smiled. "You have good endurance and a natural sense of rhythm."

The other girls looked at me with surprise. It was common knowledge that Mrs. Sprislova didn't throw compliments around freely, and as soon as the class was over, I was surrounded by a group of girls who wanted to know who I was. They told me their names as we changed out of our costumes, and I tried to remember them all. Their mothers made polite conversation with my mother and then we had to run and catch our tram. As we rattled back toward Prague Castle, I sat in my mother's lap, looking across the river at the blue light in the windows of the Frantisek Hospital. I could see the silhouettes of people, and imagined that one of them was my grandfather. I was proud that he was a famous surgeon who had saved the lives of many people.

For the next six months, I worked very hard and became one of Mrs. Sprislova's favorite students. I think she had a soft spot for me because of my size. I was too small to work properly at the bar, but I would assume my position with a lot of enthusiasm, balancing against the mirrored walls whenever my arms were too tired to grasp the bar above my head. On the occasions when we were allowed to improvise, I would position myself as close to Miluska as I could. I would stand on the tips of my toes and use the steps that Mrs. Sprislova had taught me, letting Miluska's music carry me along. More often than not, when the music stopped, I would open my eyes to find myself on the opposite side of the room, with the whole class, Miluska, and Mrs. Sprislova watching me. I may have been small, but I was one of the most expressive dancers in the class, and as the seasons changed and December approached, Mrs. Sprislova rewarded me for my efforts. I was invited to perform the "Waltz of the Marionette" from *Coppelia* in my very own segment of the Christmas show.

"Normally, I get my girls to perform in groups," she told me, "but I think we might let you dance this one by yourself. I'll show you the steps, and then you can practice at home with your mother accompanying you on the piano. What do you think?"

"I'd love to!" I cried. "Could I bring Mrs. Liskova and Mrs. Sokolova from my street?"

"You can bring anyone you like," Mrs. Sprislova smiled.

I triumphantly told the ladies about my solo, and my father agreed to drive everyone to North Prague on the night of the performance. My mother and I practiced the "Waltz of the Marionette" in the living room until I had all the steps memorized, and then I would go to school and beg Miluska to play the music at the end of class, so that Mrs. Sprislova could see how I was coming along.

"I'm getting very good at this," I would tell her. "See? It's like there are strings attached to my arms and legs!"

"Well, that's the idea," she would say. "Okay everyone, we'll see you next week, and for those of you whose parents are making costumes, please bring them with you. *Ahoj!*"

On those evenings after class, as my mother and I caught the tram back into Prague, I would always look for the blue light in the hospital windows and imagine inviting my grandfather along to see me dance. How could he say no, if he loved ballet as much as I did? As the weeks passed and the night of the performance drew closer, I became more and more convinced that if he did come and see me, he might change his mind and want to be part of our family once again.

One afternoon, on the way to school, I led my mother down Parizska Street, the nicest street in the Jewish Quarter. We walked past the Jewish cemetery and around the back of the Staronova Synagogue, and a couple of narrow streets later, we came out at the corner of the Frantisek Hospital. We had walked this way a few times before, and I knew how nervous the hospital made my mother feel. As we passed the massive wooden doors of the main entrance, I pulled at her sleeve.

"Mum, can we go inside and visit Granddad?" I asked.

"No!" my mother said reflexively. She seemed frightened by the suggestion, but I could also see that she was yearning to speak to her father. "I don't think so, little one. He's probably too busy, and even if he isn't, he might not want to speak to us."

"Yes he will," I insisted. "When I tell him that I'm going to be a dancer."

"I don't think so," my mother replied. "The court case made my parents very angry, and it's possible that my dad will still be upset."

"Please, Mum. I just want to say hello to Granddad." I looked up at her with a big, hopeful smile. "Please," I begged. "I'm sure he'll be happy to see us."

"All right," my mother said reluctantly. She took a deep breath and led me through the doorway.

The Frantisek Hospital had once been a monastery, and it was a very grim and imposing building. We crossed the cathedral-like lobby and climbed a crumbling stone staircase to the second floor. My mother led me down a long corridor, and the sound of her heels striking the tiles echoed through the whole building. When we stopped in front of her father's door, our hearts were beating loudly in our chests.

My mother gently rapped on the door.

"*Vstupte!*" an authoritative voice called from inside. "The key's in the latch. Come right in."

I clutched my mother's hand as we entered the office. A thin, stern-looking man with a shock of white hair was sitting at a desk, hunched over a pile of paperwork.

"Yes?" he said, without looking up.

My mother opened her mouth but no words came out. There was an uncomfortable pause, and as my grandfather continued to rustle through his papers, I thought he might have forgotten we were there.

"Hello, Granddad," I said finally. "We've come to see you!"

The old man dropped his pen and looked across the room. When he saw my mother, all the blood appeared to drain from his face. If it was possible, he looked even more frightened than she did.

"I'm your granddaughter, Dominika," I told him. "And I got Mum to bring me here so I could tell you that I'm going to become a ballet dancer when I grow up."

A wave of conflicting emotions appeared on Dr. Cermak's face. His hands started to shake and he dropped them in his lap.

"I have no granddaughter," he finally managed to say.

"Dad, please," my mother spoke now. "Dominika begged me to come and visit you. It's terrible that she doesn't know her grandparents. She's really proud of you. She talks about you all the time."

Dr. Cermak shook his head slowly and gathered his resolve. The corners of his mouth turned down, and when he spoke again, it was quietly and firmly.

"I only have two grandsons," he said.

My mother let out a deep sigh and tears rolled down her cheeks. She looked terribly hurt, but so did my grandfather.

"That's not true," I told him. "I'm your granddaughter and so is my sister, Klara. And we're very sad that you never come to see us. Mum has told us so many good things about you. How you save lives and play the violin. She really loves you, Granddad. We all do!"

I walked over to his desk and took one of his hands in mine. It was a big, delicate hand, and the skin was smooth. Dr. Cermak looked down at me in astonishment.

"I always wanted to have a granddad," I told him. "And I would really like you to come and see me dance. I have my own solo in Mrs. Sprislova's Christmas show, and Mr. Slavicky has said that he will wait for me to dance Odette in *Swan Lake* with him when I am older!"

"Jaroslav Slavicky?" My grandfather looked up at my mother.

"Yes! He really said he would dance with me, didn't he, Mum? Didn't he say he would?"

"He really did," my mother sniffed.

Dr. Cermak took off his glasses and rubbed his eyes with the back of his hand. I could tell that he was very moved, even though he tried not to show it. I climbed up onto his lap, and when I pressed my head against his chest, I could feel his heart slowly warming. He sat helplessly in his chair while I put my arms around his neck, and chattered away until the wall of his resolve crumbled.

"Can I offer you a cup of coffee or tea?" he asked finally.

"A cup of tea!" I replied. "Do you have any biscuits?"

My grandfather rummaged through his desk drawers, pulling out a packet of biscuits, some tea bags, and a jar of instant coffee, and then he went to fill his kettle. There was a hot plate on the windowsill along with a number of porcelain cups and saucers, and as the water began to boil, Dr. Cermak put tea bags in two of the cups and started to spoon some coffee into the large cup he kept on his desk. His hands shook as he handled the cups, and when the kettle gave out a sharp whistle behind him, he accidentally knocked his special cup off the desk. It fell on the floor and broke in half.

"I've got it, Dad!" My mother sprang from the couch.

She crouched at her father's feet to gather the broken pieces of his cup, and my granddad crouched down, too, and grabbed her hands. Then he put his arms around my mother and both of them burst into tears.

"I missed you, Honza," my grandfather whispered.

"I missed you, too, Dad," my mother sobbed.

They embraced for a short but intense moment as the kettle continued to whistle above them.

"The kettle!" my mother finally managed to say.

Dr. Cermak stood up, switched off the hot plate, and poured water into our teacups while my mother collected the broken pieces of his cup.

Then she swept up the spilled coffee and helped her father carry the tea to the couch. They sat down beside each other and I quickly climbed back up in my grandfather's lap.

"It's been a long time since I've seen you," he said to my mother as she poured milk in his coffee. "You look as beautiful as ever."

"Thanks, Dad," she smiled. "You're looking good, too."

"I'm going to be seventy next week," he told her.

"I know," my mother sighed.

"Are you going to have a party?" I asked. "We could come and bring you a present!"

"I'm going to have a small celebration at home," he replied. "But perhaps you could come to the hospital next Wednesday afternoon and we could have a small party right here."

"We'll come, won't we, Mum?"

"Of course," my mother said. "How are things at home?"

"All right," Dr. Cermak shrugged. "You know how it is."

For the next half an hour, he, my mother, and I had a wonderful time together. I asked him questions about his work as a surgeon, and he told me about some of the patients whose lives he had saved. He also told me about his love of classical music and the symphonies of his favorite composers, and promised to bring his violin and play for me the next time we met, and we shook hands on it. I invited him to my Christmas show and promised to bring him a present the following Wednesday, and then a nurse knocked on the door.

"Excuse me, comrade surgeon," she said. "But we have an urgent case in Theater Four."

"Tell Comrade Vacek I'll be right there," Dr. Cermak replied. He turned to my mother and took her hands in his.

"I'm sorry, but I have to go now," he said. "I'm so happy you came. I had a lovely time with you and your daughter, and I'm really looking forward to seeing you next week."

"Thanks, Dad," my mother smiled tearfully. "Say hello to Mum and Auntie Mary from me."

"Yes, yes, I will," he said distractedly. He got up, and as he ushered us out of his office, he bent down to kiss me on the cheek. "You're a very special girl, Dominika," he told me. "I'm very glad you asked your mother to bring you here to see me."

"Me, too," I said. "I knew you'd be our friend again. I just knew it!"

After we left the hospital, my mother called Mrs. Sprislova to explain why I had missed my ballet lesson, and then she took me up to the famous Hanavsky Pavilion at the top of the Letna Gardens, and bought me a caramel ice cream as a special treat.

"Thank you, Trumpet," she said. "I've wanted to talk to my dad for such a long time. You did a really great thing for me today."

"He's nice," I told her. "And look, we can see his hospital window from the gardens. And we really know that he's in there saving someone's life right now! Isn't that good?"

"Yes, it's very good," my mother smiled.

When we got home, I worked hard on the "Waltz of the Marionette," so that my grandfather would be impressed. My mother made me a costume for the show, which was a black leotard with a little lace tutu and lots of pretty blue rhinestones sewn into the material. On the Monday before my grandfather's birthday, I nagged her until she agreed to leave the Economic Institute early so that we could go shopping in Wenceslaus Square. I wanted to buy Dr. Cermak a present.

"We'll get him another big cup for his desk," I declared. "He looked very sad when he had to drink his coffee out of a teacup, didn't he?"

"He did," my mother agreed. "Your grandfather has always had a big cup for his coffee. Surgeons drink lots of coffee because it helps them stay awake when they work long hours."

We walked up Wenceslaus Square to a store called the Diamond. Czechoslovakia has always been famous for its porcelain and crystal, and the Diamond was one of the best places to buy kitchenware. We took the escalator to the second floor and found the part of the shop that sold cups and saucers.

"How about this one?" my mother suggested.

"It's not big enough," I told her.

"You're right," she laughed. "So which one do you think we should get?"

"This one!" I said. "It's big, but it's also the same color as his teacups. This way, they all match."

I selected a cup covered in tiny pink roses, and we carried it to the cash register at the front of the shop.

"Hello," I said to the lady behind the counter. "This is a present for my granddad, Dr. Wenceslaus Cermak. He's going to be seventy years old the day after tomorrow!"

"Is he now?" the lady said. "Would you like me to wrap it up in special paper?"

"Yes, please!" I told her. "He's a famous surgeon and he broke his special cup, so we're buying him a new one."

The saleswoman smiled at my mother and pulled a box out from beneath her counter. The box contained the same cup as the one I had selected, and she wrapped it up in a sheet of crepe paper.

"I'm sure he'll appreciate such a lovely present," she said as she tied the package with a ribbon.

"I hope so!" I said. "I only met him for the first time last week, but he's going to come and see me dance in the Christmas ballet."

"He'll be very proud of you, I'm sure," the lady told me.

FOR THE NEXT TWO DAYS, I was dizzy with excitement. All I could think about was how happy my grandfather would be when he opened his present. I pictured him with his violin in his hands, playing me snatches of Mozart and Handel. My mother and I would visit him regularly. And I imagined how once the Cermaks were friends with my parents again, the whole family would come and see me dance Odette at the Smetana Theater when I was older. My grandmother Kveta, Auntie Mary, and my granddad would sit next to my parents and Klara in the nicest box in the theater and watch me through their opera glasses.

On Wednesday morning, I put Dr. Cermak's present in my backpack and carried it carefully to the Economic Institute. The day passed very slowly, but when it was over, I took my mother's hand and excitedly led her down through Mala Strana to the little bakery near the bridge, where we had ordered a cake for my grandfather's party. We picked up the cake and crossed the Charles Bridge, walking up the quay until we came to the Frantisek Hospital. This time, we weren't afraid to go inside. We climbed the steps and walked along the corridor to my grandfather's office. It was five o'clock, the time we had arranged to meet, and my mother knocked briskly on the door.

There was a long silence.

My mother knocked again, and as she did, I suddenly noticed that the key wasn't in the latch like it had been the last time.

"Mum," I whispered. "The key's not there."

The most abject look passed across my mother's face. She knocked again, and this time we heard someone moving around inside the room. A key turned in the lock and the door swung open a little bit, and my grandfather's face appeared in the crack.

"Happy birthday, Granddad!" I exclaimed.

Dr. Cermak's eyes were red-rimmed and glassy, and the lines around his mouth were very harsh. He tried to close the door in our faces, but my mother planted her foot inside the gap.

"What are you doing, Dad?" she cried.

"Go away!" My grandfather hissed. "You're not welcome."

"What?" my mother gasped.

"But Granddad, we've brought you a cake and a present!" I said, taking off my backpack to try to show him the package. "We've bought you a cup to replace the one you've broken!"

"I don't want any presents from you," Dr. Cermak snapped.

My mother's foot was still jammed between the door and the door-frame, and she was pushing against the knob with all her might. She looked angry and determined, and my grandfather looked absolutely miserable.

"You can't do this," I heard my mother say. "This is your grand-daughter!"

"I have no granddaughters," Dr. Cermak said again. "Don't you understand? I have one daughter and two grandsons."

I stared at my grandfather in amazement. The man in the doorway was nothing like the kind, music-loving gentleman I had met the previous week.

"Get your foot out of my door or I'll call hospital security!"

My mother continued to struggle against him.

"Mum has made you do this, hasn't she?" she said.

My grandfather's face twisted up in pain. His lips started to quiver and his eyes were full of tears. "Let me be," he begged. "Go away, please."

"Why?" my mother asked.

"You know why, Jana," he replied. "I'll always love you, but please, just get out and never come back!"

They looked at each other for a long moment, and then my mother removed her foot from the door and Dr. Cermak slammed it shut in our faces.

I held my little backpack in my hands and tried to understand what had happened. For some reason, my grandfather couldn't be friends with us anymore. He had wanted to, but something had made him change his mind. I thought the Red Countess must be very strong indeed to make her good husband act against his will. It would be many years before I understood this properly; before I learned that my grandmother's power came from a regime that could crush her husband as surely as it was trying to crush her daughter, and that this power was like fire. It was a good servant but a bad master. One of the most insidious things about communism was that it pushed good people to the brink of immorality and then required them to cross the threshold. Thousands of families would be torn apart at this brink, for the simple reason that some people are capable of sacrificing their ideals while others aren't. But the ones who crossed over—even music-loving surgeons who saved people's lives—would forever be at the service of the party, even if the party was supposed to be serving them.

I looked up at my mother.

"Let's go," she said quietly.

She led me out of the hospital, threw my grandfather's cake in the first trash can she could find, and we walked in silence to the Old Town Square. We sat on the steps of the Jan Hus statue. My mother was oddly calm, but her knuckles were white and her hands were balled into fists.

"Come here, little one," she said. "Come here and sit on my lap." I threw my arms around her neck and she pressed her face into my jacket, and after a few moments, I felt her shoulders heave.

"Don't cry, Mummy," I said. But she cried and cried, and soon enough I cried, too.

I looked up over her shoulder and could see Jan Hus towering above us. The incorruptible priest who had said no to the pope. Five hundred years earlier, he had stood at his own moral brink and chosen the worst kind of death instead of sacrificing his ideals, and my grandparents had been so moved by his courage, they gave their daughter his name during the German occupation. They had wanted an idealist, but they had got more than they bargained for. Because as terrible and hurtful as the family split was, the likelihood of my mother crossing the Communist threshold was as impossible and remote as their ever being able to cross back.

Some things you simply can't do or undo.

f i v e

THE LITTLE
COGNAC PEAK

 THAT CHRISTMAS, I danced the "Waltz of the Marionette" in Mrs. Sprislova's show, and while it was exciting to be the center of attention for an evening, I could tell that my parents and Mrs. Sokolova were forcing themselves to be happy for me. My mother was devastated by her father's behavior, and Mrs. Sokolova was upset because Mrs. Liskova had gone away. Both Mrs. Liskova and Mrs. Noskova had been confined to their beds in the weeks before they disappeared, and I had visited them many times. They had both seemed very calm, and Mrs. Liskova had told me that she was really looking forward to joining her friends. In my mind, the ladies had gone somewhere nice and warm to get better, and while I couldn't wait for them to come home, it occurred to me that wherever they had gone might have been so nice and so warm, they might not be coming home anytime soon. At least not in the middle of winter.

After the performance, we dropped Mrs. Sokolova off, and then we went down to our kitchen for a snack before dinner. I was still wearing my costume and had changed back into my *piskoty* slippers.

"Dad, do you think we could go and see Mrs. Liskova and Mrs. Noskova?" I asked. "I was thinking that maybe we could take Mrs. Sokolova with us, and we could all have a holiday together."

"That would be one hell of a holiday," my sister laughed.

"Klara," my mother snapped. "We won't have any of that kind of talk, thank you."

My sister sighed mightily and threw her tea in the sink, and then she stalked from the room with my mother right behind her. I listened to them arguing all the way up the stairs. My mother's temper had been very short ever since our disastrous visit to her father, and I really hated it when she became angry, because she wasn't an angry person. She was usually very sweet.

I looked at my dad, and he shook his head glumly.

"She's still upset," he shrugged.

"I was hoping my dancing would cheer her up," I told him. "But what do you think about us going to visit the ladies? Do you think we have enough money to go on holiday?"

The expression on my father's face was serious, and it looked like he was about to say something important. But the second I asked if we had enough money to go on holiday, his eyes lit up and he flashed me one of his wheeler-dealer smiles.

"It's funny you should ask," he said.

He crossed the room and closed the kitchen door, and then he opened the window so he could smoke a cigarette.

"Can you keep a secret?" he asked me.

"You know I can!" I was, in fact, a terrible keeper of secrets. "I won't tell anyone. I promise!"

"All right, then," my father grinned. "An interesting thing happened in the cab the other day. I was driving an old man who lives in Semily, which is a little town near the mountains in the north. His family had a nice big farm, and an agricultural cooperative came and took it from them almost thirty years ago. The Communists who did the collectivizing were the worst farmers around, and this poor fellow was forced to hand everything over to a group of village thugs he had known since childhood. When he tried to say no, they threatened to throw him in prison and send his sons to the military service, so he lost a property that had been in his family for over two hundred and fifty years."

My father blew a jet of smoke out of the window and lowered his voice confidentially.

"Now. Up in the hills above the farm is a little mountain chalet, which the man tells me is just wonderful. It's perfect for skiing and it's great in summer, and the men who run the cooperative have basically been going there every weekend since the fifties. The cooperative forced him to sign a thirty-year lease on the chalet in 1950, so from the first of January, 1980, the property will belong to him again. And he's desperate to sell it."

"Do you think he might sell it to you, Dad?" I asked excitedly.

"Well, this is what we were talking about," my father said. "The man is afraid that if he doesn't sell it, the cooperative will force him to sign another lease. The men are a bunch of old drunks now, but the fellow in my cab is old as well, and he's still afraid of them. The head of the cooperative has made his life hell for thirty years. But there's a slight chance the cooperative will forget to re-sign the lease before the first of January, and if that happens, the man can sell me his chalet and walk away."

My eyes widened. "We would have our own holiday house!" I exclaimed. "I could practice my skiing."

"Yes, you could," my dad agreed. "I'm going to drive to Semily next week to have a look, and if the chalet is as wonderful as the man says, I'm thinking of making him an offer. Apart from anything else, it will be a good investment."

"What does Mum think?" I asked.

"Your mother doesn't know. That's why it's a secret," my dad replied. "She will only worry herself silly about what the cooperative will do if we buy the chalet from under them. The best thing is to just wait and see what happens. A bunch of Communists I can handle. Your mother's nerves, I can't. So, can I count on you to keep this a secret for the next couple of weeks?"

"Yes!" I cried. "I won't say a word to anyone. I swear!"

I MANAGED TO KEEP my father's plans to myself for the rest of the holidays, and, even more amazingly, everything worked out the way my father had hoped. The agricultural cooperative did forget to renew their lease, so my dad bought the chalet on New Year's Day. The ex-farmer had only wanted ten thousand crowns for it, but my father ended up paying him sixteen so that he and his family would have some compensation for the hardship they had suffered.

"You realize you're going to have some trouble with the cooperative," the man told my dad after the deed had changed hands.

"Oh, yes," my father said happily.

As my dad suspected, my mother reacted to the surprise with a mixture of happiness and trepidation. When her back was against the wall, she could fight with as much ferocity as my father, but her style was to avoid conflict, and there was no escaping the fact that there would be plenty of conflict when we went to Semily to take possession of our chalet. The way she saw it, we were setting ourselves up for the same kind of problems we were having in Cernosice. If the cooperative controlled the balance of opinion in the town, they could make our holidays very unpleasant. Not to mention the fact that they could simply refuse to respect the change of ownership. They did, after all, have the State behind them.

"The trick will be to go in with a total show of force," my father

growled. "The outcome of most disputes is decided in the first five minutes, so we'll give these old drunks five minutes they'll never forget."

"If you say so, dear," my mother sighed.

The first week of January was notorious for unofficial holidays, and
after my sister and I made it very clear that we weren't prepared to wait
for the weekend, my mother agreed to break her perfect attendance
record at the Economic Institute. We loaded the car while she worked up
the nerve to call in sick, and as my dad attached Barry's trailer to the back
of the Skoda, I ran down the street to tell Mrs. Sokolova the news.

"Hello, Mrs. Sokolova! Guess what?" I hollered as I kicked the snow
off my boots on her front landing. "We've bought a chalet in the mountains and we're going there for a holiday!"

"How lovely!" I heard her call out. "Come right in. The door's open."

I found Mrs. Sokolova in her living room, sitting in an armchair with a
book in her lap. Her face looked even more wrinkled than usual. Her knees
were covered with a blanket and her shoulders were wrapped in a shawl.

"How very nice to see you, Dominika," she said. "I'm a little short of
breath at the moment, so forgive me if I don't get up."

"Are you okay?" I was worried.

"Yes, of course," she replied. "It's nothing, just a little cold."

She made an effort to smile and held out her hand for me to take. Her
hands were very small and covered in calluses from her years of working
as a railway porter.

"I asked my dad if you could come with us, but he said it might be better
to wait until next time. He has to show total force to a bunch of old drunks!"

"Yes, maybe next time would be better," Mrs. Sokolova agreed.

I started to tell her about the clever way my dad had bought a chalet from
a man he met in his taxi, but as I talked, I realized that Mrs. Sokolova was
having difficulty staying awake. Holding her hand, I felt her arm become
heavy and then she started to snore. I didn't want to wake her, so I tucked
her hand beneath the blanket and pulled the shawl around her shoulders.

"Good-bye, Mrs. Sokolova," I whispered.

I tiptoed out of her apartment and closed the door quietly behind me, and as I trotted down the steps, I saw a man walking up our street alone. It was my father's best friend, Tomas Glatz. He was carrying a large backpack and he didn't look very happy.

"Hello, Mr. Glatz!" I called out. "Did you catch the train to Cernosice?"

"Yes, what a nightmare," he replied. "Are your parents at home? I was going to drop in and see them."

"I'm going home, too, so we can walk home together," I told him. "What are Andy and Monika up to?"

"They had to stay home," Mr. Glatz said quietly.

We walked up the street to our garage and found my father and Klara tying our skis to the top of the car. Barry was eyeing the trailer suspiciously.

"*Ahoj,* Jarda!" Mr. Glatz called out from the doorway. "What are you up to? It looks like you're going somewhere."

"*Ahoj,* Tomas!" my father bellowed back. "We're off on holidays, believe it or not. What are you doing here on foot? Has something happened to your Skoda?"

Mr. Glatz dropped his backpack on the ground and stared at his shoes for a long time. He looked as though he was going to burst into tears.

"Oh, no," my dad said. "Don't tell me."

"It's serious this time," Tomas muttered. "She wouldn't even let me take the car."

My father walked over to his friend and threw an arm around his shoulders.

"Well, luckily for you I have more beer in my trunk than I know what to do with," he said. "Let's go down to the kitchen for a quick drink, and you can tell me all about it."

"Thanks, Jarda," Mr. Glatz sniffed.

My dad pulled a couple of Pilsner bottles from the trunk and led his dejected friend down the front steps to our house. Klara and I inspected Mr. Glatz's backpack, which looked as though it contained all of his worldly possessions. Even his sleeping bag and bedroll.

I looked at my sister.

"They've been fighting for years," she explained.

She leaned against the car and watched me as I persuaded Barry to climb into the trailer. As easygoing and lazy as he was, Barry hated this trailer with a vengeance, and getting him to climb inside was a major operation. In his movie star years, when my dad used to chauffeur him to and from work, Barry always sat in the front. My dad had even gone so far as to remove the passenger seat entirely so that Barry would have more space. Whenever the family would go on holidays, my mother and Klara would sit in the back while Barry assumed his position beside my dad, sticking his head out of the window to soak up the adulation of his fans. After I was born, he was banished from the front seat, and despite the fact that I was the cause of his misfortune, I was the only member of the family who could get him to climb into the trailer.

"Come on, Barry!" I told him. "We're going to the mountains! You can't just sit around in Mr. Kozel's apartment all the time. You have to get out and see new things."

By the time I managed to coax Barry into the trailer, my parents and Mr. Glatz came up from the kitchen and announced that Mr. Glatz would be coming to Semily with us. My father picked up his friend's backpack and loaded it onto the roof. He and Mr. Glatz sat in the front of the car while my mother, Klara, and I squeezed into the back. As we drove down our street, I turned around to look at Barry. His fur wasn't as glossy and his eyes were less alert than they had been when he was younger. Poor old Barry was getting on in years. He huddled miserably on the floor and prepared himself for an undignified trip as we rumbled down the hill and into Prague. We reached the city and followed the quay through Mala Strana to North Prague and the road that would take us to the mountains.

The road to Semily was lovely. Baroque church towers dotted the hills, and we saw the snowcapped ruins of several medieval castles. Brilliant white fields lined the road, and if I looked carefully, I could see deer and hares digging for roots in the snow. It took us two hours to reach the Krkonose Mountains, and by the time we arrived in Semily, I could hardly contain my excitement. My dad stopped in the small town square so that he and Mr. Glatz could attach snow chains to the tires. The chains rattled and the engine shuddered and howled, but the Skoda steadily climbed the slippery, steep road, and as we rounded a curve at the top, an enchanting green cottage appeared in front of us.

"This is it," my dad announced.

We stopped next to a matching green fence that was buried in a snowdrift, and I was out of the car before my father had time to switch off the engine. The cottage was made of wood and stone, and it must have been a couple of hundred years old. The wooden rafters were hand-carved and the gaps between them were filled with blackened mortar and lime. A tall hat of snow sat on the roof, and icicles hung down from the gutters like a row of jagged teeth. The house was surrounded by a pristine blanket of snow, and here and there, a trail of deer footprints lazily crisscrossed before disappearing into the forest. As the sun broke through the clouds, the chalet windows began to shimmer and dance in the light.

"This is just like The Grandmother's cottage!" I breathed. "It's exactly like the pictures from my book."

"Isn't it?" my mother said behind me. "It really is from another time. I can't believe it's ours!"

Klara, my dad, and Mr. Glatz climbed out of the car and took a deep breath, savoring the fresh mountain air. As we stood together in a kind of stunned silence, the mountain was so quiet and peaceful, I could hear an underground stream gurgling beneath the snow.

"Wow!" my sister said finally. "This is a really nice cottage, Dad."

"Yes, Jarda," Mr. Glatz agreed. "You've scored yourself the bargain of the century."

I ran to unlatch Barry's trailer. "Come on, Barry!" I urged. "Come and have a look! It's much nicer here than it is in Cernosice."

Barry climbed down and began to suspiciously sniff his way around the side of the cottage. When he was satisfied that the new environment was safe, he lifted his leg and casually peed in the snow.

"Come on," my dad said. "Let's get everything in from the car."

He got a shovel from the trunk and cleared a path to the door, which he unlocked with a big, old-fashioned key. My mother, Klara, and I took a suitcase each and followed him inside, walking down a narrow hallway with a stone floor, past an ancient wooden staircase that led up to the attic. There was a single square room with a cooking stove in the corner. Both the ceiling and floor were made of big slabs of wood, and the walls were whitewashed. A big oak table stood to one side of the room, and there were two double beds beneath the windows. It was freezing cold, and the first thing my father did was light the stove and send Mr. Glatz out into the backyard to fetch some firewood. I followed him outside, and waded through the snow to inspect a little hut that stood near the fence. It was tiny and charming, with a heart-shaped peephole cut into the door, and I was disappointed to discover that all it contained was a wooden bench with a hole in the seat.

"Just like the old days, eh?" Mr. Glatz laughed as he came outside for more wood.

I shut the outhouse door and went upstairs to help my mother. While the outside of the cottage was picturesque, the inside resembled the front bar of the Rotten pub in Cernosice. A greasy deck of playing cards sat on the table, and over a hundred empty beer bottles stood on the floor around the stove. Soot covered everything, and the windows looked like they hadn't been wiped in years. Klara and I stacked the bottles on the porch while my mother swept the floor, and, once the cottage was clean, she cooked us lunch. The room quickly filled up with the delicious smells of pinewood and caramelized onions. We spent the rest of the afternoon transforming the chalet into our second home, and, once the sun had set, my father lit an oil lamp and we sat around the table, playing cards or reading. A big enamel pot warmed up on the stove, its lid chinking as the steam lifted it up. Barry snored at my feet as the wind sighed through the forest. After dinner, my mother gave me a hot bath in the sink, and I fell asleep in my red-and-white sleeping bag, listening to the crackling fire and the sound of my parents talking and laughing.

The following morning, my father rose early and boiled some water so that he could shave. I crawled out of the double bed I shared with my sister and stepped over Mr. Glatz sleeping on the floor. I put on my boots, my thermal underwear, and my fleecy jacket and hat, and made a quick trip to the little hut. It must have been at least minus twenty degrees outside. I dashed through the snow, pulled down my pants, and climbed up onto the wooden bench, which stuck to my bum like a block of dry ice. It was so cold it took me ages to pee, and my hands were so frozen by the time I finished, I could hardly hold the paper to wipe my bum. When I unlatched the door, I saw a car driving up the mountain. It was a Soviet-made jeep called a GAZ, and two men in green overcoats sat inside it. There was no mistaking the fact that they were headed for our house, so I ran inside to alert my father.

"Dad!" I cried. "There's a car outside!"

My father got up and looked through the window.

"That will be the men from the cooperative," he said calmly. "News travels fast in the country."

"*Ježis Marja*," my mother sighed. "What do you want us to do?"

"Nothing," my dad replied. "Barry and I can take care of it. Can't we, Barry? Come on, boy!"

Barry raised his head from the floor and slowly climbed to his feet. I ran to the window and looked outside in time to see the jeep stop at our front gate. Two men got out, and I could tell by the way they barged through the yard that they considered our cottage to be theirs. The driver was tall and stocky, with a head that sat on his shoulders like a log, but his companion was obviously the tougher of the two. He was short and surly-looking, with the red, lumpy nose of a heavy drinker, and a beer gut that strained the buttons of his overcoat. My father opened the door and intercepted them.

"Good morning, gentlemen," he growled. "What can I do for you?"

"*Cest praci,* comrade," the shorter fellow barked. "I'm Comrade Berka, the division chief of the local agricultural cooperative here in Semily, and I've come to rectify an unfortunate mistake that has been made concerning the ownership of this cottage."

My father pulled out his cigarettes and took his time lighting one.

"An unfortunate mistake, you say?"

"That's right," Comrade Berka said, puffing out his beer gut. "The man who sold you this cottage had no authorization to do so. The cottage has been requisitioned for state use by the state, and it's technically the property of the collective."

"Requisitioned for state use by the state," my dad said thoughtfully. "And what kind of state use would that be? I found a deck of playing cards and a mountain of empty beer bottles inside, but I had no idea that important state work was going on. To my eye, the place looked like the weekend house of a bunch of small-town apparatchiks."

A look of outrage appeared on Comrade Berka's face, quickly followed by a look of fear. The only people who talked insolently to party officials were other party officials or people with serious party connections. By using the phrase "small-town apparatchiks," my father was not only pulling rank from Prague, he was also alluding to the possibility that his connections within the party were better than those of Comrade Berka.

"What's that you've got there?" my dad asked, indicating a slip of paper the cooperative chief was carrying.

"This is a lease renewal form that has been stamped and notarized by the National Committee," Comrade Berka replied. "As I said, the man who sold you this cottage had no authority to do so. The cooperative therefore requires you to sign this document and vacate the property immediately."

He handed the paper to my dad while his driver nodded officiously. My father scanned the document, then folded it in half and put it in his pocket.

"Oh, I don't think so," he said. "You and I both know that the man who sold me this cottage was its rightful owner. My paperwork is in order. If you would care to file an official request via the National Committee, I'll have my notary send you a copy of the deed. In the meantime, you're trespassing on my property . . ."

He shook his head and smiled regretfully at the comrades.

". . . so piss off," he added.

Comrade Berka let out an involuntary gasp of rage and strode furiously to the bottom of the steps. His driver followed, and the two men looked ready to attack my dad. They both had the thick wrists and battered faces of experienced bar fighters, but they were also thirty years older than my father, who himself was no stranger to fighting. He flicked his cigarette into the snow and descended until he was nose to nose with the comrades.

"You want to take this further?" he asked quietly.

"I don't see why not," Comrade Berka replied. "You city folk are all show and no go. You want us to leave your yard? Go ahead and make us."

"Very well," my father growled. "Barry! *Pocem!*"

At the mention of his name, Barry lumbered out through the front door and trotted heavily down the steps, his tail wagging the whole way down. He took up his position beside my father and proceeded to drool in front of the comrades, staring up at them with his red-rimmed eyes.

"*Vem si je!*" my father commanded.

Barry swivelled his big head to look up at my father, and if the expression on his face could have been translated, it would have been, "You're kidding." But loyal as he was, Barry let out a deep sigh and recomposed his body on the steps, and I watched in amazement as he lifted his head and began to growl. It was a sound unlike anything I had ever heard him make. There was no mistaking the danger. The two men took a hasty step backward, but while Comrade Berka continued to glare at my father, I noticed that his driver was staring at Barry with amazement.

"That's . . . Bohousek, from the movies," he said finally. "The Dog Who Eats Everything."

"That's right," my father growled. "And he'll eat you in a minute if you don't get off my property!"

Barry continued to snarl, and then he worked himself up into a fit of frenzied barking. His voice echoed up and down the mountain, sending the comrades running for the safety of their jeep.

"If you think this is over, you are very wrong," I heard the cooperative chief shout at my dad. "Your entertainment connections mean nothing up here. To us, you're just a man with a dog, and I tell you this: dogs can have accidents, just like people."

"Oh, so now you're threatening Bohousek, are you?" my father roared. "I'm sure your grandchildren would be delighted to hear that."

The rest of the exchange was muffled by the sound of the jeep's engine, but as the two men drove away, I glimpsed the driver craning his neck to take one last look at our famous dog.

For all of his unpleasantness, he was obviously a fan.

My dad and Barry stood at the gate and watched the comrades drive down the hill, and then came back inside to a hero's welcome. Mr. Glatz bustled around the kitchen, whistling cheerfully as he heated a saucepan of mulled wine to fortify us for our first day on the ski slopes. My mother was relieved, and even Klara was impressed. While we all knew that my father could take care of himself, the party was so unpredictable, small conflicts like this could easily get out of hand.

"'Your entertainment connections mean nothing up here!'" my dad laughed. "That was a bit of a giveaway, wasn't it? Let's just hope they keep thinking we're connected!"

I ran over to Barry and gave him a pat. "Aren't you a good boy?" I told him. "You were so brave, you can have the rest of my breakfast sausage!"

Barry rolled his eyes and swallowed my sausage in one gulp, then he crawled under the table and watched us get ready. We had heard that one of the families in Semily operated a homemade ski lift, so we walked half a kilometer up the hill until we found a small group of people standing around a log cabin that housed a generator, an engine, and a rickety-looking contraption designed to pull skiers up a nearby slope. The slope was quite steep, so my mother, who had lent her skis to Tomas Glatz, insisted on acting as both my private ski lift and instructor, taking one end of my ski pole and pulling me up the shallow incline at the foot of the hill. For the best part of the day, she wore herself ragged while my dad, Klara, and Mr. Glatz had a great time on the slope. Every time they whizzed by, my mother and I would cheer them on, and then my mother would release my pole and I would ski down the bottom of the hill behind them. By the end of the day, my dad agreed to take me to the top of the slope. He positioned me between his legs so that we could catch the lift together, and we wobbled our way to the top of the hill.

"What do you think?" he asked me. "It's pretty steep. Do you think you can handle it?"

"Yes," I told him. "Even if I fall over, it doesn't hurt because I'm so small!"

"Very well," my father smiled. "You go first, and I'll ski right behind you."

"Okay!" I said. And promptly skied down the hill.

We had such a wonderful time in the mountains, we completely forgot about the morning confrontation, and so it was with some surprise that we arrived home to find our Skoda completely buried beneath a snowdrift that had been caused by a snowplow driving up and down the road beside it. My dad laughed at the petty nature of Comrade Berka's revenge, but he stopped laughing after it took him and Mr. Glatz the best part of a day to dig the car out of the snow. We kept the car in our yard after that, but when we returned from skiing a few days later, someone had dumped a full pile of horse manure in our driveway. And then there was the problem with the people in the village. While the mountain folk on the ski slopes were friendly enough, whenever my mother and I went shopping in Semily, the villagers could be quite rude. One day, I accompanied my dad and Mr. Glatz to the pub to buy some cigarettes, and the room fell silent when we entered, just like in the Rotten pub in Cernosice. Comrade Berka and his driver were sitting at a table near the bar, and they met my father's fierce smile with ferocious grins of their own. As we left, Comrade Berka muttered something to his friends, and the whole pub exploded in laughter.

"I'm going to have to do something about this," my father growled as we walked to our car.

"What? Now?" Mr. Glatz asked nervously.

"No. But I'm going to have to confront this idiot publicly, otherwise he's going to keep nipping at my heels."

"What are you going to do, Dad?" I asked.

"I don't know," he said. "But I'll think of something."

We drove back to the cottage and hung our jackets to dry on the wooden rack above the stove, then we gathered around the table in our pajamas. It was the second to last day of our vacation, and my father spread his big map of the mountains out in front of us.

"I was thinking we might climb to the plateau tomorrow," he said. "It's supposed to be the best cross-country skiing in the region."

"We could take Barry," I suggested. "Poor old Barry has spent his holiday indoors and hasn't even seen the mountains!"

"I don't see him complaining," my sister pointed out. "Do you?"

"We could tie a barrel of rum around his neck like a proper Saint Bernard," Mr. Glatz laughed. "It might come in handy in an emergency."

"Well, who will guard the cottage if we take Barry?" my dad asked.

"I don't mind," my mother volunteered. "I've never been particularly good at cross-country skiing. I'd just as soon stay at home with a book."

"Hear that, Barry?" I dove under the table. "You're coming to the mountains with us. Won't that be good?"

I put my arms around his neck and buried my face in his fur. He looked up and wagged his tail a few times, and then he lowered his head onto his paws and fell right asleep.

We awoke before dawn the following morning and waxed our skis for the climb. I didn't have cross-country skis, but I insisted on coming along. I balanced my little yellow skis across my shoulder as we followed the forest trail to the steep slope that led to the plateau. We finally climbed up through the clouds where the sky became blue and the sun shone brightly overhead, and a large white plain spread out in front of us.

"The hardest part is over," my father said cheerfully. "From here, all we have to do is follow the blue markings to the mountain lodge."

We put on our skis and set off across the plain. It was much easier skiing across the soft plateau snow than climbing the hard snow of the mountain, but as we rounded a patch of dwarf pines and saw the lodge in the distance, my father noticed that Barry was limping. We stopped to inspect his paws and discovered they were encrusted in ice. The soft snow had worked its way in between his toes, forming big packs of ice that turned his feet into hooves. We cleaned the snow out, but his paws were quickly covered with ice again, and after the third or fourth time they started to bleed. Saint Bernards are a famous breed of mountain dog, but their feet are not designed for soft snow. It took us a long time to reach the mountain lodge, and by the time we did, poor old Barry could hardly walk.

The lodge was a handsome wooden chalet surrounded by a fence of skis and a gathering of skiers sitting at the long, beer garden–style benches out front. As we staggered into view, the skiers became very excited by the appearance of Bohousek, and Barry was quickly surrounded by a group of admirers, all of whom were brandishing sausages and bread. Despite the pain in his feet, he rose to the occasion and theatrically ate all the food he was offered, and the manager of the lodge was eventually called outside to pose for a photograph feeding Barry a pot of goulash. By the time the photos had been taken and the manager had gone back to work, we discovered that Barry's belly was twice its original size. He lay on his side panting heavily and groaning, and after my dad put him on the leash, he started to limp along behind us. The sun was low now, and the wind had turned sharp, blowing snow into our eyes. The ice continued to stick to Barry's paws, and after half a kilometer, it was obvious that he could go no farther.

"Come on, Barry!" I cried, but the poor dog was having a terrible time. His paws were bleeding and his stomach was fit to burst. He fell over on his side and began to whimper miserably.

"I don't think he's going to make it down the mountain," my father said worriedly.

"What do you want to do?" Mr. Glatz asked.

"I don't know," my dad said. "The snow is picking up and it's starting to get cold. Maybe you should take the girls and I'll try to get Barry down on my own."

"I'll help you, Dad," I volunteered. "I'm not cold!"

"Don't worry about me, I'll be fine," my father said. "Tom, if you could carry my backpack and poles, that would be a great help. Take Klara and Dominika down to the cottage, then get the car and meet us in the village."

"Are you sure?" Mr. Glatz asked doubtfully.

"Not really, but I don't see any alternative, do you?" my dad replied.

"I'll stay!" I insisted. "I want to help."

"Now is not the time, little one," my dad said. But then he unexpectedly relented, and as Klara and Tomas skied away across the plain, we crouched down beside Barry.

"What are we going to do, Dad?" I asked. "I don't think he can walk."

"No. His paws are frostbitten," my father agreed. "I think I'm going to have to carry him down on my back."

"On your back? But he's even bigger than you are!"

"He's as big as a house," my dad laughed ruefully. "And I'm wearing cross-country skis. But at least we're going down instead of up. Do you think you can stay with me the whole way down the mountain?"

"I'll try," I said. "Will we be going very fast?"

"With Barry on my back? I don't think so. Just stay ahead of me so that I can see you, because once we get started, I don't think we're going to be able to stop."

"I bet I can do it," I said confidently. "I've had lots of practice."

"Yes you have," my dad agreed. "Just stay in front of me, okay?"

He squatted down like a weightlifter, and we somehow managed to get Barry to climb onto his back. The dog must have weighed at least seventy kilos, and my father's skis sank deeply in the snow as he straightened his knees and took the weight on his shoulders. He rose slowly and took a couple of experimental steps. Satisfied that he could ski with Barry on his back, he told me to flatten the snow ahead of him by skiing across it as heavily as I could.

"All right. Let's get this over with," he growled.

The wind howled across the plain as we began our descent. When we finally reached the edge of the plateau, my knees were shaking and my face was frozen, but it was nothing compared to the challenge of skiing the whole way down the mountain without stopping. I quickly realized that the trail was steeper than the pleasant slopes I had been skiing on all week, and as we progressed, we gathered speed like a train without brakes. I desperately tried to keep my balance, concentrating harder than I had ever concentrated in my life. My little yellow skis were made of cheap plastic, and my dad's cross-country skis were completely wrong for fast skiing, but somehow we hurtled through the forest like a couple of downhill racers. Looking back, it was a miracle that we made it to the bottom in one piece. Suddenly, we were out of the trees and whooshing down the slopes that overlooked the village, and just when I thought the worst was over, I found myself trying to brake on the icy street that led straight to the local pub. But the road gradually leveled out and we finally came to a halt in the middle of the village. The pub door flew open and a group of drinkers came out onto the balcony. Comrade Berka was with them, and as my dad crouched down to let Barry off his back, the cooperative chief let out a hoot of derision.

"Look, it's the famous film-star family from Prague!" he jeered. "Their dog is so special, they carry him everywhere!"

I turned to look at my dad, and he was so exhausted he could hardly stand up again.

"Having a bit of trouble there, comrade?" the cooperative chief threw his beer glass in the snow and lurched down the stairs.

"You think you can just breeze into town and we're going to kiss your ass because your dog was in a couple of films?" he laughed. "I'm afraid it doesn't work like that around here."

"Who's we?" my dad panted. "The only person I see kicking up a stink is you, you fat bastard."

He drew himself to his full height, but he couldn't hide the fact that his legs and arms were shaking. Barry lay in a shivering heap at his feet and, as I watched, a few of the local villagers followed Comrade Berka as he swaggered over to my dad. I was much more afraid than I had been on the mountain.

As I stood trembling in the middle of the road, the side of the pub was lit by car headlights, and before I knew what was happening, my mother had swept me up in her arms and carried me over to my father's side. She thrust herself between him and the cooperative chief, whose eyes were bloodshot and puffy and whose breath reeked of cigarettes. His fists were up and he was glaring at my dad, and he didn't register my mother's presence until she was standing right in front of him.

"Excuse me! Can't you see that my husband is exhausted?" she snapped. "Our dog has had an accident, so he has just skied down a mountain with a Saint Bernard on his back!"

"You're kidding!" one of the men from the pub said incredulously.

"It's true!" I cried. "Barry's paws were bleeding and he couldn't walk, so my dad had to carry him the whole way down from the plateau."

"The whole way down track two?" another villager gasped. "That's the steepest slope on the mountain. Why on earth would you go down track two?"

"I didn't know there was any other way," my dad admitted.

"That's incredible," someone else said. "I can't ski that slope on a good day!"

"You could probably use a shot of rum, comrade," a fourth man said. "Your dog looks like he could use a shot of rum, too. He really is Bohousek, right? From the movies?"

As Comrade Berka looked on in disbelief, his drinking companions insisted that we accompany them to the pub for a shot of rum. We were really too tired to accept, but we accepted anyway, and my father won his public confrontation. He sat shivering near the fire with a stunned look of triumph on his face. Even the toughest-looking drinkers were charmed by Barry, and the story of my father carrying him down the mountain passed into local folklore. From that moment on, we were characters, not enemies, and as we left the pub and Mr. Glatz drove us home, it was as though half the town had gathered outside to see us off.

"*Hezky vecer!*" they called out as we drove away. "Have a good evening!"

We arrived at the cottage where Klara was waiting anxiously, and hurried inside to the warmth of the stove. My mother wrapped me up in a blanket and boiled some water for my bath.

"Poor Trumpet," she whispered. "I do hope you're not going to catch a cold."

After my bath, she tucked me up in bed and piled sleeping bags on top of my blanket. I floated deliriously in a sleepy haze, listening to my father tell Klara and Mr. Glatz about our trip down the mountain, and as I listened, I could see his words floating through the air and piling up beneath the ceiling like balls of wool. Just before I drifted into a feverish sleep, I had a vision of the little god from the Czech fairy tales. He sat on top of the wool as though it was Heaven, and contentedly blew smoke rings from his pipe. I wasn't sure if I was dreaming or not, but there was no mistaking the barefoot old man with a white beard and piercing blue eyes.

"Hello!" I said. "Are you the little god?"

The old man smiled delightedly, and my body was filled with the most incredible warmth.

"Thank you for watching over us all the way down the mountain," I told him.

He nodded and waved his arm as if to say "Not at all," and as I tried to think of some more questions to ask him, his wool cloud drifted into the distance and I fell asleep with the smell of his tobacco in my nostrils. It was the only time I ever saw the little god, but I spent a great deal of my childhood trying to see him again. Every time I went to sleep, I would secretly hope that he would appear and smile at me once more, and I often found myself talking to him, especially when I was sad and lonely.

I woke up with a fever the following morning, and my dad and Barry were very sick, too. Tomas Glatz had to drive us home. I snuffled and coughed the whole way back to Cernosice, watching poor Barry through the window as he lay in his trailer. When we finally arrived at home, he crawled out of the trailer and slunk down to his kennel. My father and I went straight to bed, and Mr. Glatz carried his backpack down to the train station and went home to try and patch things up with his wife. It was a disappointing end to a wonderful vacation, but there would be many other opportunities for us to go back to the cottage and talk and laugh around the stove.

On Monday morning, my father forced himself to get up and go to work, and my mother took me to the local pediatrician, who took my temperature and ordered me to stay in bed for the whole week. My mother was due back at the Economic Institute, so Klara was delegated the responsibility of looking after me, which she did with surprising tenderness, feeding me a steady diet of chicken soup, camomile tea, and fairy tales. I lay in bed for the full five days, but as soon as I was back on my feet, I hurried down to tell Mrs. Sokolova about our adventures up in Semily.

"Hello, Mrs. Sokolova!" I knocked on her door. "I've been sick for the whole week. I had to stay in bed because my dad and Barry and I skied the whole way down a mountain without stopping, and the three of us caught a nasty cold!"

There was nothing but silence.

I knocked again but nobody answered, and when I tried the door handle, it was locked. I pounded some more, and then I raced around the side of the house and up the stairs to the apartment of Mrs. Sokolova's daughter and her husband.

"Hello!" I called out desperately. "Is anybody home?"

"Who is it?" a voice replied, and after a few moments, Mrs. Sokolova's daughter came outside. Mrs. Bendova was a worried-looking woman in her late forties, and while I was always welcome in her mother's apartment, I could tell she disapproved of my frequent visits.

"Why, it's Dominika." She sounded worried. "What are you doing up here?"

"I'm looking for your mum," I sobbed. "She hasn't gone away, has she?"

Mrs. Bendova smiled bravely. "I'm afraid she has, sweetie," she said. "She had a nice long rest and then she went peacefully."

"But I didn't get to say good-bye!" I wailed. "She was sitting in her chair and then she fell asleep. I should never have gone to the mountains!"

As I stood on Mrs. Bendova's balcony, I suddenly noticed that the floor was covered with trays of food. There was smoked salmon and hors d'oeuvres and many different kinds of cheeses, and even though I didn't know much about the preferential system of shopping under communism, I knew enough to understand that this was the kind of food that ordinary people couldn't buy.

I stopped crying and looked at the food in amazement.

"That's a lot of food," I sniffed.

"Yes, it is," Mrs. Bendova agreed. "We're having a—" she faltered.

"Our West German relatives will be here tomorrow, and this is the food I couldn't fit in the fridge. Please try not to step on the trays. In fact, maybe it would be better if you went home now."

"Okay," I whispered. "Do you know when your mother will be back?"

Mrs. Sokolova's daughter shook her head and sighed. "Perhaps you should ask your parents to explain this to you," she said. "You're old enough. You're not a baby anymore."

I retreated down the stairs, and as I walked home past Mrs. Noskova's and Mrs. Liskova's empty apartments, I felt terribly sad. My three fairy godmothers had gone, and the abruptness of their departure made me think that I might have done something wrong. As I opened the front gate and wandered down to Barry's kennel, the full realization hit me: I had no one to talk to and no one to play with. My mother and father were frantic with work, and my sister was spending more and more time away from home. All I had was Barry, and while I loved him very much, all he ever did these days was sleep and eat.

"Hello, Barry! How are you feeling?" I asked him.

Barry looked up and slowly wagged his tail.

"Mrs. Sokolova has gone away and I didn't say good-bye to her properly," I crawled inside his kennel and wrapped my arms around his neck.

"I shouldn't have gone to the mountains," I whispered. "I should have stayed home and seen her off."

Barry lifted his head and began to lick my hand, and I pressed my face into his fur and started to cry. There wasn't much space in the kennel with Barry inside it, but as I patted him, I suddenly realized how sick he really was. His breathing was labored, and he had lost a ton of weight, and he had left his food untouched, which was something he rarely did.

"Why aren't you eating?" I asked him. "You have to eat your food, Barry, otherwise you won't get better."

I pushed the bowl in front of his nose, but he just stared at it listlessly.

"Please, Barry," I begged. "Please eat some food. Just for me, okay?"

I reached into the bowl and picked up a handful of dog food pellets. Barry sniffed disinterestedly at first, but then he started to lick a few pellets from the palm of my hand.

"Good boy," I said. "When Mum gets home, I'll ask if she can cook you something special. Would you like that? Maybe she could make you something really yummy, like the food I saw at Mrs. Bendova's house. Oh, Barry, you should have seen it."

As I described each tray to Barry, his eyes lit up and he licked the pellets from my hand as though they were the exotic meals I was describing. By the time my mother came home, he had eaten many handfuls and was snoring contentedly in his kennel, like a bear.

That evening, my dad finally gave in to the flu that had been plaguing him all week and declared himself too sick to drive his taxi, so we ate an early dinner and went to bed after the Radio Free Europe news broadcast. I snuggled in my sheets and drifted off to sleep, only to be woken in the early hours of the morning by the sound of our telephone. It seemed to ring forever, and then my father picked it up.

"Hello? Any idea what time it is?" I heard him growl, but he was silenced by a female voice that shrieked so loudly from the receiver I could hear it through the wall.

"*Ježiš Marja*, Mrs. Bendova!" my dad finally said. "I'm sick as a dog, but I'll come over as soon as I can throw on some clothes."

I leapt out of bed and ran into my parents' bedroom.

"Was it Mrs. Bendova?" I asked. "Has her mother come home?"

My father was stepping into his pants. He looked very tired and his forehead was drenched in sweat.

"I have no idea," he replied. "She was hysterical, but I gather she wants me to go over there right now."

"I'll go with you!" I cried, and before he had time to say no, I dashed into my room and threw on one of my sister's flannel shirts. A few seconds later, I joined my dad at the front door. We walked down the road to

Mrs. Bendova's villa, which was the only house in the street with its lights on. Her husband met us at the front gate, wearing a striped bathrobe.

"Come with me," he motioned us up the stairs in the solemn manner of a policeman inviting two detectives to witness the scene of a spectacular crime. When we reached the balcony, there was Barry lying in the middle of the floor, surrounded by a vast number of empty dishes and trays. His belly was even bigger than it had been up in Semily, and his nose and mouth were covered in whipped cream. My father and I stared at him in astonishment, while Mr. Benda shook his head and Mrs. Bendova sobbed hysterically from behind her French doors.

"Oh, Barry," my father sighed. "What have you done?"

Barry looked up, and despite the fact that he was obviously in a lot of trouble, he also seemed rather pleased with himself. He had eaten every scrap of food that Mrs. Bendova had left on the balcony.

"I had to buy this food on the black market," Mrs. Bendova wailed. "Our rich relatives are coming for my mother's funeral. You have no idea how much trouble I've gone to!

"I'm terribly sorry," my father apologized. "I will of course pay for all the food Barry has eaten."

"That's going to cost you a fortune," Mr. Benda said grimly.

"Your stupid dog has ruined everything!" Mrs. Bendova cried. "I have to feed more than twenty people tomorrow evening! How on earth am I going to do that now?"

"We'll have to take them to a restaurant," Mr. Benda added. "And I'm not even mentioning the emotional damage—"

"Yes, yes," my father cut him off. "How much?"

Mrs. Bendova blew her nose. Her husband thrust his hands in the pockets of his bathrobe and looked inquiringly at his wife.

"Four thousand," she sniffed.

"Four thousand?" my dad gasped. "I don't suppose you have the receipts?"

Mrs. Bendova burst into tears again, and my father let out an exasperated sigh.

"Okay, I'll square this with you before your guests arrive," he said. "But we'll work out the price tomorrow morning, okay? Right now, I've got to get my kid and my dog home."

He slapped the side of his leg and clucked his tongue. "Come on, you silly beast!" he commanded.

Barry let out a huge groan and climbed to his feet. His belly was so swollen, he dragged it down every single one of the steps and it took us a very long time to walk him home. By the time we reached the gate, he was wheezing like a steam train, and he looked up at my dad as though he expected to be told off.

"So, my old friend," my father snorted. "It looks like you just ate the most expensive meal of your life."

He patted Barry behind the ears and the old Saint Bernard licked his hand gratefully. They had had so many adventures together, it was impossible to treat this disaster as anything more than another chapter in Barry's extraordinary life. Barry really was like an aging Hollywood star. We took him down to his kennel and tucked him up in his blankets, and his eyes twinkled briefly with amusement as though he was somehow reliving the glories of his past.

The following morning, my father paid Mrs. Bendova three thousand crowns for Barry's dinner, which turned out to be the last big meal of his career. For the whole month of January, he lay in Mr. Kozel's apartment and failed to recover from the cold he caught on the mountain. I would visit him every day after ballet, but he became progressively thinner in spite of my attempts to nurse and feed him, and whenever I pressed my ear to his chest, it sounded as though he had bagpipes instead of lungs. By the middle of February, he was too sick to eat the food or the medicine we had bought him, and we had no choice but to take him to the animal hospital in Prague. My father wrapped him in a blanket and carried him up to the garage, and let him ride in the front seat, like old times. We drove quickly to the hospital and carried him straight into the surgery to be examined by one of the best dog-men in the city.

"Look, it's Bohousek!" I heard somebody whisper as we carried Barry through the waiting room.

"Are you kidding?" someone else whispered back. "Bohousek was huge. This dog is all skin and bones."

My eyes filled with tears and I followed my dad into the surgery.

"All right, old fellow," the vet said as he motioned my dad to put Barry on the table. "Let's have a look at you then."

I was frightened yet hopeful as I watched the vet examine Barry. He was an older man with a halo of white hair, and he seemed very competent as he examined Barry's eyes and throat with a penlight and listened to his chest with a stethoscope. But when he took the stethoscope off, his expression was very grave. He turned and muttered something to my dad, and my father swallowed heavily and lifted Barry's head up so that he could look the old dog directly in the eyes. They stared into each other's eyes for a long while, and then my father nodded calmly. I could see though that he was very upset. He threw his big miner's arms around my shoulders.

"We're going to have to put Barry to sleep," he told me.

"Okay," I whispered. "Will it hurt?"

"No," my dad replied. "He won't feel a thing."

He told me to keep stroking Barry's paws while the vet pulled a vial from a glass cabinet, broke its neck, and filled a syringe. My dad sat on the edge of the table and put Barry's head in his lap, then he nodded at the vet, who quickly plunged the needle into Barry's neck. My father lovingly scratched his famous dog behind the ears while I stroked his paws, and we watched his eyelids grow heavier and heavier until he finally closed them.

Then the wheezing stopped and Barry lay still.

My father thanked the vet, and then he took me by the hand and led me out of the surgery. We walked through the hospital and down to the car park. I was so overwhelmed by what had just happened, I wasn't able to cry. We climbed into our Skoda and drove back to Cernosice, and as we followed the Berounka River home to our little valley, I turned to look out of the rear window, half expecting to see Barry's trailer bumping along behind us. Huge wet snowflakes fell from the sky like dandelions. It was the last snow of the winter, and while I knew that the snow would soon melt and leaves would suddenly appear on all the trees, I also understood that my three fairy godmothers wouldn't be coming home that summer. They and Barry had gone away forever.

I stared helplessly at the road behind the car, watching the trees and houses receding into the distance as the tears finally spilled down my cheeks. My three old friends and my dog were gone, and no matter how much I loved them, no matter how much I missed them, there was nothing I could do to bring them back.

For this is the way it works in life, as opposed to fairy tales. Time marches on, turning our hopes and wishes into memories.

THE PUNCHER

 THE THREE THOUSAND CROWNS we had to pay
Mrs. Sokolova's daughter put us in a difficult
position. We were broke again, and my father
was determined to finish the house that summer. The exposed brickwork needed to be
covered, and he had already ordered materials to build an internal corridor from the garage to the living room. The materials were due at the end
of April, and since Barry's eating spree had cleaned out our savings, his
choices were to postpone the work for another year or sell the chalet and
put the money into the house. We were heartbroken when he decided to
sell the cottage earlier than planned, but he argued that since Barry was
the unofficial hero of the mountains, the place wouldn't have been the
same without him.

"Every time I'd go to ski, I'd just imagine that big, silly dog sitting on
my shoulders," he sighed. "Poor old Barry. I really do miss him."

"I miss him, too," I agreed. "But I still wish we didn't have to sell the
chalet."

"Right now, it's either the house or the chalet," my dad said firmly. "We have a lot of work ahead of us, but if we can get the corridor and the facades out of the way this year, we can start looking around for other cottages later. I don't know about you, but I'm sick of walking through a mud pile every time I go to the garage."

In the end, he sold the chalet to a well-known actor for more than three times the price he had paid, and the rest of the year was spent in a frenzy of construction. On the days that I didn't have ballet and so didn't go to work with my mother, I made sandwiches for the workers, and sometimes even helped them shovel sand into the two cement mixers my dad kept in continuous rotation. I made a lot of sandwiches that year and fed a large collection of willing and unwilling workers, the latter being the many boys from the neighborhood who came to visit my sister.

Klara had recently turned fifteen, and while she had inherited our mother's slim and willowy figure, her genes had also conspired to endow her with a pair of our grandmother Hilda's enormous breasts. She found herself receiving a lot of attention from the boys who had previously ignored her because of my father's bad status. My sister may have been an enemy of the state but she was also one of the prettiest girls in Cernosice, and as her breasts swelled and the interest in her swelled with them, she wasted no time in transforming herself from a shy outsider into the village bombshell.

In 1980, the year in which her breasts became truly huge, my sister's early attempts at self-reinvention were actively hindered by my dad. My father was investing all his money in the house, so buying Klara nice clothes was very low on his list of priorities. But more frustrating, whenever a boy would come over to ask Klara out on a date, my dad would immediately put him to work.

"Ah, you're here to see my daughter," he would growl. "Grab a spade and throw some cement in this foundation trench, will you? When you're done, I'll tell her you're here."

The boy would reluctantly start to help my father in the yard, and many hours would pass before my sister was summoned. Sometimes, if my father didn't like the look of him, my sister wouldn't be summoned at all, and the only thing the young man would receive for his troubles was one of my messy, homemade sandwiches. Needless to say, it was only a matter of time before the local boys started avoiding our house like the plague.

In the early months of summer, Klara made an already difficult working environment even more difficult by throwing regular tantrums, slamming doors, and locking herself in the bathroom for hours at a time. After it became apparent that this wasn't going to stop my father from treating her young suitors as anything other than a handy source of unpaid labor, she retaliated by squeezing herself into the tightest clothes she could find and spreading mascara around her eyes in the "raccoon look" that was very popular in Prague. She teased her hair so that it stood on end, and perfected a number of haughty facial expressions that would have served her well at the local discotheque had she been allowed to visit it. Unfortunately, the disco was at the Hotel Kazin, so my dad had forbidden Klara to go there on the (not unreasonable) grounds that it would make it a lot harder to keep track of all the people who were informing on us. Throughout the five years it took us to reconstruct our house, scarcely a month would pass without a National Committee delegation arriving on our doorstep to investigate some anonymously made claim about the legitimacy of my father's building permit or the source of his materials. The license plate of every delivery truck was religiously taken down and reported, often by several neighbors at a time, and people were always complaining about the unorthodox hours he kept as a taxi driver. The way my father saw it, the kids who went to the Rotten pub disco all lived with their parents, and my sister could easily be pumped for information, deliberately or unwittingly. To Klara's chagrin, not only was she not allowed to go to the disco, but my dad also imposed an early curfew on her, and it went without saying that she was expected to spend most of her free time working on the house with the rest of us. Her early experiments with hair and makeup were therefore confined to our backyard, where she would mix cement and work on her haughty expressions. But it was also around this time that my father came up with an unusual money-saving scheme that gave my sister her first means of liberation.

My dad had met a woman who lived on the other side of our hill, and it turned out she was running a small farm on her property. The woman's name was Mrs. Backyard, and she was the wife of a very prominent gynecological surgeon who was one of the best cancer specialists in the country. Despite the deprivatization of the medical profession (which was single-handedly overseen by the Red Countess in the fifties and sixties), good doctors could command a lot of money under communism by offering their services under the table to whomever could afford them. While the rank and file tended to die on operating tables with astonishing frequency, the party elite privately engaged the best of the doctors whose practices they had collectivized, which resulted in the creation of a medical elite devoted to keeping the party elite in good health. Dr. Backyard was the gynecologist of their choice, so when he wasn't operating on the wives of high-ranking party members, he could usually be found in the Slovakian mountains shooting deer with their husbands. He kept his practice (and, word had it, many mistresses) in Prague, and rarely came out to Cernosice where his wife and family lived. Dr. Backyard's only interest in the farm his wife was running out of her own initiative was the family of badger dogs he had instructed her to breed. Badger dogs are small, ferocious dachshunds that are valued highly by hunters, and Mrs. Backyard had over twenty on her farm, along with three horses, three cows, two peacocks, two pigs, countless cats and chickens, and a goat. It was an unusual farm, and it provided the inspiration for my father's unusual money-saving scheme, which was hatched the morning he drove home from Prague and saw Mrs. Backyard carrying a feed bag up the hill. He offered her a lift home and was surprised to learn that she was milking her own cows.

"Just out of interest, what's the difference between milk straight from the cow and the milk you buy in shops?" he had asked.

"The milk in the shops is pasteurized, but it's also full of preservatives," Mrs. Backyard explained. "The secret to really good milk is to get your cows to calve every year. The more calves they have, the better the quality of their milk. In the milk cooperatives, the cows have few calves, they don't go outside as much as they should, and their feed is full of chemicals and steroids."

"Can you pasteurize milk yourself?" my dad asked.

"Of course," Mrs. Backyard told him. "You just pour it into a large pot and heat it to seventy-two degrees Celsius to kill the microbes. All the cream floats to the surface, which is handy if you want to churn your own butter."

"I see," my father said thoughtfully.

When he arrived home, he was carrying a large enamel pot in one hand and a pail full of Mrs. Backyard's milk in the other. Klara was at school, and my mother was off to work, so it was my job to help my dad pasteurize the milk and churn the cream into butter, which, like most of the projects he embarked upon, turned out to be a lot harder than it looked.

"That went well," he said cheerfully after several hours. "I think we can do this on a regular basis."

My arm ached from stirring the cream with a wooden spoon, and it was hard to determine whether we had indeed heated the milk to 72°C, but we did have butter and we did have fresh milk, and the milk, I had to admit, tasted much better than the milk we bought in plastic bags down at the local grocery store.

"How will we get the milk, Dad?" I asked. "Will the lady with the cows bring it over?"

"No, we'll send Klara across the hill," he replied. "She can carry the milk home in the pail, and then we can pasteurize and bottle it here in the kitchen. Not only is it healthier, it's also much cheaper, and if we play our cards right, Mrs. Backyard might also sell us some fresh bacon every winter!"

That evening, Klara and my mother were less than thrilled when they learned about my father's latest project.

"You want to pasteurize milk and churn butter. In the twentieth century," my mother said. "Don't we have enough to do without making more work for ourselves?"

"He wants me to be . . . a milkmaid!" my sister sobbed. "I won't do it! I'd rather mix cement."

It wasn't often that my mother and Klara sided with each other, yet whenever they did, they were a formidable combination. But my father had already committed himself to buying milk from Mrs. Backyard, so buy milk we would, and no amount of door-slamming and complaining would convince him otherwise. From that day on, we bottled our own milk three times a week, and Klara was sent to Mrs. Backyard's farm every Tuesday, Thursday, and Saturday afternoon. She hated this job at first, until word of her thrice-weekly pilgrimage spread like wildfire through Cernosice, and the road to the farm was suddenly filled with loitering boys. After that, Klara couldn't wait to fetch the milk, and the hour it took her to fulfill her duties quickly stretched out to two hours, and then three. She would rush home from school and spend a lot of time dressing and making herself up for the occasion. Then she would seize her pail and disappear into the late afternoon, only to return around sunset smelling strongly of peppermint and complaining about the long delays she had experienced at the farm. Tuesday and Thursday afternoons weren't so bad, but her Saturday milk runs always seemed beset by a lot of strange-sounding problems that required her to stay out until very late in the evening, and after she had missed three dinners in a row, my mother decided enough was enough.

"Klara, I was thinking that maybe Dominika can go with you to the farm from now on," she announced. "She could keep you company during these long waits you keep having."

A look of alarm appeared on Klara's face.

"Oh, it's okay, Mum. I don't mind," she replied.

"I think it's a good idea," my mother said firmly. "Certainly, if there's a problem and it doesn't look like you'll be here in time for dinner, she can run home and tell us, can't you, Trumpet?"

"Yes! I'd love to go to Mrs. Backyard's farm." I was oblivious to my sister's furious glare across the table. "I'd love to say hello to the cows and help you get the milk."

"Well, it's settled then," my mother smiled. "You'll go together to-morrow afternoon."

We finished dinner and I put on my pajamas and curled up with my brand-new copy of *Sleeping Beauty*. My mother had recently taught me the alphabet, so I was working my way through the easy sentences, most of which I already knew by heart. My sister took her time in the bath-room as usual, and after she had finally finished, she came into the bed-room and slumped down upon her bed.

"Come here, Little Trumpet," she said pleasantly. She patted the sheets and motioned me to sit on the bed beside her. "Come and sit next to me. I want to tell you something."

Klara hardly ever called me Trumpet and she never invited me to sit on her bed, but I was curious to see what she wanted, so I sat down be-side her.

"What is it?" I asked.

My sister waited until I was sitting on the bed; then she grabbed my head and pushed my face between her breasts and then she rolled over and lay on top of me. I tried to wiggle out, but she was too big and heavy. She smothered my face with her cleavage until I ran out of breath.

"I can't breathe! Let me go!" I begged. "Let me go!"

Klara rolled onto her side and let me take a big gulp of air, and then she rolled back on top of me again. I could hear her laughing as I strug-gled helplessly beneath her, and after what seemed like an eternity, she fi-nally rolled off me.

"What was that for?" I sobbed. "What did I do to you?"

"It's not what you did, it's for what you're not going to do," Klara snapped. "When we go and pick up the milk tomorrow evening, you're not going to snitch on me."

"I won't! I don't even know what 'snitch' means!" I said angrily.

"Snitch means, 'Tell Mum and Dad,'" my sister replied. "The trouble with you is that you can't keep your mouth shut. If you're going to come with me, you're going to do exactly what I tell you, otherwise—"

She pushed me down on the bed and rolled on top of me again.

"Get off me!" I gasped. "Let me go or I'll tell Mum you're hurting me!"

"Where's your evidence?" Klara laughed. "You have no bruises to prove I've even touched you. It's your word against mine."

"All right! I won't tell!" I cried. "I won't tell! Now get off me!"

"You'd better not," my sister said sharply. "Because if you do, I'm going to take you to bed with me every evening and turn you into my new teddy bear. *Capisci?*"

"Okay," I sniffed. "I understand."

The next day was Saturday, so Klara and I had to get up early and work in the yard as usual. We mixed and shoveled cement all day, and it was a great relief when my mother finally announced that it was time to go and fetch the milk. After Klara had changed and attended to her makeup, we grabbed the pail and left the house, turning left and walking up the track that led into the forest. As soon as we were hidden by the trees, Klara wedged the pail between the roots of a massive oak tree and then led me down a trail I had never seen before. We pushed our way through a dense thicket of elderberry bushes and came out onto the main road that led down to the local shops.

"I didn't know that trail was there," I said excitedly. "It's like a secret path!"

"There are lots of things you don't know," my sister snorted.

We walked past the grocery store and the beauty salon, and then, to my great surprise, we crossed the street and hurried through the front gate of the Hotel Kazin. There was a small parking lot in front of the pub, and a collection of teenagers were standing around beneath the chestnut trees. The girls were dressed in tight jeans and sleeveless home-knitted sweaters, and they chewed gum and talked with the same bored and haughty expressions I had seen my sister practicing at home. A few of the older boys had tiny motor scooters known as "goat's breath," on account of the stream of yellow exhaust smoke they spewed. The boys stood around their bikes and tried to look as Italian as possible, calling each other *volé*, which is the Czech way of saying "man" but actually translates as "you ox."

"Here comes trouble," one of the boys drawled when he saw us. He kicked his scooter to life and rode it in a lazy circle around Klara and me until his goat ran out of breath and spluttered to a halt.

"Ciao, bambina!" he nodded at my sister. "I see you've brought an actual *bambina* with you this time."

"Ciao, volé," Klara blushed. "This is my little sister, Dominika."

"Hello!" I said. "We're not supposed to be here. We've snuck away without telling our parents!"

"Have you now?" the boy on the bike smiled. He pulled a comb out of his pocket and began to comb his hair. "And where do they think you are?" he asked me.

"They think we're collecting milk from Mrs. Backyard's farm!" I told him. "But I promised Klara I wouldn't tell, because otherwise she'll lie on top of me and squash me!"

"Shut up, you idiot," my sister snapped.

"She's a noisy little thing, isn't she?" the boy laughed. "Hey, Martin! Come here, will you, *volé*?"

He snapped his fingers and summoned a short, nervous-looking boy who was standing nearby.

"This is Klara's sister," he said, handing the boy a ten-crown note. "How about you take her inside and buy her a lemonade or something."

"Sure, *volé*," Martin shrugged.

He pocketed the money and led me inside the ballroom at the back of the pub. The room had been set up for the weekend disco, with a mirrored ball rotating from the ceiling, casting an array of colored light across the walls. Two rows of pillars supported a small balcony on either side of the room, and the dark space between the pillars and the walls was filled with tables and chairs. As Martin led me to the bar and bought me a lemonade, I noticed that my sister and the boy she had been talking to had ducked behind the pillars and were standing very close to each other. Before I had the chance to investigate further, Martin handed me my lemonade and took me over to the jukebox. He studied the catalog briefly and slotted a crown into the machine.

"Would you like to dance?" he asked wryly.

"Yes, I love dancing!" I told him. "In fact, I'm going to be a dancer when I grow up."

The words had scarcely left my mouth when the jukebox began to play a popular song by Olympic, a government-sanctioned rock band that dominated the charts during the normalization era by writing the most politically harmless songs imaginable. As the raspy voice of the lead singer burst out of the speakers, I ran to the middle of the room and began to dance. The music and the colored lights were very atmospheric, and it was easy to imagine that I was dancing on the stage of the Smetana Theater. I stood on my tiptoes and pirouetted and kicked my legs to the great amusement of the boys and girls who were sitting at the tables, and as I danced, I was surprised to notice that my sister was easily the most popular girl in the room. Every time she finished her drink, a boy would rush over to the bar and buy her a new one, and after a while her breasts were heaving voluptuously beneath her blouse as she laughed delightedly at all the jokes the boys were telling her. Martin continued to feed the jukebox, and I drank my lemonade and practiced my ballet until Klara glanced at her watch and leapt out of her chair.

"*Ježiš Marja!*" she cried. She dashed across the dance floor and grabbed me by the hand. "We're going to have to run to the farm, otherwise there'll be hell to pay at home!" she told me. "*Ciao!*" she called out to the boys. "See you next weekend!"

We ran out of the pub and retraced our path through the forest, collecting the milk pail and hurrying across the hill.

"That was fun!" I panted as I trotted behind Klara. "I would like to do that again! Do you think we can?"

"That depends on you," my sister replied. "If you snitch, Dad will definitely stop us, and I'll lie on top of you every night for a month. Do you think you can keep your mouth shut?"

"I won't say a word," I declared as we arrived at Mrs. Backyard's front gate. "I promise!"

MRS. BACKYARD'S FARM had once been an expensive Art Deco villa, and it was surrounded by a lavish and overgrown garden. Cow sheds and stables stood at the bottom of the yard, and a long row of dog kennels lined the side of the house.

The second we walked through the gate, we were besieged by a yapping pack of badger dogs.

"Mrs. Backyard!" my sister called out as we fought our way to the house. "It's Klara! I've come for the milk!"

A few moments later, a tired-looking woman appeared at the door. She was tall and bony, and with her close-cropped hair, she looked like a man in her dirty overalls and boots.

"Shut up!" she snapped at the dogs.

"Sorry we're late," my sister told her. "We were held up at home again."

"It's true," I agreed. "We were very, very busy!"

"Were you indeed?" Mrs. Backyard frowned. "And who are you?"

"I'm Klara's sister, Dominika," I told her. "I've come to help Klara get the milk."

"I see," Mrs. Backyard sighed. "Well, follow me to the cow shed, then."

We walked down to the bottom of the yard, and Mrs. Backyard took our pail into the shed to fill it from a milk can. The cows lazily shooed flies with their tails, and I could hear the horses stamping in the stables next door. As we waited, I tried to make friends with some of the badger dogs, but they scampered away whenever I tried to pat them. In the end, I crouched down beside a very old dog who was too slow to avoid me. I scratched his ears and he began to wag his tail.

"His name is Maximilian Ferdinand von Ackerman, but we call him Max," Mrs. Backyard told me as she finished pouring the milk. "He's the granddad of the whole litter."

"Hello, Max," I said. "Aren't you a handsome fellow."

The old dog rolled over on his side, and I stroked his tummy.

"That will be ten crowns." Mrs. Backyard handed Klara the milk.

My sister's jeans were so tight she had trouble extracting the money from her pockets. As she fished around, one of the badger puppies darted over and lifted its leg and peed on her socks.

"Oh, no!" my sister shrieked. "He's done it again!"

"*Fuj,* Argo!" his mistress scolded. The puppy ran away before she could punish it, and Mrs. Backyard tried very hard not to smile. "Isn't that strange?" she said. "He's never peed on anyone else. He must be attracted to your smell."

"He does it every time," my sister moaned.

She took off her socks and wiped her feet on the grass, and Mrs. Backyard led us back to the front gate.

"I'll carry the pail home," I told Klara. "It can be my job."

"Whatever you say," my sister shrugged.

I said good-bye to Mrs. Backyard and Max, and followed Klara home across the hill. The milk pail was very heavy and I had to hold it in both hands and rest it on the ground many times as I walked, but whenever my sister offered to help, I proudly refused. It was almost dark when we reached the house, and as I kicked off my sandals, Klara reached inside the shoe chest and pulled out a bag of strong mint candy called *haslerka*s.

"Not a word to Mum and Dad," she reminded me sternly.

"Okay," I promised. "I won't say a word."

Klara gave me a *haslerka* and slipped one in her mouth, then she zipped the candy and her cigarettes inside one of her old winter boots. "All right, let's get this over with."

We went down to the kitchen and found my dad smoking and listening to Radio Free Europe, while my mother stood beside the oven and looked tired and unimpressed.

"It's not my fault!" Klara blurted before my mother could get a word in. "Dominika had to pat every single animal. It took me ages to get her out of there!"

"It's true," I told her. "Mrs. Backyard has lots and lots of dogs. And guess what? One of them peed on Klara's socks!"

"Again?" my mother said. "That's the weirdest thing I've ever heard."

She reheated our dinner, and as we ate she emptied the pail into the big enamel pot, stirring the milk until it pasteurized and then skimming the cream from the top. After the news broadcast had finished, my dad threw on his jacket and drove off to Prague. Klara ladled the milk into glass bottles, and my mother took me upstairs.

"So," she said casually as she ran the bath and helped me take off my clothes. "You and Klara went straight to the farm. You didn't stop anywhere else along the way?"

"No, Mum," I said nervously. "We went straight there."

My mother lowered me into the water and poured some shampoo onto my head. "Your hair smells funny," she observed. "It smells like you've been sitting in a pub."

"No!" I cried. "We didn't go anywhere near the Hotel Kazin! We didn't!"

"The Hotel Kazin," my mother frowned. "I see."

WHEN WE FETCHED THE MILK the following Tuesday and Thursday, Klara and I were very careful to be home in time for dinner. I was worried that I might have accidentally snitched, but as the week passed, it looked like my mother and father really didn't suspect anything. We worked in the yard on Saturday as usual, and when it was time to get the milk, I ran to the bathroom and washed my face and brushed my hair. Klara framed her eyes with black eyeliner and checked herself approvingly in the mirror, and then we grabbed the pail and disappeared into the forest, taking the secret trail down the hill to the Hotel Kazin.

"Ciao, bambina!" the boys called out as we appeared in the parking lot.

"Hello, *volé*!" I exclaimed. "Is Martin here today?"

"No, he had to stay at home," Klara's friend with the bike said regretfully. "But maybe you can dance with one of the girls. Hey, Martina! You want to look after Klara's little sister?"

"Sure, why not?" the leader of the gum-chewing girls shrugged. "We'll take good care of her, won't we, Sarka?"

"You bet," one of her friends laughed.

The two girls slouched over and made a show of examining my cheap skirt and cheap sandals.

"You Furmans really know how to dress," they observed.

"What you need is some makeup," Martina suggested. "Come with us and we'll have you looking terrific in time for your afternoon performance."

"That sounds good!" I said excitedly.

I followed them to the ladies' bathroom where they sat me up on the sink and went to work with the lipstick and eyeliner. Then they rubbed several handfuls of styling gel into my hair, teasing it so that it stood on end like I had jammed my fingers into an electric socket.

"What do you think?" they smirked.

"I like it!"

We emerged from the bathroom to a round of ironic applause from the boys, and Martina and Sarka led me to the dance floor. The mirrored ball rotated lazily above us as we danced to the Communist rock on the jukebox, the girls shaking their bottoms and wiggling provocatively. I noticed that their haughty smiles were gradually replaced by genuine ones. The room filled up with cigarette smoke, and more and more couples ventured out onto the dance floor until everyone, including my sister, was dancing. Song after song thundered out of the jukebox, and right at the point where I was sure that this was the happiest moment in my life, the door of the ballroom flew open and my mother and father walked in.

Everyone immediately froze.

"Klara! Dominika! What kind of masquerade is this?" my dad growled.

Within seconds, the dance floor was empty. My sister and I were the only people left standing.

"Get your things," my father ordered.

My sister collected her handbag while her friends stared intensely at their shoes. A few of the boys who had worked in our yard muttered, "*Dobry den,* Mr. Furman," but my dad ignored them and took Klara by the elbow and led her from the room. We drove home in silence, and Klara and I were sent down to the kitchen, which was where the family conferences took place. Except for the time I had run away from home, my parents had never been angry at me directly, but I had seen my father yell at Klara, and it was a terrible thing to behold. We were both on the verge of tears as we stood in the kitchen and waited for the ordeal to start. My dad wasted no time in laying down the law.

"If you have time to sneak away from your duties at home, you have time for a proper job," he told my sister. "We understand that you want to be independent, but independence has to be paid for. From now on, during the summer holidays and every weekend, you'll be working at my mother's buffet at the Florenc bus station."

The blood drained from Klara's face.

"Hilda's buffet?" she said incredulously.

"Your grandmother has kindly offered to employ you," my mother said. "Dominika will take over your milk run and you can start earning your pocket money like everyone else."

"But I don't want to work at Hilda's buffet," Klara spluttered.

"Well that's the price you pay for being dishonest and setting a bad example for your sister," my mother snapped. "Maybe in the future you'll think twice about lying to your parents."

Klara burst into tears and ran upstairs in an absolute rage, and when she came into our bedroom that evening, she wordlessly threw herself on top of me and read a book for half an hour. I struggled beneath her and tried to explain that I hadn't meant to snitch, but she not only ignored me for the rest of the week, she continued to ignore me for the rest of the year. As the seasons merged and we adjusted to our new routines, Klara made a ritual of punishing me every day she had to work at the buffet by smothering me while she read her book the same evening. After a while, I learned to stop fighting and conserved my breath instead.

Sending my sister to work with my grandmother actually turned out to be a huge mistake, but it would be many years before my parents understood this. Once Klara and Hilda got past their personal differences, my sister not only received a crash course in under-the-table capitalism, she also picked up a few of my grandmother's more cynical personal philosophies and found them more to her liking than the strict moral code my mother preached at home. Hilda was a wheeler-dealer like my dad, but she had spent her young adulthood raising a family in poverty, and her view was that she had wasted a golden opportunity by failing to exploit her sexuality when she had it. Like Klara, my grandmother had been stunning as a girl, and after she had married (and been unhappy with) my granddad, she had seen many less attractive women marry for money instead of love and profit greatly as a result. Hilda thought that women like my mother were naive, and had never gotten over my mother's walking away from such great wealth to marry her son. My mother and Hilda were polar opposites, but in Klara, my grandmother found a willing protegée. So, by the time the leaves had fallen, Klara had completely replaced her old wardrobe with a new one, bought with the money she was earning, and these new clothes were a constant source of conflict between her and my mother. She had enough money to buy her own drinks now, too, so she went to the Hotel Kazin whenever she felt like it. The unexpected result of my father's attempt to discipline her through work was that she acquired the means to do whatever she wanted. With Hilda's encouragement, she became fiercely independent.

As the arguments between Klara and my parents grew louder, I quietly gained some independence of my own. My dad bought me two little milk pails to carry over across the hill to Mrs. Backyard's farm. The distance couldn't have been more than five hundred meters, but it was as though I had discovered a whole new world outside my doorstep. Apart from the farm, which was a wonderful source of entertainment, I was quickly introduced to the local children, and it turned out that Mary Hairy and Petr Acorn were just the tip of the iceberg: Cernosice was crawling with baby-boom kids like me.

Since I was a friendly and confident little girl, my natural instinct was to say hello to everyone, and it was only a matter of time before I knew the names of all the local boys and girls. As I carried my milk pails back and forth from the farm, I would always try to visit one of them. I would knock on their doors and ask their parents if they could come out and play, and while the children themselves were quite happy to see me, I began to realize that their parents were not.

"Ah, you're Furman's little girl," they would say. "Aren't you a bit young to be knocking on our door?"

"I don't think so," I would reply. "Is Petra home? Can she come out and play?"

"Petra's busy," they would tell me. "You should probably go home."

The parents who discouraged their children from playing with me were the same parents who had discouraged their older children from playing with Klara when she was my age (and whose sons were presently falling over themselves to buy her drinks at the Rotten pub). But whereas Klara had become shy and withdrawn as a result, the disapproval only made me more determined. If Petra couldn't play today, could she play tomorrow? I was forever asking, and as the Christmas season approached, more and more parents became wearily resigned to the sight of me playing in their yards with their children.

Despite the initial resistance of their parents, I became quite good friends with Petr and Mary. The Acorn and Hairy families were next-door neighbors who lived two houses down the street from mine. Their villas had been converted into communal housing, but like most people in the region, they lived with their relatives instead of complete strangers. The Hairy house was occupied by the Hairys and the Caesars, Mr. Caesar being Mr. Hairy's brother-in-law.

Everyone in the street was afraid of Mr. Caesar. He was extremely fastidious when it came to noise and litter. He was one of the few neighbors who kept his house and garden in immaculate condition, but his fussiness also extended to the forest, where he could often be found dismantling local treehouses and forts on the grounds that they were unsafe. Barking dogs enraged him, and excessive snowball-throwing or shouting in the street would also drive him nuts. It was a well-known fact that if you made a lot of noise outside the Hairys' villa on the weekends, Mr. Caesar would come out and chase you away. As far as the older kids in the neighborhood were concerned, playing cat and mouse with Mr. Caesar was even more fun than re-creating famous battles in the forest, but this was one game I would never join in. Deep down, I liked the way Mr. Ceasar kept his garden neat and tidy, and I longed for the day when our own house would be finished, because I secretly hoped it would look as nice as his.

MY SISTER AND MY PARENTS declared a truce over Christmas, and Klara made the festive season the best one I had experienced so far by contributing a lot of food to my mother's pantry and promising to stop lying on top of me when she came home from work. The Baby Jesus brought me a set of wax pencils and a Russian recording of *Swan Lake,* and we

saw in the New Year by singing around the piano like old times and remembering Barry by watching him on TV.

It was a perfect start to an important year in my life. I would be attending school for the first time that summer, but I was also old enough to
audition for the National Ballet Preparatory School, and this audition had
been on my mind ever since the day I had met Mr. Slavicky. After the Christmas show, Mrs. Sprislova had taken my mother aside and explained that
while I was one of the most expressive dancers she had ever trained, my size
was going to be a problem at the audition. And now that the February date
was approaching, she seemed even more nervous than my mother and I.

On the morning of the audition, my mother crisply ironed my best
dress and put my hair up in pigtails. I was too nervous to eat, so I had a
glass of milk for breakfast and checked my backpack several times for my
leotard, legwarmers, and *piskoty* slippers. Then we stood outside the house
and waited for my dad to return home from work. Just after sunrise, he
rattled up our street, performed his famous three-point turn, and drove
my mother and me back to Prague.

"Good luck," he winked as we hopped out of the car.

I followed my mother through the big revolving door at the rear of
the Federal Parliament building, and we walked into a crowded lobby.
There must have been at least five hundred little girls applying for the
preparatory school, and all of them seemed to be wearing dresses that you
could only buy in Tuzex, an exclusive chain of shops that sold Western-
brand products to the party elite or people who could get their hands on
U.S. dollars or deutsche marks. The mothers wore fur coats and seemed
even more glamorous than the well-to-do women whose daughters attended Mrs. Sprislova's school. Everyone checked out my mother's outfit
and hat, before looking down at me and smiling with relief. I was easily
the smallest girl, and I could tell that none of the women considered me a
threat. I clutched my backpack and waited nervously in the crowd until
Mrs. Saturday appeared at the head of the stairs.

"*Dobry den!* Thank you very much for coming," she announced. "We have a long day ahead of us. The way the selection process will work is that I'll call everyone's name in alphabetical order, forming groups of thirty that will audition together."

She began to read from a long list of names, and the girls she selected kissed their mothers good-bye and climbed the stairs like a flock of sacrificial lambs. Once the first group had been formed, the girls followed Mrs. Saturday down the hall, while the rest of us had to wait in the lobby until they finished. The wait was unbearable. After what seemed like an eternity, Mrs. Saturday reappeared and began to read more names from her list. I prayed that my name would be called because I wasn't sure that my nerves would hold out. Fortunately, I was the last girl in group two, and my knees began to shake as I heard my name echo through the lobby. I let go of my mother's hand and followed Mrs. Saturday to a small dressing room opposite one of the studios. The girls and I changed quickly and then were ushered across the hallway, walking past the five-person auditioning committee that sat at a long table at the front of the room. The studio was freezing cold, and we all warmed our backs against the radiators that lined the walls. The fat pianist I had seen in Mrs. Saturday's class two years earlier strode into the room and sat behind her piano, while Mrs. Saturday divided us into three lines. I looked up as she passed me, hoping for a glimpse of recognition, but her face betrayed nothing and I felt sick with fear. Even though we were only five or six years old, everyone in the group knew that the school only accepted one student in ten, and each of us desperately wanted to be chosen.

"Very well, we will begin!" Mrs. Saturday boomed. "We will examine you individually at first, so when we call your name, please step forward and let us take a good look at you."

One after the other, we stood in front of the committee and let Mrs. Saturday examine us like horses, measuring and testing the elasticity of our limbs, pushing our legs up as high as they would go. Whenever a girl was able to touch her forehead with her foot, the committee members would whisper to each other and nod approvingly. No one said a word as I was examined. I could hear the vertebrae cracking in my spine as Mrs. Saturday forced my legs up and down.

When the individual examination was over, we were told to exercise at the bar. The pianist played a cheerful waltz, while Mrs. Saturday made us kick our legs in time, and while I kicked each leg as high as it would go, the bar was still slightly too high for me to reach, and it was obvious that the taller girls were doing a much better job. To make matters worse, I could see the reflection of the committee in the mirror, and none of the ladies were even looking in my direction. I felt like crying, but I gritted my teeth and persevered to the end.

"Very well," Mrs. Saturday said as the pianist finished her waltz with a flourish. "Now step out onto the floor and we will end the audition with five minutes of improvisation."

The girls scattered around the studio, splaying their feet into the fifth position and raising their arms like professional ballerinas. The pianist walked over to the record player in the corner of the room and was about to put the needle on the record.

"Maybe not the Prokofiev this time," Mrs. Saturday stopped her. "Could you please put on side two of the other record?"

The pianist looked vaguely surprised and she removed the record from the turntable and replaced it with another.

After a short pause, the urgent sound of an oboe warbled into the studio, and as soon as the first notes crackled from the speakers, my body was electrified. It was the final act of the Moscow Symphony Orchestra's famous recording of *Swan Lake*. My heart heaved with emotion, and I stood up on my toes and took control of the space. While the other girls danced more or less on the spot, I began to dance through the studio in search of my prince. I knew every bar of this ballet by heart, but more important, I knew the story behind the music. In the last act of *Swan Lake*,

Odette waits for her prince to arrive, knowing that if he doesn't show up in time, she will turn back into a swan and die of a broken heart. In the populist version, the prince does arrive in time, but in the classic version, he is delayed, and Odette's climaxing dance is filled with desperation. As Mrs. Saturday and the committee looked on in amazement, I re-created this desperation, dancing frantically across the room from the window to the door and listening for the sound of Mr. Slavicky's steps. The music thundered and roiled like a stormy sea as I searched every corner of the room for my prince, knowing all too well that if I couldn't find him, I was doomed to turn back into a swan.

When the music stopped, I opened my eyes to see the whole class staring at me. One of the girls actually giggled with embarrassment, until Mrs. Saturday cleared her throat loudly. She walked across the room to the auditioning committee, and after a hushed conference, she clapped her hands.

"Would you ladies please step back against the wall?" she said, indicating the majority of the girls. Then she looked directly at me. "We'll try that again and give you a little bit more space," she told me. "Just try to relax and let it come, okay?"

"Okay," I said nervously.

The other girls moved back, glaring daggers at me as Mrs. Saturday instructed the pianist to replay the record, and for the next five minutes I danced as though my life depended upon it, letting the music carry me through the room. I searched for my prince and was heartbroken by his absence, and before I knew it, the audition was over.

"Thank you very much, ladies—that will be all," Mrs. Saturday announced. "We'll notify you of our decision at the end of the school year."

The class left the studio and returned to the dressing room. As I passed Mrs. Saturday, I felt her hand briefly brush against my shoulder, but when I looked up, her face was as impassive as ever. I'll never know for sure, because I never had the courage to ask, but I've always believed that Mrs. Saturday deliberately changed the record to give me a chance in the audition. The committee hadn't even looked at me when I first entered the room, but as I left, I could feel their eyes burning into my back.

I changed out of my leotard and slippers in a daze, and hurried down to the lobby.

"How did it go?" my mother asked.

"I think I got in!" I whispered excitedly. "Mrs. Saturday played the final act of *Swan Lake,* and she asked me to dance Odette by myself in front of the committee!"

"Really?" she said. "That sounds promising. I guess sending you to Mrs. Sprislova's school must have really paid off."

"I hope so," I told her. "All the other girls were so much taller than me. And they had proper leotards and everything."

"We'll buy you a proper leotard, don't worry," my mother sighed. "But in the meantime, how about I take you down to the Florenc bus station and we can have lunch with Klara at the buffet?"

"That would be great!"

Now that my nerves had settled, I discovered that I was terribly hungry. When we arrived at the station, we joined a large crowd of customers and waited to be served. I couldn't help noticing that most of the customers were men.

"Klara's going to be very surprised when she sees us!" I said.

My mother smiled as we worked our way through the crowd, and then her smile suddenly vanished. Hilda's buffet was fronted by a large glass counter, and while the counter contained an eye-catching array of little cakes and sausages, the main attraction appeared to be my sister's breasts. Klara stood behind the counter in a low-cut stretch T-shirt, and she had taken off her bra underneath it. Most of the customers appeared to know her by name, and whenever they placed an order, Klara would lean revealingly forward as she scooped up their purchases and poured them their drinks. The men watched her in amazement, and after Hilda had rung up an arbitrary total on the cash register (the prices were written illegibly in chalk, so she cheerfully charged whatever she liked), the men would round the bill up to the nearest five or ten crowns and give it to Klara as a tip. Judging by the size of the crowd and the amount of money changing hands, my grandmother and sister were making a small fortune.

Klara continued to lean forward and smile at the men until she met my mother's eyes across the counter. She leaped in the air as though a wasp had stung her.

"Mum!" she gasped. "What are you doing here?"

"Dominika had her dancing audition today," my mother said coolly. "We thought we'd celebrate by visiting you."

"That's . . . that's great!" My sister blushed. "What can I get you? Hey, Hilda, look who's here!"

My grandmother looked up from her cash register, and it took her a few moments to place us.

"Ah, Jana!" she said finally. "How surprise I am to see you!"

"I bet," my mother agreed. "I see you're selling more than just food."

"Of course," Hilda replied smoothly. "May I offer you a glass of wine?"

"No, thank you," my mother shook her head. "It's a little early in the day for drinking, don't you think?"

The two women glared at each other while my sister retreated to the far side of the counter, but before things were able to get completely out of hand, I stood up on my tiptoes so that Hilda could see me.

"*Ahoj*, Grandma!" I called out. "Guess what?"

"Why, it's little Dominika!" Hilda was grateful for the diversion. "What is it, sweetie?"

"I think I got into the National Ballet Preparatory School," I told her. "I danced all by myself in front of the judges!"

"Really? That's wonderful!" my grandmother smiled. "It sound like it might be a call for a celebration. Why don't you come here and I'll give you a treat?"

"Yes, please!" I said eagerly.

I started to push my way through the crowd, but before I made it around the side of the counter, my mother's hand landed firmly on my arm.

"I think we might keep going," she told Hilda and me. "We just dropped by to see how you are doing. And now we've seen," she added ominously.

"Suit yourself," Hilda shrugged.

"But Mum!" I cried. "I'd like a little cake. I'm hungry!"

"I'll buy you some fruit," my mother replied. And before I could argue, she took my hand and pulled me away from all the delicious food my sister was selling. I couldn't believe it. There was so many cakes at Hilda's buffet, and they all looked much nicer and more exotic than the little cakes at our local bakery. She even had the hard-to-find cakes, like the swan and the puncher, which was a sponge cake soaked in punch. I could see that my mother was angry at Hilda for letting Klara dress so provocatively, but I was terribly upset that she had declined Hilda's offer for me. I didn't have nice clothes like Klara and I hardly ever got to eat little cakes or sweets, and now it suddenly turned out that my sister was working at a place where there were better cakes than the ones in Cernosice, and even then I still wasn't allowed to have one. It really didn't seem fair. To add insult to injury, my mother took me to a fruit stand and bought me the same stringy, bitter Cuban orange she always bought me as a treat. I really hated these oranges.

I ate it sullenly as we rode the train home in silence.

THE NEXT COUPLE OF WEEKS were spent in an uproar. My mother was furious at my sister's "immorality," and our family dinners were tense and formal affairs. My dad's cheerful optimism had no effect on either party, and around the time of my birthday, we were both beginning to think that the rift between Klara and my mother might never be mended. But then two things combined to provide a strange resolution: my mother received a phone call from Mrs. Sprislova, and my sister began to complain of a pain in her spine.

Mrs. Sprislova's phone call was both encouraging and daunting. She had spoken to Mrs. Saturday, and the word from the auditioning committee was that my improvisational dancing had been viewed very favorably, but there were serious concerns about my height and my weight. The height issue was something that could resolve itself later. I would either grow or I wouldn't. But the weight issue was something Mrs. Saturday suggested we look into immediately. I wasn't fat by any means, but I was broad-shouldered and muscular, and according to the Russian height-to-weight ratio the preparatory school was working from, my body was unsuitable for ballet. Mrs. Saturday had said that she would see what she could do, but she strongly suggested that I try to lose as much weight as possible before the start of the school year.

My mother thanked Mrs. Sprislova for the news, and she had just put down the phone when my dad and Klara returned from Prague where they had spent the day consulting a specialist about my sister's back problems. The specialist had run many tests and concluded that Klara's back pains were caused by bad posture on account of her large breasts growing larger as a result of the extra weight she had gained at the buffet. In his opinion, Klara needed to lose eight kilograms, which was roughly twice the amount Mrs. Saturday wanted me to lose.

"Well, that settles it," my mother said decisively. "It looks like I'm cooking light meals from now on."

"For everyone?" my dad asked nervously.

"Of course. It's not fair to expect Klara and Dominika to cut down on their food while we are eating heartily. The only fair thing to do is put the whole family on a diet."

My dad and Klara looked at each other in alarm. Whenever my mother set her mind on doing something, she could be counted on to keep going long after everyone else was desperate to stop.

"What do you think, Trumpet?" she smiled. "Shall we try and lose some weight together?"

"Yes!" I said excitedly. "We can eat lots of salad and get very very thin, and maybe I'll grow taller, too, so that I can reach the bar in Mrs. Saturday's studio. I'd like that very much!"

"I bet you would," my sister groaned.

AS IT TURNED OUT, my mother's diet really affected only my mother and me, as we were the only ones who stayed on it. My sister would visit Hilda's buffet before and after school, and my dad snacked at the various taxi stands in Prague. We would get up in the mornings and eat the bland hot cereals my mother prepared, and then my dad and Klara would hurry away to eat their real breakfasts in town, leaving me to count the hours until lunch, when my mother would serve such delicacies as half a cauliflower in tomato sauce or a plate of dry lettuce. On the days when I would accompany her to work, she would prepare our ham-and-cheese sandwiches using a special kind of low-fat cheese that tasted like wax, and we stopped visiting the little bakery in Mala Strana, which made me very sad. The fridge was always empty and the pantry door was always locked, and sometimes I was so hungry I would chew the uncooked spaghetti my mother kept in a jar. My father would sneak food home from Prague on the days when he was looking after me at home, but I would always be helping him in the yard, and the work made me even hungrier than usual.

The worst part of being hungry was that it took the fun out of dancing.

I'd put on my *Swan Lake* record and practice my steps in my bedroom, but my tummy would be grumbling the whole time. In the end I would give up and go outside to either forage for nuts and wild berries in the forest (the forest was full of food, it turned out), or carry my pails to Mrs. Backyard's farm a couple of hours early. After I had patted her dogs and filled my pails, I would carry the milk to the front gate and surreptitiously drink half of it. Then I spent the rest of the day making a tour of the neighborhood, dropping in on the families of my friends, usually around the time they were having afternoon tea.

By the time Mrs. Sprislova arranged for Mrs. Saturday to weigh me privately, I had indeed lost three kilos, and I was delirious with joy as I thought this would mean the end of my mother's diet. I spent the next couple of days dancing with renewed enthusiasm until I realized that the reduced meals were not going to stop.

I didn't think I could stand it another day.

"I'm hungry!" I complained to my mum as she served me another plate of lettuce. "Ever since you put Klara and me on that stupid diet, I'm hungry all the time!"

"There, there, Little Trumpet," my mother said soothingly. "I know it's very difficult, but you'll have to watch your weight if you're going to dance in *Swan Lake*. Otherwise, Mr. Slavicky won't be able to lift you above his head, will he?"

"I guess not," I mumbled. "But I miss little cakes!"

"You still want to be a dancer, don't you?" my mother suddenly became serious.

"Yes," I whispered.

"Well, that's good," she said. "Because I've just received a letter from Prague."

I looked up in surprise, and she pulled an envelope from the pocket of her apron. She opened it up and handed me the letter inside.

"What does it say?" I asked.

"It's from the auditioning committee," she told me. "You've been accepted to study at the preparatory school next year."

"Really?" I cried. "I got in?"

"Yes, you got in," my mother smiled.

I jumped up and down and began to dance around the kitchen, laughing with happiness and relief. My dream had come true. I had made the first step in the long and difficult journey to become a professional ballet dancer. I may have been an outsider, but I was on my way to the National Theater.

"Don't get too excited," my mother said sternly. "Now that you've gotten in, you're going to have to watch your weight even more than before. Which means an even stricter diet and lots and lots of exercise. You understand this, don't you, Trumpet?"

I let out a deep sigh.

"Yes, Mum," I said. "I understand."

seven

THE LITTLE INDIAN

 AS IT TURNED OUT, my mother didn't have to worry too much about my diet. Our summer vacation would solve the weight-loss problem with unexpected efficiency. Our family went on holidays to Pisek, the town my father used to visit as a boy, and we rented a room from an old woman with ten cats. The woman's name was Mrs. Nova, and her house was near the banks of the Otava River, which were overflowing with campers from Prague. The local pubs were packed to the rafters and the air smelled faintly of rotten apples. It was August 21, 1981, the thirteenth anniversary of the Soviet invasion of Czechoslovakia, and the town was decorated with flags in celebration. Sausages sizzled on barbecues, and the radio played love songs. Everyone was having a wonderful time.

We were on holiday because my dad had finally been fired from his job driving taxis. At the end of his shift one evening, two secret policemen in gray suits were waiting for him in the dispatch office, to tell him that taxi drivers were now required to become STB informers.

"Given your papers and record, comrade engineer, we assume you wouldn't be interested in working for us," the policemen had smiled. Then they stopped smiling and confiscated my dad's license.

This kind of thing happened regularly to my father. Somewhere in the Ministry of Interior, there was a huge dossier on his activities that was kept up to date by smiling men in gray suits, and he had been fired from over thirty jobs since the Russian invasion. The secret police hated my dad for many reasons, but one of the things that infuriated them most was that whenever they tried to break his spirit, they usually achieved the opposite effect. My father was the kind of person who would be nervous about losing a job when he had one, but as soon as he was fired, he would become defiantly cheerful and take us out to dinner with what little money he had.

"The good thing about hitting the bottom is that you can't fall any farther," he would declare. "From here, the only way is up!"

The problem with my father's optimism was that it often flew in the face of reality. When he lost his taxi license, he packed us off on holiday the very next day, and we arrived in Pisek to discover that all the good houses had already been rented. Mrs. Nova's was the best we could find, and it was a shabby building at the end of a shabby street. The rent was cheap, but so was Mrs. Nova. There wasn't any soap or hot water, which proved to be disastrous.

The week had passed slowly. My parents would relax in the house until midday, while my sister would dash outside the second the sun rose. She would throw on her bikini and trot down to the river, where the local boys swarmed around her like wasps as she reclined on a towel and rubbed suntan lotion into her massive cleavage. Like most of her clothes, Klara's bikini was several sizes too small, but none of the boys was complaining. A few of the braver ones would grab her by the arms and legs and swing her into the river, and afterward they'd all go off for ice cream. It looked like a lot of fun, and I'd go down to the river and try to join in, but my sister and her friends weren't interested in babysitting a six-year-old girl. As there weren't any kids my age to play with, I had no choice but to make my own entertainment. There was an old wooden bench in Mrs. Nova's backyard, so what I ended up doing was playing school with the cats.

I was due to start first grade in a couple of weeks, and my mother had bought me a very nice purple dress to wear. I couldn't wait. I had heard all about school from my sister (she didn't like it), and I had even been to the schoolyard a couple of times, so I was pretty confident I knew what I was doing when I rounded up the cats.

Of the ten cats that Mrs. Nova fed regularly, more than half were wild. Every day after lunch, I would bring a bowl of milk-soaked bread rolls out into the backyard, and the wild cats would come in from the fields and beat up the four house cats who were my favorite students. The poor house cats were big and fluffy, and had no chance against their thin and hungry class-mates. There was one particularly mean, young tomcat whose black-and-ginger fur looked like a flannel shirt, and he took great delight in disrupting my class. Every time I tried to put him on the bench, he would hiss and try to scratch my arms. The afternoons were very hot, so the four house cats and a couple of the friendlier wild ones were happy to sprawl and fall asleep. I would pat them and tell them all the things I knew. I could count to twenty. I could write my name on a piece of paper. I could name all the colors, even purple and orange, and I knew that Prague was the capital of the Czech part of Czechoslovakia, while Bratislava was the capital of the Slovak part. All in all, I was a very good teacher.

On the last day of our vacation, I held class in the morning, bringing bread and milk out early and watching with satisfaction as the house cats licked the bowl clean. The wild cats were caught off guard by my change of routine, which meant four favorite students were able to study in peace. I had just lifted them onto the bench and was about to start the les-son, when I saw the red tomcat sneaking through the back fence with a live mouse in his mouth.

"Hey!" I called out. "What's that you've got there?"

The tomcat dropped the mouse and pounced on it again. I ran to the fence and cornered him. He had the mouse between his teeth and his orange fur was standing on end.

"Stop that!" I cried.

I knelt down and tried to get him to drop the mouse.

"Come on, kitty," I said soothingly. "Let the poor mouse go."

I reached for the mouse and the cat sank a claw into my finger. I yelped with pain and grabbed the mouse by its tail, and tried to pull it out of the tomcat's mouth. The cat hissed and scratched, but I hung on with all my might until the tail snapped and came away in my hand.

"You naughty cat!" I sobbed. "Look what you've done!"

The cat dropped the mouse and batted it around on the grass until he was satisfied that it was really dead. Then he lost interest in both of us and slunk away into the fields.

I dug a small hole and was in the process of burying the mouse, when my mother called me in for lunch. I filled the little grave with dirt and patted it down properly, and then I walked back to the house to join my parents and sister at the dining table. A tray of roast chicken sat steaming in front of them.

"One of the cats just scratched me!" I showed my mother.

"Well, you should be more careful," she scolded. "Now hurry up and wash your hands. Your lunch is getting cold."

I could only wash my hands in Mrs. Nova's laundry sink, because the sink in the downstairs bathroom was too high for me to reach. There was no hot water (Mrs. Nova had turned it off), and I patted the soap tray, reaffirming that it was empty. Mrs. Nova had hidden all the soap and laundry powder, so I had no choice but to rinse my hands in cold water and wipe them on my pants before I hurried off to lunch.

At the table, I followed my father's example and ate the chicken with my fingers. Ever since he had been buried in the Ostrava coal mines, my dad tended to eat every meal as though it might be his last. We made short work of the chicken and saved the bones for the cats, though I made sure that the red tomcat didn't get any. Later that afternoon, we packed our bags and returned to Prague.

But by the time we arrived in Cernosice, I was terribly sick. I ran straight to the bathroom and threw up in the sink. My mother came in to help me, then she took me to my room and tucked me up in bed.

"You'll feel better in the morning," she assured me. "You've probably just caught a bit of sunstroke."

My mother was usually right, but on this occasion she was wrong. I woke up the next morning to discover that my tummy had swollen to the size of a melon. I climbed out of bed and tried to walk to the toilet, but my legs shook and I barely made it in time.

"Mum! Help!" I cried out.

My mother came in and put her hand on my forehead. My temperature was very high, and she could see that this was no ordinary sickness. She watched as I was wracked by a series of great heaving spasms, and quickly ran off to call Dr. Polakova, my pediatrician.

I stayed on the toilet for the next two hours, wiping my bum with nasty Polish toilet paper. It was a particularly bad time to have diarrhea, as regular toilet paper was in short supply. The state-run paper factory had burned down the previous year, and toilet paper was so scarce, shop assistants were selling it under the counter. We had wiped our bums with newspaper for a few weeks until my dad used his connections to get his hands on some toilet paper from Poland. It was cheap and had the same waxy coating as baking paper. The sheets were slippery yet abrasive, and from constant use my bum started to bleed.

My mother spent the morning trying to call Dr. Polakova until she found out that the doctor was on vacation and wouldn't be back until Monday. The emergency room in Radotin was famously bad, so she decided to nurse me through the weekend herself. She made me swallow black pills that tasted like charcoal, and bathed my bum with chamomile tea. By Sunday night, my fever was even higher, and when I awoke the next morning, I was wrapped in a blanket, sitting with my mother in the car.

We drove down to the local health-care center, which was one of the nicest buildings in Cernosice. It had once belonged to a famous Czech actor, but now housed an assortment of local doctors and dentists. Dr. Polakova's office was on the ground floor, and my father carried me through a waiting room crowded with mothers and children. We went straight in to see the doctor, a nice old lady who knew the senior staff at many of the big hospitals in Prague. She did what she always did, which was take my temperature and weigh me.

"Thirty nine and a half." She frowned at the thermometer. "That's very high. Can you put her on the scale for me?"

My dad transferred me to the old-fashioned scale that stood in the corner of the room.

"Eighteen kilos," Dr. Polakova muttered. "That's very low. And she has bad diarrhea, you say? What do you think we should do?"

"Can you refer her to someone at the Bulovka Hospital?" my mother asked. "Is there anyone there who might be able to help?"

Dr. Polakova opened her desk drawer and scratched her head thoughtfully.

"Jiri Kopecky owes me a favor," she said. "His assistant is Dr. Bartos. I'll write you a referral and give them a call while you drive there. How does that sound?"

She scribbled a referral while my mother wrapped me back up, and a few minutes later we were driving frantically to the Bulovka Hospital.

My father took the direct route through Prague, using all of his taxi-driving skills to pilot us through the narrow streets of the Jewish Quarter. We drove up the quay past the Manes Bridge, and then my dad suddenly jammed on his brakes. An old man with a nylon bag in his hand was standing near a pedestrian crossing. My father excitedly wound down his window.

"Lada Stern!" he called out. "The STB have fired me again. I've been trying to contact you all week."

The old man turned around and his face lit up.

"Jarda Furman! *Ahoj!*" he called back. "You're not going to believe this. I just found Kriegel's ashes! They were in the toilet at the Central Railway Station!" He held up the nylon bag.

"You're kidding!" my dad exclaimed. "Are you heading home?"

The man nodded and my father swung open the passenger door.

"We're driving to the Bulovka Hospital. Dominika has come down with something nasty, so we're in a hurry. But I'll drop you off on the way if you like."

Mr. Stern was at least twenty years older than my dad. He was short and stocky and his skin was wrinkled and gray, but his deep-set blue eyes radiated an almost ethereal calm. Mr. Stern and his wife had been part of the Czech resistance during the Second World War, and had spent many years in German concentration camps. They were dissidents, like my parents, and close friends of future Czech president Vaclav Havel. In 1984, Mrs. Sternova would become the official spokeswoman for Charta 77, Havel's protest group, and the secret police would routinely interrogate her in the old Gestapo headquarters in the middle of Prague, where she had been tortured by the Nazis four decades earlier.

Mr. Stern climbed into the car and put the bag between his knees.

"Hello, Dominika. You're not looking so good," he said kindly.

"Hello, Mr. Stern. I don't feel so good, either," I whispered.

He patted my hair with his big hand and began to tell my parents the story of how he came to find the ashes of one of the greatest Czech patriots in a public toilet at the Central Railway Station.

FRANTISEK KRIEGEL was a doctor who worked with Mr. Stern in the resistance and later became a member of parliament during the Prague Spring. When the Russians invaded in 1968, all the important Czech politicians were arrested and flown to Moscow, where they were presented with the normalization agreement that authorized the Soviet Union to take control of Czechoslovakia. Fearing for their lives, nineteen men signed the agreement. The only man who didn't sign was Kriegel. He said no to General Secretary Brezhnev, expecting that the Russians would probably shoot him. To everyone's surprise, they allowed him to return to Prague, where he was quietly and systematically hounded to death by Czech collaborators. He was fired from his job, interrogated regularly by the STB, and denied medical treatment until he died of a heart attack in 1979. Even after his death, the secret police didn't leave him alone. First they tried to ban his funeral, and when it was reluctantly approved, a group of agents rode their motorcycles to the cemetery and revved their engines loudly in the street to disrupt the service. A few days later, they stole his urn from the cemetery and erased his name from the tombstone in much the same way that they would erase it from the history books. By 1981, few Czech people even knew that Mr. Kriegel had existed. The cremation urn that sat on Mr. Stern's knees was symbolic of the way our country could so easily dispose of its bad conscience.

"It took me a year and half," Mr. Stern said grimly. "I kept plugging away at the Ministry of Interior until I received an anonymous phone call yesterday, advising me to check the toilets in the major railway stations. I had to go to five different stations before I found his ashes."

"Ježiš Marja!" My father shook his head. "Those guys are such assholes! They've got a new rule that says all taxi drivers have to work as informers. It's getting ridiculous. I'm at the point where I'm thinking I might as well sign the Charta. I've got nothing to lose!"

Charta 77 was a human rights document drafted by Vaclav Havel and Pavel Kohout, demanding that the Communist government respect the basic laws of the Geneva Convention. By signing it, my father would add his name to Radio Free Europe's official list of dissidents, which would make the secret police focus on his activities even more than before.

Mr. Stern turned to look at me in the backseat of the car, wrapped up in a blanket and shivering in my mother's arms.

"Don't be silly, Jarda. You have a lot to lose," he said quietly.

THE BULOVKA HOSPITAL was on top of a hill that overlooked the Vltava River. When we finally arrived, my father rolled down his window and presented our referral to the guard at the gate. The man waved us in and we drove up to the emergency room, which was a dilapidated building surrounded by a fleet of rusty ambulances. We trooped into the building and asked a nurse to help us find Dr. Bartos. It turned out that he had just left for the day, so I was examined by an overworked intern instead. The young doctor was very tired. He suppressed his yawns as he prodded my belly, and when a nurse handed him the result of my blood tests, he looked them over and sighed. He told the nurse to make him a strong coffee, and called my parents into the room.

"Your daughter has dysentery," he said flatly. "How she managed to catch it, I don't want to know. Technically speaking, it doesn't exist anymore."

"It doesn't exist?" my father growled.

"Not under the Socialist Health Care System," the doctor explained. "We cured it years ago. It's one of the diseases our five-year plans have officially wiped out."

"But that's terrible!" my mother cried. "What can we do?"

"You can't do anything," the young doctor told her. "It doesn't exist. The fact that there's a ward full of Gypsy kids crawling with it down in the Infection Pavilion is beside the point. If I take your daughter down there, she will simply become unclassifiable until she gets better. That's the way it works with diseases we've already officially cured."

"The Infection Pavilion?" my father said anxiously.

"It's a bunch of isolation wards that specialize in contagious diseases," the doctor said. "They'll put your daughter on an IV and shoot her full of drugs for a couple of weeks. It won't be pleasant, but you should have brought her to us earlier. People die from dysentery, you know."

The blood drained from my mother's face.

"How long will she have to stay there?" she asked.

"Two weeks, a month," the doctor shrugged. "No solids, lots of fluids, and lots of rest."

"I don't want to go," I whispered. "I want to go home."

"Does a Dr. Kopecky work in these isolation wards?" my mother wanted to know.

"Yes, he's the head of the unit," the intern replied. At the mention of Dr. Kopecky's name, he suddenly became a lot more attentive.

"What's your daughter's name?" he asked.

"Dominika," my mother told him.

"Well, Dominika," he said more cheerfully. "Let's find you a bed and get your treatment underway. We'll give you some medicine and I'm sure you'll be back on your feet in no time."

"I don't want to go," I said miserably.

The doctor called a nurse over and asked her to prepare some paperwork for my father, and then he picked me up and carried me to the elevator at the rear of the emergency room. I tried to protest, but I was too weak to cry. The best I could do was wave sadly at my parents, who looked very worried.

"Visiting hours are on Wednesdays and Sundays," the doctor told them. "And don't worry. The pavilion is mostly made up of pediatric wards, so the nurses down there are very good with children."

THE INFECTION PAVILION was at the bottom of the hospital. It was built into the side of the hill and looked like a big concrete bunker. The doctor carried me out of the main building and through the hospital gardens, and his mood seemed to change as he approached the pavilion. He walked through the front door and carried me downstairs.

"You're not going to believe this," he said to the admissions nurse. "I've got a white kid here with dysentery."

"Dysentery? You're kidding!" the nurse said.

"No," the doctor sighed. "Is Dr. Kopecky here?"

"He's on a break," the nurse said. "Take her down to the Gypsy Ward and I'll let one of the nurses know you're coming."

She buzzed us through the door and the doctor carried me down a long corridor to the dysentery ward. The doctor lowered me onto a bed and a nurse removed my clothes and sealed them in a plastic bag. She took the bag away, presumably to burn it, and then wheeled in an IV drip, which she attempted to insert. She jabbed me repeatedly with a needle, trying to find my artery. I whimpered with pain.

"She's got arms like matchsticks," the nurse grumbled.

She pulled the IV out of my arm and tried again and again.

"Try the other arm, Magda," the doctor suggested.

He gave me a vitamin B shot as Nurse Magda finally found an artery and hooked my left arm up to the IV drip.

"Turn her over," the doctor ordered, and Nurse Magda flipped me onto my belly. The next thing I knew, the doctor was using my bum as a pincushion, jabbing it quickly with a variety of needles. He then got the nurse to flip me back over and tapped my tummy with a little hammer. I cried out with pain and he looked satisfied. He put the hammer back in his coat pocket, and Nurse Magda put a bag of ice on my tummy. And that was it. They covered me with a sheet and hurried out of the ward.

Yellow bruises covered my arms, and as the ice in the bag began to melt, the sheet soaked through and started to freeze to my body. It was awful. I didn't think I'd survive the ordeal, but the doctor must have given me something powerful, because I was asleep before I knew it. I drifted off for what seemed like a couple of minutes, but it was dark when I awoke and the hospital was silent. I opened my eyes and looked around the ward. A lamp on the observation deck outside the window cast a bleak light inside the room, and I could hear a faint rustling near the foot of my bed. A trickle of sweat ran down my spine. I tried to sit up and the rustling grew louder. Suddenly, a pair of black eyes snapped open beside me.

"Hello," the eyes said. "What's your name?"

"My name?" I cried out. "Who are you?"

"Shhh," the voice whispered. "You don't want to let Nurse Magda catch you talking."

"You've been asleep for three days," another voice said. "We thought you were never going to wake up."

"Three days?" I gasped. "But I was supposed to go to school on Monday!"

I hoisted myself up on my elbows and someone slid a pillow behind my neck. When I finally was able to sit up properly, I found myself surrounded by four more pairs of eyes.

"You're not going anywhere if they don't want you to," they whispered. "There isn't even a handle on the door."

I had to bite my lips to stop them from trembling.

"My name is Dominika," I said.

"I am Zoltan," the first voice replied. "This is Lucie, Mirka, Erika, and Gejza. We've all got tummy bugs, like you."

I could tell they were Gypsies, because they spoke with a Gypsy accent. Their eyes were huge, and blacker than the night, and they wore filthy pajamas with buttons missing. As my eyes adjusted to the darkness, I could make out their faces. Behind them, near the wall, two toddlers stared at me through the bars of their cots.

"What kind of tummy bugs?" I asked. "I've got dysentery."

"I've got dysentery, too," Zoltan said.

"Me, too," whispered Mirka

"So do we," said Erika and Lucie.

"I don't," Gejza declared proudly. "I have typhus."

"What's that?" I asked.

"Oh, it's just like dysentery," Zoltan said. "He's just showing off."

Heavy steps echoed in the corridor and the lights snapped on in the ward next to ours. The Gypsy kids scurried back to their beds, and through the big glass window, I could see Nurse Magda shaking a young boy awake. She rolled him over, pulled his pants down, and smeared his thigh with a yellow liquid. Then she jabbed him with a needle. The boy immediately started to cry, but Nurse Magda said something that made him stop. Then she pulled his pants back up and switched off the lights.

As soon as the slap of her footsteps died away, the Gypsy kids reappeared at my bedside.

"That was Magda. She's nasty," Lucie whispered. "She hits you if she catches you talking after dark."

I was horrified at the prospect of being hit by Magda. Her work with the IV had been punishment enough.

"What about the other wards?" I asked. "Are they allowed to talk?"

"We don't know," Lucie replied. "We can see them, but we can't hear them."

"And they're allowed to eat," Erika added.

"What? We're not allowed to eat?" I cried.

"Shhh," Zoltan whispered. "Eating just makes you shit harder, you know?"

"Measles, mumps, and smallpox get biscuits and fruit," Lucie said miserably. "Jaundice are allowed to have sugar in their tea, and the kids with heavy colds get whatever they want."

"Well, what do we get?" I asked.

"Black tea and dry rolls," Lucie and Erika said together.

"That's it?" I couldn't believe it.

"The nurses don't like to come in here much," Erika shrugged.

"I don't think they like us," Mirka whispered.

I lay down and pulled the sheet over my face, listening to the Gypsies as they returned to their beds. The room became quiet, except for the toddlers crying near the wall. They must have just soiled their nappies, because a terrible smell wafted across the room. No wonder the nurses didn't like to come in. I blocked my nostrils with my fingers and tried to fall asleep, thinking about my nice purple dress and how I had missed the beginning of school.

The following morning, a row of lights snapped on across the ceiling, one after the other, like falling dominos. I sat up and looked around. Through the big glass window at the side of our room, I could see a pretty young nurse distributing pills and thermometers to children in the other wards. She seemed much nicer than Nurse Magda. She smiled and even patted one or two of the children on their heads. Behind her, an even younger nurse with glasses pushed a tea trolley through the room, filling chipped enamel mugs with a steaming liquid. I noticed that many of the kids were reluctant to drink, but the pretty nurse made sure that they did.

"The nurses are bringing something to drink," I called out to Zoltan. "It looks like the other kids hate it."

"Oh, no!" Zoltan groaned. "Nurse Zdena's coming! She's going to make us drink the *vitakava*!"

"*Dzungalo! Vitakava* is disgusting!" said Gejza, sticking his tongue out for effect.

"Is that malt coffee?" I asked worriedly. "My mum always makes me drink malt coffee when I'm sick."

"Yeah," Zoltan said grimly. "Nurse Zdena says *vitakava* is better for us than black tea. She makes us drink it three times a week, even though it makes us shit like crazy."

"Can't we just say we don't want any?"

"We've all tried," Zoltan said. "Nurse Zdena says we have to put on more weight before the doctors will let us go home."

The key turned in the lock and the two nurses wheeled their trolley inside our room.

"Good morning, children!" they said cheerfully.

Nurse Zdena made a circuit of the room, handing thermometers to the Gypsy kids, along with little cups of charcoal tablets. As she walked past my bed, she saw that my eyes were open.

"Hello there!" she smiled. "Welcome back!"

"Hello," I said nervously. "Can I go home now?"

Nurse Zdena laughed good-humoredly and slid the thermometer under my armpit.

"It's not up to me, my dear," she said. "First we have to make sure that your tummy bugs have gone."

"But I feel much better!" I said. "Really! I think I'm well again!"

"That's for the doctors to decide," Nurse Zdena smiled. "In the meantime, here's a nice cup of malt coffee!"

"I'm not very thirsty," I said in a small voice.

The young nurse filled a cup with *vitakava,* and Nurse Zdena brought it over with a stern expression on her face.

"Now, now," she said, pressing the cup to my lips. "You need to put back all the weight you've lost."

The vitakava smelled like wet bedsheets, and it was covered by a thin layer of skin. It tasted even worse than my mother's malt coffee, but I drank it down without complaint.

"Good girl," Nurse Zdena said approvingly. "And let's have another one! You're all skin and bones!"

The young nurse refilled my cup and Nurse Zdena made me drink it. When I had finished, she wiped my mouth with a cloth.

"When can I see my mum and dad?"

"On Sunday," she said brightly. "They came to see you yesterday, but you were still asleep. They left me a package for you."

"A package?" I said breathlessly.

Nurse Zdena smiled and asked the young nurse to hand her my package, which was on the bottom shelf of the trolley.

"Would you like me to open it for you?" she asked.

"Yes, please," I said.

"I wish my parents would send me a package," Lucie grumbled. "I've been here for three weeks and I haven't got a thing."

"Now, now, Lucie," Nurse Zdena frowned. "At least your family come and see you. Look at poor little Fedor and Aranka. They don't have parents. We'll have to send them to the orphanage as soon as they're better."

She unwrapped my package and pulled out a pair of pink pajamas and a pair of wooden clogs.

"How lovely," she said. "What a pity you won't be able to keep them."

"I won't be able to keep them?" I cried.

"Of course not," Nurse Zdena said. "We'll have to burn them when you leave, because they'll be full of nasty microbes. I'm sorry, my dear, but this is a quarantine ward. Someone should have told this to your parents when they brought you here."

"But they're so nice!" I moaned. "Couldn't we just wash them?"

The clogs were the kind of clogs I had always wanted. They had thick cork soles and green leather straps with buckles. I couldn't believe that the nurses would burn them.

"It doesn't work like that," Nurse Zdena explained. "Microbes are very small and they live inside the material. But maybe your parents will buy you another pair of clogs when you go home."

"Maybe," I said doubtfully. My parents didn't have much money. Buying me this pair would have been difficult enough.

"Breakfast time!" the young nurse called out.

She gave us each a dry bread roll, collected our cups and thermometers, and pushed her trolley to the door.

"We'll be back tomorrow morning," Nurse Zdena smiled. "The doctors will be along shortly, so please try and tidy up your beds before they come. Nurse Magda will be very disappointed if you don't."

She smiled sympathetically and left the ward, closing and locking the door behind her. I put on my new pajamas and admired my new clogs. The Gypsy kids were very impressed.

"Nice clogs," they muttered. "Really nice. Ve-ry nice."

Half an hour later, a group of student doctors appeared at the head of the corridor. I could see them through the row of big glass windows. A short doctor with a beard appeared to be in charge, and Nurse Magda was with them, wheeling a trolley of clean white towels. As the group slowly worked its way through the pavilion, the Gypsy kids were frantically trying to tidy up their beds. None of them was very good at it, and by the time the party of doctors arrived, their sheets were very messy and covered with breadcrumbs.

"Good morning, children!" the short doctor boomed.

"Good morning, Dr. Kopecky," the Gypsy kids replied.

The doctor sniffed the air and frowned at Nurse Magda.

"You know, it still smells really bad in here."

Nurse Magda threw an angry look at Zoltan and went to open a window with a special key.

"So . . . Dominika." Dr. Kopecky read the plate on the bottom of my bed. "How are you feeling?"

"Much, much better, comrade doctor!" I said. "Is there any chance I could go home soon?"

The young doctors laughed, but Dr. Kopecky was very serious. He removed my sheet and prodded my tummy with his fingers.

"A classic case of dehydration, but nothing to worry about," he told his colleagues.

He forced my eyelids open and shone a penlight in my eyes.

"The pupils are slightly dilated, but her temperature is back to normal," he said. "I think we can disconnect the drip and continue with medicinal charcoal and regular doses of penicillin."

The doctors nodded in agreement, and one of them helped Nurse Magda remove the IV from my arm.

"The rest of the children are on diets, so there's no problem there. I think that might be it for today," Dr. Kopecky said. "Now, then, I wonder what's for lunch!"

"Good-bye, children!" He waved cheerily.

"Good-bye, Dr. Kopecky." We waved back.

As Dr. Kopecky and his colleagues hurried off to have lunch, Nurse Magda stayed behind and fiddled with the IV. As soon as the doctors were out of earshot, she wheeled around and started shouting at Zoltan.

"The next time I tell you to keep your beds clean, you do it or I'll give you a good spanking!" she roared. "And what have I told you about the smell? We make three trips a day and that's it. If the babies soil their nappies, it's not my problem, it's yours. We don't have time to clean up after you Gypsies! We're understaffed as it is!"

"Yes, Nurse Magda," Zoltan said in a thick voice.

"Well, you see to it!" she snapped. "Here are your towels. I'll be back at midday to change your bedpans. Not a minute earlier, you understand?"

"Yes, Nurse Magda," Zoltan fumed.

We huddled meekly in our beds as Nurse Magda gave us each a fresh towel, and then she left her trolley at the door and stalked out of the room.

"What are the towels for?" I asked Zoltan.

"I don't know," he shrugged angrily.

I could see he was upset and I wanted to say something nice to cheer him up, but before I could think of anything to say, I suddenly felt very sick. My bowels churned horribly, and I climbed down from the bed and slid my feet into the clogs.

"What are you doing?" Zoltan asked.

"I have to go to the loo," I whimpered. "Where is it?"

"There." Zoltan pointed to an enamel pot that sat on a little ledge beneath my bed. "You have to use that."

I tried to pull the pot off the ledge, but my legs and hands were trembling violently.

"Oh, no!" I moaned. "I'm not going to make it!"

Zoltan leaped out of bed and handed me his pot.

"Here," he said. "Use mine."

The Gypsies crowded around me as I pulled down my pants. As soon as my bottom touched the rim of the pot, I filled it with a nasty explosion of diarrhea. The Gypsy kids nodded approvingly.

"Couldn't you at least turn around?" I begged.

"Why?" they asked. "We're all going to shit in a minute or two."

As if to prove the point, they grabbed their own pots and noisily emptied their bowels a few minutes later.

"See?" Gejza cried. "It's the *vitakava!*"

The toddlers rattled the bars of their cots and started to howl. They had both soiled their nappies, and I could see the diarrhea running down their legs. The smell inside the room was overwhelming. We were shitting the malt coffee Nurse Zdena had fed us, and to my great embarrassment, I could see that some of the kids from the other wards were looking in at us and laughing.

A few minutes later, Nurse Magda burst into the room.

"What's the meaning of all this noise?" she demanded.

She strode over to the babies, cursing loudly when she saw their dirty nappies. She carried them roughly to the sink and hosed the babies down. As she soaped their bums, I could see that their buttocks were chafed and their thighs were covered with a nasty rash. So this was why they cried all night. Nurse Magda shook the babies dry and laid them on an ironing board that served as a changing table. She put a clean nappy between each one's legs, folded another into a triangle, and wrapped it expertly around their hips.

"What time is it?" she snarled at Zoltan.

Zoltan shot a frightened look at the big clock on the wall. His lips moved and I could see that he was trying to tell the time.

"It's ten o'clock, Nurse Magda," I answered for him. "We're sorry. We really couldn't help it!"

Nurse Magda collected our pots and put them on her trolley. She shot me a black look, but spoke less harshly to me.

"I can't understand it," she said. "You eat nothing but fill your pots to the brim. I hope your parents aren't sneaking you food. If I find out, there'll be hell to pay!"

No one said a word about Nurse Zdena's *vitakava*. When Nurse Magda finally trolleyed our dirty pots out of the room, I looked over at the pile of clean nappies and cotton pads on the changing table, and suddenly had an idea.

"Listen," I said. "Why don't we take care of the babies by ourselves?"

"By ourselves?" Lucie gasped. "But we're too small. We can't reach them."

"Yes, we can," I told her. "If we push a chair over to the cots, we can get them out. And we can reach the sink that way, too."

"I don't want to change their nappies," Zoltan grumbled.

"Would you rather have Nurse Magda yell at you all the time?" I asked.

"No," he said. "But are we allowed to change the babies' nappies?"

"We don't have to tell Nurse Magda, do we? We could do it without telling her. It would be like a game."

The Gypsies pricked up their ears.

"We're the partisans, and Nurse Magda and Zdena can be the Germans," I suggested.

"But I like Nurse Zdena," Mirka whispered.

"She's the one who makes us shit, stupid," Zoltan reminded her.

"Go on!" Gejza said excitedly. "So what do we do?"

"Well, the first thing we'll need is a couple of lookouts."

FROM THAT MOMENT ON, we waged a defensive war against Nurse Magda. Zoltan and I were the joint leaders of the partisans, and Mirka, Erika, Lucie, and Gejza were our lieutenants. Our primary objective was to keep the toddlers out of Nurse Magda's hands. We couldn't wait for them to soil their nappies. We had a whole procedure worked out.

Whenever Fedor or Aranka started to cry, we would push a chair over to their cot and pull them out. Gejza and Lucie would stand lookout, while Mirka and Erika brought the chair to the sink. Then I would roll up my pajama cuffs and climb up into the basin, which was wide and deep enough for me to stand in. Zoltan was the strongest, so he passed each baby up to me. There was a rubber hose at the end of the tap that I used to wash the babies' bums. Then Mirka and Erika dried their bottoms with the cotton pads. Last, I would climb down and supervise the folding of the nappies. It was actually a lot of fun. We got to play with live dolls and pretend that we were in a German prisoner-of-war camp. As we refined our operation, I noticed that the kids from the other wards were watching us with interest instead of their usual scorn.

As the days slowly passed, it became apparent that Nurse Magda had no idea about the *vitakava*. It was typical of the way communism worked. The left hand didn't know what the right hand was up to. Our work with the babies kept Nurse Magda from yelling at Zoltan, but she was still grumpy about our full chamber pots and suspicious that our parents were sneaking us food. She was particularly vigilant on the days our parents came to visit. We were taken from the ward and washed in a large communal shower, and after we had made our beds, she let us climb up onto the radiator by the window and press our noses to the glass.

"Don't forget to smile at your mummies and daddies," she said ominously. "We don't want them to worry about you, do we?"

"No, Nurse Magda," we replied.

"Well, then," she tightened her mouth into the most gruesome smile. "Make sure you look happy."

Then she stood beside us for the whole hour that our parents came to visit, making sure it looked like we were having the time of our lives.

The Infection Pavilion was built like a bunker, so that parents could look in on their children without entering the building. There was also the large observation deck that ran past the six big windows at the back of the pavilion, and from the outside, the wards must have looked like a miniature zoo. A wrought-iron staircase led up to the deck, and I squealed with excitement as I saw my mother's hat. She was climbing the stairs with my father and sister behind her.

"Hello, Mum!" I cried.

"Hello, little one," she called back. "How are you?"

"I'm okay," I said bravely. "Can I come home soon?"

"Of course you can, my love," she said. "You look awfully thin. Are they feeding you properly?"

I shot a look at Nurse Magda, who was watching me like a hawk.

"I think so," I replied.

My mother opened her mouth to say something, but a huge Gypsy family swarmed onto the deck behind her; old women, children, and girls with babies in their arms.

"Zoltan! *Mro cho!*" a young woman with the most amazing hair cried out. She ran to the window and smothered it with kisses, while Zoltan made an embarrassed face and tried not to cry.

"Mirka! Lucie!" two teenage girls shrieked. "*So tuke? Soske tut o Del marel!* Guess what, Gejza? You have a new baby sister!"

The Gypsies were making so much noise it was impossible to hear what anyone was saying. Some of them danced and sang to entertain the kids. Lucie had at least ten relatives in front of her, and my parents were pushed aside by her extended family. In the end, I found a tiny square at the bottom of the window and pressed my face against it. My mother touched the window with her fingers and smiled, but I couldn't hear what she was saying. My breath fogged up the window, and I choked on a big lump in my throat. I drew a picture on the fogged-up glass with my finger, and my mother got teary. She wiped her face and hid it under the brim of her hat. I rubbed the picture out with my pajama sleeve and breathed some more mist onto the glass. Then I wrote on the window: please bring biscuits. My parents looked puzzled at first, but then they signaled okay and my mother blew me a kiss.

"End of visiting hours!" Nurse Magda said, clapping her hands.

The Gypsy kids began to cry and my own eyes filled up with tears.

Nurse Magda helped us down from the radiator and tucked us up in our beds. I watched my mother's hat as it drifted down the hill, disappearing behind the row of chestnut trees that lined the path to the hospital gate.

Later that afternoon, Nurse Zdena appeared at my bedside with a big bag of *piskoty* biscuits my father had sweet-talked her into sneaking into the ward. These were the same sponge biscuits my mother fed my sister and me when we were dieting. They were small and plain, but there would have been at least sixty in the bag.

"I shouldn't be doing this," Nurse Zdena said. "But I don't think they'll do you any harm."

"Thank you, Nurse Zdena," I said gratefully.

"You're welcome," she smiled. "If I were you, I wouldn't let Magda catch you with them. Maybe you could put them in your bedside drawer."

"Okay," I nodded.

The second Nurse Zdena had left the room, the Gypsy kids leaped out of bed and surrounded my bedside table. They stared at the drawer with their hungry black eyes.

"Would you like some biscuits?" I asked.

"Yes, please!" they all exclaimed. Gejza stuck his tongue out and nodded so hard he almost bit it in half.

I opened the drawer and gave a sponge biscuit to each of the kids. Then I ate one myself. Piskoty biscuits were my least favorite in the world, but in the ward that afternoon, they were an incredible treat. Some of the kids actually groaned as they ate them. I handed out a second biscuit, then a third one, then a fourth. We really were starving. All we had to eat was one bread roll three times a day, as well as dry mashed potatoes and semolina pudding. I had lost so much weight, my legs looked like broomsticks. All the children in the wards were on the verge of starvation.

"Can I please have another one?" Mirka whispered after she had eaten her fifth.

The packet was now half empty.

"We should save some for later," I told her. "I'm not sure if I'm going to get any more, and we don't know if they'll make us go to the toilet. How about if we have some more in the morning?"

"In the morning?" Gejza cried. "But that's a long time away!"

"Can't we just have one?" Lucie whined.

After a lot of protesting, the kids grudgingly returned to their beds and spent the rest of the afternoon whispering to each other in Gypsy language. They were angry, and our nappy changing was less fun than usual. When Nurse Magda finally switched out the lights, I put the bag under my pillow just in case. I could hear Zoltan and Gejza creeping around in the darkness as I tried to go to sleep. Every so often, my bedside drawer would creak open, and one of them even put his hand on my pillow.

"Go away!" I whispered. "Leave my biscuits alone!"

The following morning, we didn't have to drink Nurse Zdena's *vita-kava*. The young nurse with glasses brought us a jug of black tea instead and told us that we would have to wait for breakfast, because an American boy with meningitis was on his way to the pavilion. The head of the hospital had come down and insisted that a good impression be made. The kids in the ward next to ours were relocated to other parts of the hospital, and the staff had to drop whatever they were doing and help the doctors get ready. Nurse Magda mopped the floor and changed the sheets on the one remaining bed, and then a fleet of doctors came in and surrounded it with surgical tables and lots of expensive equipment.

The Gypsy kids and I watched with interest, waiting for the American boy to turn up.

"Is he going to speak American?" Lucie wanted to know.

"Americans only speak American," I said. "They don't speak anything else."

"Why not?" Mirka whispered.

"They won the war," I told her. "When you win a war, everyone has to speak your language."

"That makes sense," Gejza nodded approvingly.

A few minutes later, there was a loud clattering in the corridor and we all rushed over to the window and peeked under the blinds in time to see the young nurse with glasses pushing a bed into the room. A boy was lying on the bed, and a very well-dressed man and a woman walked in behind him. Dr. Kopecky and a team of doctors and nurses followed.

"Nice sweater," Gejza whistled. "These people must be rich!"

"Is that Mickey Mouse?" Mirka wanted to know.

"No, it's not Mickey, it's Yerry," I told her, pronouncing the J the Czech way. "The cat is called Tom and the mouse is called Yerry."

A huge doctor with a sausagelike mustache entered the room. He smiled politely at the boy's parents and laid a thin metal suitcase on the table.

"*Kurva fix,* I knew it!" Zoltan swore under his breath. "It's Dr. Horvath! They're going to give the kid a spinal tap!"

Zoltan shuddered. "See that suitcase?" he said. "There's a huge needle inside it, and Dr. Horvath is going to stick it all the way in the boy's spine!"

"You're just saying that to scare us!" I cried.

"No, I'm not. I've seen him do it to three kids already. They bring in a special chair and make you sit backward, and then he sticks you with the needle!"

I thought Zoltan was making this up until Nurse Magda brought in a big silver chair. Dr. Horvath opened his suitcase and pulled out a syringe with the longest needle I had ever seen. The blood drained from the American woman's face as she stood behind the chair and stroked her son's hand. Then Dr. Horvath stuck the tip of the needle into the boy's spine. The American kid screamed so loudly, the doctor jumped away. When he tried again, the boy squealed like a pig being slaughtered. This went on for five minutes, until Nurse Magda whispered a few words to Dr. Horvath and then led the boy's parents out of the room.

Once they were gone, three nurses pounced on the boy and held him down while Dr. Horvath drove the needle into his spine. The kid screamed even louder than before, but all of the doctors and nurses ignored him. Finally, Dr. Horvath removed the needle, and the nurses laid the boy on his belly and then his parents were allowed to return. The father thanked the doctors and nurses, and the mother rushed over to her son. She stroked his hand, but he furiously pushed her away; then she opened a big cardboard box and started to pull out an assortment of toys.

The Gypsy kids and I watched in amazement. She was like a magician pulling rabbits out of a hat. There was a toothbrush with Mickey Mouse on the handle (I pointed him out to Mirka), and a little music box that played "Silent Night," but the best toy by far was a miniature BMW that the woman put on the floor. She picked up a remote control and made the little car drive all by itself. When it crashed against the side of the bed, she handed the control to her son, but he threw it across the room. In desperation, the woman pulled out a plastic bag filled with candy. There were Kinder Eggs and Swiss chocolate, as well as pralines and nougat and Mars bars. The American woman offered the sweets to her son, but he angrily pushed the bag away.

The sight of the sweets made me sick with hunger. Saliva flooded my mouth and I pressed my lips to the window, trying to taste a bit of sweetness on the glass.

"You know," I said miserably, "I would have a spinal tap if they gave me a bag of chocolate at the end."

Lucie's eyes widened. "Is that true?" she asked. "Will they let you?"

"Probably not," I sighed.

"Aren't you frightened of needles?" Gejza asked. "I am!"

"I am, too," I said. "But I've always wanted a Kinder Egg."

"You have biscuits!" Gejza said accusingly. "At least you have something. We have nothing!"

I was about to point out that I had offered to share my biscuits in the morning, when the door crashed open and Nurse Magda walked in. The young nurse with glasses followed, pushing a trolley with our dry rolls. She handed them around while Nurse Magda distributed charcoal pills and thermometers. Then she collected our pill cups and loaded them onto the trolley, and would have left had Lucie not stopped her.

"Can I please have some chocolate?" she asked.

"What was that?" Nurse Magda turned in the doorway.

"Can I please have some chocolate!" Lucie whined. "Dominika said we could have chocolate if we let the doctors spine our taps!"

"I didn't say that," I said.

"Yes, you did!" Gejza cried. "And you have biscuits under your pillow!"

Nurse Magda's eyes narrowed. She strode across the room and whipped the pillow off my bed. There was a very long pause when she saw the biscuits lying there.

"Who gave these to you?" she demanded. "Who gave you these biscuits?"

I looked up at her, too terrified to answer.

"Where did these biscuits come from?" Nurse Magda roared.

"Nurse Zdena brought them," Zoltan said. "She told Dominika to hide them in her drawer."

"Did she?" Nurse Magda snapped. "We'll see about that. You're supposed to be on a diet! You Gypsy kids are more trouble than you're worth!"

She snatched up my packet of biscuits, and as I listened to the sound of her storming down the hallway, I realized that the real source of her anger was Nurse Zdena, not us.

The young nurse shook her head unsympathetically.

"Well, I guess that's the last time Zdena sneaks food to you kids," she said. "Magda will make so much trouble for her, she'll be lucky if she ends up working in one of the cancer wards."

She ignored our crestfallen faces and left the room, leaving us to grapple with our hunger and the consequences of Gejza's and Zoltan's denouncement.

"Now we all lose," I said miserably. "Now we all go hungry."

"Serves you right," Zoltan muttered.

"If you had waited, I would have given you the biscuits!" I cried. "I would have! Really!"

"No, you wouldn't," Zoltan sneered. "You would have eaten them yourself! You *Gadže* are all the same!"

Suddenly we weren't partisans working against a common enemy anymore. It was me versus the Gypsy kids, and the babies howled as their nappies went unchanged. Our tummies rumbled with hunger for the rest of the day, until Nurse Zdena came in with our dinner. She had survived Nurse Magda's attack, but I could tell that she was very upset, and she didn't say a word to us. We had not only turned against each other, we had managed to turn our allies against us as well.

Fortunately, Dr. Kopecky pronounced me fit to leave the hospital the very next day. Dr. Polakova had had a word with him on the phone, and he was happy enough to sign me out. Nurse Zdena sent my pajamas and clogs away to be burned, then handed me some new clothes and led me out into the garden where my parents were waiting. My father gave her a bunch of flowers and thanked her profusely for taking such good care of me, and I threw my arms around my mother's neck, fighting back the tears. As we walked to the car, I looked back at the pavilion and could see the Gypsy kids pressing their faces to the window.

When we arrived home, my father made me close my eyes and led me upstairs. When I opened them again, I was standing in the middle of my brand-new bedroom that he had finished while I was away. He had made a chest of drawers and a little bookshelf out of fiberboard, and painted them red and white, which were my favorite colors. A new pair of green clogs stood beside the bed, and the smell of roast chicken wafted up from the kitchen.

"This is your own bedroom now," my father told me. "After lunch, we'll carry your books in from Klara's room."

"Lunch is ready!" I heard my mother call.

I was so hungry I could have eaten the whole chicken, but I had to be careful as my stomach had shrunk after two weeks in the hospital. My mother served me a small portion of chicken and a tiny piece of the chocolate cake she had made in celebration of my recovery.

My sister nudged me in the ribs.

"The house was quiet without you," she smiled. "It took me about a week to get used to it."

After lunch, I looked in the large mirror that stood in our hallway and it took me a few seconds to realize who was the incredibly skinny girl I saw. My head seemed too large for my body, and my arm and leg joints seemed huge. I tried to stand on the tips of my toes, but I couldn't manage it. I was very weak, and would have to work tremendously hard to catch up to the other girls at ballet school. In spite of this, I was secretly glad that I had lost so much weight. Losing weight is an important part of dancing.

After I had rested and seen Dr. Polakova, my father drove my mother and me to the preparatory school to have a chat with Mrs. Saturday. I weighed fifteen kilos, the average weight of someone half my age, and Dr. Polakova had urged my mother to help me try to gain five kilograms as quickly as possible.

"Five kilograms?" my mother frowned. "That seems a bit much. Wouldn't three be more appropriate?"

"Whatever you think is best," Dr. Polakova replied.

But Mrs. Saturday had a different opinion. She put me on the scale and told me to stand on the tips of my toes. Then she got me to do a set of kicking and stretching exercises. She narrowed her eyes and told my mother that my build was still a little heavy for her liking.

"If she's serious about ballet, she could still afford to lose half a kilo," she said briskly. "You might want to think about reducing her dinners."

eight

THE LITTLE BANANA

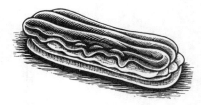

As soon as she was sure I had fully recovered, my mother put ribbons in my hair, a new satchel on my back, and sent me down into the valley for my first day of school. Falling leaves and gossamer floated in the breeze, and swallows perched on the telephone wires, chirping along with the excited chatter of children. The first thing I noticed when I arrived at the schoolyard was that everyone was standing in a group. I didn't have a group to stand in, because I had missed the start of school and all the first-grade kids had formed their friendships without me. I saw Mary Hairy surrounded by a bunch of girls I didn't recognize, and caught a glimpse of Petr Acorn standing in the yard with a couple of older boys. I waved at him and was sure that he saw me, but he didn't wave back. I couldn't see anyone else from my street, and I realized that the only way to preserve my dignity would be to stand in my own group alone and pretend I didn't envy the children who had friends.

When the bell finally rang at a quarter to eight, the school caretaker,

Mrs. Vincentova, unlocked the front doors. Mrs. Vincentova reminded me of a sheep. Her eyes were filled with suspicion and her blond hair looked like fleece. She stood on the steps and took careful note of who did and didn't wipe their shoes on the doormat. As I tried to walk past, she blocked my way with her broom.

"I haven't seen you before," she said.

"That's because I've had dysentery," I replied. "I've been in the hospital."

Mrs. Vincentova regarded me with horror. "Last name?" she demanded.

"Furmanova," I said. "I'm Klara Furmanova's sister."

Mrs. Vincentova's eyes narrowed. "Look at your shoes!" She tapped my sandals with her broom.

The soles of my sandals were covered with mud from the construction site.

"This is a school and not a pigsty!" Mrs. Vincentova snapped. "Take your shoes off and wash them in the bathroom. Next time, make sure they are clean or I'll send you back home!"

The ground floor of the Cernosice elementary school was divided between Mrs. Vincentova's apartment and the two first-grade classrooms. Grades two and up were located on the first floor, along with the toilets and the headmistress's office. There was a miniature gymnasium in the attic, although we usually went out to the garden. Instead of lockers, we had large communal changing rooms, which were cages made of wattle fencing. Each was furnished with benches and coatracks, and everyone had to leave their shoes and coats inside before the bell rang at the beginning of class. If you forgot your homework or left a textbook in the cage, you were in big trouble, because you would have to ask Mrs. Vincentova to unlock the cage, which would result in a lot of sighing and grumbling. She was very obsessive about the state of your shoes, and took great pleasure in pointing out that mine were always dirty. Years later, I would learn that she was not only a friend of the Nedbals but also part of the information network the Red Countess used to keep tabs on my father.

Running into her on my first day of school was unfortunate, because I didn't yet know where my classroom was. I had hoped to follow some of the younger children inside, but by the time Mrs. Vincentova had finished with me, they had disappeared. I had to find the room all by myself.

I was very nervous when I walked into the classroom. I held on to my satchel, trying to avoid the pieces of paper, chalk, and school slippers my classmates threw at each other. Boys and girls ran around the room shrieking like monkeys. A few quiet girls were gathered at the front bench, but after looking me over quickly, they went back to braiding pigtails in one another's hair. The bell rang and the class continued to make noise until a fat boy in a denim jacket who was stationed by the door whispered, "Okay! Shut up! Comrade Humlova is coming!"

Everyone quickly returned to their seats as Comrade Humlova strode into the room. She shut the door behind her, and the class immediately fell silent. Comrade Humlova was a big woman who wore green trousers with a broken zipper. Her belly stretched the fabric of her pants, and I caught a glimpse of white bloomers through her fly. Her face was round and friendly, but she had the unfortunate habit of standing too close and spraying her students with saliva when she spoke. She surveyed the classroom and noticed me standing near the window.

"You must be Dominika," she said.

"Hello," I said nervously.

Comrade Humlova gave me a friendly smile and patted me on the head.

"Dominika has been sick for the past two weeks," she told the class. "She's behind with her studies, but I'm sure she'll catch up quickly. Everyone say hello to Dominika."

"Hello, Dominika," the class droned.

"Now. Where will we seat you, my dear?" Comrade Humlova grabbed me by the hand and led me around the classroom. It was a bright room divided into three rows of benches. Each bench had two seats, and most of them were occupied by other children.

"How about here?" Comrade Humlova said, pointing to an empty bench where a big girl, obviously a few years older than everyone else, was sitting by herself. The girl looked at me with big sleepy eyes.

"This is Romanka," Comrade Humlova said. "She's a little slow, but I'm sure you'll get along very well."

"Hello, Romanka," I said, offering her my hand. "I'm very happy to be sitting next to you."

Romanka stared at me blankly.

The class giggled.

Comrade Humlova patted me on the head again and then moved to the front of the classroom to start the lesson. I had to squeeze into my seat, because Romanka took up three quarters of the space. I opened my writing pad and tried to follow what Comrade Humlova was saying, but Romanka continued to stare at me with her mouth slightly open and it was very hard to concentrate. The other kids kept looking at us and trying not to laugh, and I started to feel very uncomfortable.

The class was halfway through the alphabet, so Comrade Humlova was writing very easy sentences on the blackboard and getting everyone to read along with her.

"M-y . . . m-other . . . m-akes . . . m-ustard," she would say.

"M-y . . . m-other . . . m-akes . . . m-ustard," the class would repeat.

This went on for an hour, and my nervous discomfort gave way to boredom. I already knew the alphabet. The walls of our house were covered with my writing. My father had not yet discovered that the wax pencils the Baby Jesus gave me for Christmas could not be painted over, so he and my mother encouraged me to use the walls of our house as a canvas. Many years would pass before they realized the enormity of this mistake, by which time the walls would be completely covered with my indelible, childish scribble. In the end my father put up hideous wallpaper, vowing to remove it the second he made some serious money, which of course would not be for many years.

As the weeks progressed, I got to know all the kids in my class. The fat boy in the denim jacket was nicknamed "The Steamroller," and the most popular girls were twins Monika and Alice Rabbit, who had an aunt in Austria and access to Western clothes. Terezka Jandova and Andula Thatcher were the teacher's pets, and sat in the front row. The tough girls from the bottom of the valley occupied the second and third rows in the middle of the class. They rarely paid attention to the lessons, and drew pictures of horses in their exercise books instead. The back of the room was reserved for the troublemaking boys. A malicious kid called Honza Tucek was the ringleader. He tormented his friend Petr Halbich mercilessly, making bullets out of chewing gum and spitting them at him through a straw. He gave Petr such a hard time, in fact, that the rest of the class joined in, and poor Petr went from being a troublemaker to a victim overnight. By the end of the year, he would be sitting in the front row with the quiet girls.

As we worked our way through the rest of the alphabet, I amused myself by reading the posters on the walls: THE COMMUNIST PARTY IS THE GUARANTOR OF WORLD PEACE! announced a picture of workers harvesting wheat in a field. THE SOVIET UNION FOREVER AND EVER! exclaimed a group of American soldiers playing balalaikas to a crowd of young women. I read the notices on the bulletin board and the graffiti carved into the neighboring benches, including the one on the back of Romanka's seat, which said, "Don't learn, the life will teach you."

I told Romanka what was written on her seat, but she wasn't impressed. She sat motionless and silent like a big, breathing log, and the only time she became animated was during the snack break, when Mrs. Vincentova burst into the classroom with a box of bread rolls and plastic bags filled with milk. For some reason, Romanka was one of Mrs. Vincentova's favorite students and she was always given two bread rolls instead of one. She slurped her milk and took big bites of her roll, while I peeled the hard and bitter Cuban orange my mother had given me, along with her weekly lecture about vitamins. Every kid in my class had milk and a bread roll, but my mother didn't have enough money to pay for a school lunch, and she also thought it was unhealthy to drink milk out of plastic instead of glass. Eating my orange and watching the other kids play with their straws, I felt sad and different yet again. I realized I was sitting next to Romanka because no one else wanted to, and that even Romanka had a bag of milk and a straw.

I wished that I fit in more easily with the other children. I wished my mother didn't work at the Economic Institute and was more like the other mothers in Cernosice, who had permed hair and didn't think drinking milk from plastic bags was bad. Mrs. Rabbit and Mrs. Thatcher didn't give their daughters lectures about vitamins, and they went to the beauty salon once a week, where all the local mothers gossiped. My mother refused to set foot in the place, even though she had the nicest hair in town.

One day, during a particularly boring mathematics lesson, I told Comrade Humlova that I had to go to the bathroom. I tiptoed past Mrs. Vincentova's door, smelling the meat and onions she was cooking for lunch, and as I walked past the wattle-fence cages, I saw her snack box sitting on a bench. A couple of leftover milk bags were in the box. The door was open, but Mrs. Vincentova was nowhere to be seen, so I grabbed a bag of milk and a straw, and I dashed upstairs to the toilet and locked myself in a stall. I sat down on the toilet seat, eagerly tearing the corner off the bag. I put the straw in the milk and took a long sip. It tasted very different from the fresh milk we bought from Mrs. Backyard's farm. It wasn't sweet and it had an industrial aftertaste, but I liked the straw, which had a joint in the middle, and I could bend it into different shapes. I was sipping the milk and playing with the straw, when I suddenly heard heavy steps. The bathroom door swung open, and beneath the gap at the foot of my stall, I saw two feet and a broom.

"Open the door!" Mrs. Vincentova bellowed. "I know you're in there!"

She started to bang on the door with her broomstick. I was terrified.

My heart was pounding so hard I could hear it in my ears. I unlocked the door with trembling hands, and Mrs. Vincentova wrenched it open. When she saw it was me, her anger tripled.

"Furmanova!" She hissed. "I might have known!"

She grabbed me by the ear and hauled me out into the corridor, pointing furiously at the floor with her broom. A long trail of milk dribbled all the way downstairs from the bathroom to the cage. With a sinking feeling, I realized that the milk had been left over because the plastic bags were leaking.

"And who do you suppose is going to mop up this milk?" Mrs. Vincentova exploded.

"I'm very sorry," I stammered. "I'll clean it up! I will! I promise!"

"No, you won't," she said grimly. "You're off to see the headmistress! We have a way of dealing with thieves at this school!"

Mrs. Vincentova dragged me up the hall and knocked on the headmistress's door. I had never even seen the headmistress before, but I imagined her to be a tough Communist bureaucrat inclined to deal harshly with criminals and dissidents. Her office door was big and imposing. After a while, Mrs. Vincentova knocked again and then opened the door without waiting for a response. She pulled me into the office and closed the door behind her. The headmistress turned out to be an attractive woman wearing a smart white suit, glamorous earrings, and bright red lipstick. She was sitting at her desk and speaking on the phone. Her eyes were friendly, and she looked at me and smiled.

"Yes, this is Comrade Richmanova," she said into the phone. "Can I please speak to the regional school committee inspector?"

She cupped her hand over the mouthpiece.

"What is it now?" she asked Mrs. Vincentova.

Mrs. Vincentova opened her mouth to explain, but Comrade Richmanova was back on the phone.

"Yes, I am still waiting," she said. "Please tell the inspector I need to speak to him urgently!"

She returned to Mrs. Vincentova with an impatient look on her face. "I'm listening. Go on," she said.

Mrs. Vincentova started to explain how I had stolen the milk, but she had hardly begun when the bell rang announcing the end of class. A loud roar erupted from the classrooms. Doors banged open and the corridor was quickly flooded with children who wiped the milk off the floor with their school slippers, destroying Mrs. Vincentova's evidence. Comrade Richmanova looked up from the phone and sniffed.

"Comrade Vincentova, do I smell something burning in your kitchen?"

Mrs. Vincentova stiffened. She looked at Comrade Richmanova and she looked at me, and then wordlessly dragged me out of the office. In the corridor, she shot a despairing look at the now clean floor.

"You had better watch out!" she snapped. "I know about your family. I know about you!"

And then she ran downstairs to her room like a witch, sweeping everyone out of her way with her broom.

EVERY DAY AFTER THAT, Mrs. Vincentova made a point of carefully inspecting my muddy sandals, but she wasn't able to get me into too much trouble, because I turned out to have two powerful allies. The best of them was the third-grade teacher, Marinka Novotna, who had once taught my sister and had known me since I was a baby. She was a little old lady who looked like a doll and was almost as tiny as I was. On a few occasions, she had even visited our house, and loved the fact that my mother called me "Little Trumpet."

My other ally was Comrade Humlova, who had also taught my sister but was very scrupulous about keeping her political records up to date and was always asking Klara to supply information about my father's work. Regardless of this, I thought Comrade Humlova was nice. I had been a favorite of hers ever since I became a member of her poetry group.

It all began one day when she asked me to read a poem called "The Great October Revolution."

The Revolution calls her children to war!
We march in the streets and say: No more!
We roll our sleeves and shake our fists . . .
To hell with the capitalists!

I had read aloud with great feeling, and as I said, "To hell with the capitalists!" I shook my fist at Comrade Humlova. She was so impressed, she asked me to become a member of her poetry group. This meant I was able to move from my seat next to Romanka and sit on the front bench next to Andula Thatcher, one of the quiet girls with pigtails. Comrade Humlova gave me a book of her favorite poetry, marking the poems she wanted me to memorize. She told me to turn up for a rehearsal the following afternoon wearing a blue Pioneer uniform, because immediately after the rehearsal we were scheduled to perform at a Red Cross reunion.

I excitedly broke the news to my parents over dinner.

"Where can I get a Pioneer uniform, Dad?" I asked, causing my father to choke on his soup. "I'm going to recite poetry for the Red Cross tomorrow, and Comrade Humlova says I need to wear a blue shirt with a red neckerchief tied around my neck."

My parents looked at me with shocked expressions while my sister burst into laughter.

"You can't wear a Pioneer uniform," my father roared. "We're dissidents! Do you have any idea what being a Pioneer means? I used to beat up Pioneers in the streets of Ostrava! I would rather die than see my daughter wearing that stupid costume!"

I showed my parents Comrade Humlova's book of poetry and the poems she had marked for me to learn, and my mother was very concerned about the violence in the passages. The poems, of course, were written in the language of Revolution. Lots of smashing and killing for the good of the state. With the same seriousness she used to explain the vitamin content of my lunchtime oranges, my mother quietly pointed out that any kind of violence is wrong, even violence advocated by the government. In the background, my dad smoked furiously and nodded in agreement.

"But I want to recite at the Red Cross reunion," I told them. "I'm the best at reciting. I have the loudest voice!"

"We don't have a problem with you reciting poetry," my mother said. "We just don't think it's a good idea for you to recite violent poetry."

"And there's no way you're wearing that uniform," my father growled. "If anyone tries to make you, I will strangle him!"

Later that evening, my sister came to my room and told me that Comrade Humlova was a bitch and the Pioneers were stupid and there was nothing more ridiculous than reciting poetry in public. She was in an oddly good mood and smelled faintly of cigarettes, and, completely out of the blue, she told me a political joke she had heard at the Rotten pub. Klara had taken to spending her late afternoons at the pub with a group of similarly disaffected young people called "*maniczky.*" *Maniczky* were basically Czech hippies. The name came from a character in a popular puppet show (and later TV series), who, in sharp contrast to the cleanly scrubbed youths depicted in the Socialist art of the time, had long hair and round John Lennon glasses. After the Russians crushed the Prague Spring uprising, a lot of young people expressed their disillusionment by imitating the protest generation of seventies America. Blue jeans, long hair, acoustic guitars. This kind of protest was passive enough to spare them the harsh treatment dealt out to men like my father. The children of both dissidents and party officials achieved common ground in the image of Maniczka. Everywhere you looked, there were long-haired young people in old sweaters and jeans, smoking and talking in the back rooms of pubs, ridiculing the stern doctrine of socialism. Hence the joke my sister told me.

"Okay. You have to swear you won't repeat this to anyone," she said. "This joke is dangerous. If someone denounced us to the secret police, we would have to go to jail, and it all would be your fault. So swear, okay?"

"Okay," I promised. "I swear!'"

"Shhh." My sister scanned the room furtively and then lowered her voice. "The day before the May Day parade, the mayor of Cernosice gave two posters to a Gypsy to put up in his window," she said. "One was a picture of Lenin and the other was a picture of Stalin. The mayor says to the Gypsy, 'I want to see these posters in your window, otherwise you're in serious trouble. Understand?'

"'I understand,' says the Gypsy. But of course, he sleeps in and misses the beginning of the parade. Suddenly, he hears the parade going past his house. In a panic, he jumps out of bed stark naked, grabs the posters, and holds them up in the window. Everyone in the parade can see his little bird. Finally, the mayor walks past. He sees the Gypsy, starts waving frantically, and yells, 'Put that prick away!' 'Which one?' the Gypsy asks. 'The bald one in the suit, or the one with the mustache?'"

My sister burst into laughter. She laughed and laughed and laughed.

"How come the Gypsy wasn't wearing any clothes?" I asked.

My sister stopped laughing. A familiar look of exasperation appeared on her face.

"That's not the point," she snapped.

"Wouldn't he have been embarrassed standing there with no clothes on?"

"*Ježis Marja!*" My sister rolled her eyes. "I can't tell you anything! It's a very funny joke, and if you weren't so busy sucking up to the Communists, you might actually understand it. Sometimes I don't know why I bother. Go ahead and read your stupid poetry then. Wear your stupid Pioneer uniform! See if I care!"

She marched out of the room, switching out the light as she left. I lay in the darkness and tried to work out what had happened. I was used to my parents reacting strongly to things, but my sister rarely became angry. Her usual style was to burst into tears. I felt ashamed that I didn't understand her joke, and worried that my decision to read poetry had caused so much trouble in our house. I didn't want to be a collaborator, but I had already said yes to Comrade Humlova.

I wasn't sure what I should do.

The next morning, I arrived at school at a quarter to eight, just as Mrs. Vincentova had opened the front door. I made myself very small and tried to sneak past her as usual, but she grabbed my satchel and pulled me back.

"Your shoes are dirty," she said. "You're going to have to go home and clean them."

I looked up and saw a malicious expression on her face. There wasn't any more mud on my shoes than usual, but Mrs. Vincentova had obviously decided to make trouble for me today. She towered above me and tapped my shoes with her broom.

"Can't I clean my shoes here?" I asked.

"No," she replied. "You'll have to go home and clean them, and afterward I'm going to write you up as being late for class."

"But that's not fair!" I protested.

"Oh, so you're talking back to me now?" Mrs. Vincentova said. "That's a detention right there! I'll have a word with Comrade Humlova and you can stay behind after school. Now get going! The later you return, the worse it will be for you."

I opened my mouth to argue, but then thought better of it. My sister had often complained about Mrs. Vincentova's deliberately making things difficult for her, and I really didn't want to have to stay behind after school and write sentences on the blackboard. I walked halfway up the hill and found a patch of dewy grass, which I used to clean my sandals. Then I ran back to school with a change of heart. I had planned to tell Comrade Humlova that I wouldn't be able to recite at the Red Cross reunion, but I realized that the poetry group would save me from detention. I was sure that Comrade Humlova would prefer me to leave school early with the rest of her group rather than stay behind for talking back to the caretaker.

I ran up the steps, showed Mrs. Vincentova my clean shoes, and dashed into the classroom.

"Does anybody know where I can borrow a Pioneer uniform?" I whispered, walking from one bench to the other. "Can anyone lend me a blue shirt and a red neckerchief?"

At lunchtime, Comrade Humlova and Mrs. Vincentova had a talk in the hallway. From a distance I could tell that Mrs. Vincentova was not very happy about Comrade Humlova's decision. When the bell rang at two fifteen, I joined the other girls in the poetry group, and we walked across town to the National Committee Building. The National Committee had requisitioned the nicest villa in Cernosice for its headquarters, and while I had often admired this lovely old villa, I had never actually been inside. I looked up and down the street, terrified that I would see my dad's yellow Skoda, and then dashed up the driveway and into the bathroom to change into Romanka's old Pioneer uniform. The other girls wore white stockings and crisply ironed uniforms, while Romanka's blue shirt was several sizes too big and made me look like a scarecrow. Comrade Humlova had bought herself a new dress, and her hair was freshly permed. She took us through a quick rehearsal, waving a wooden ruler like an orchestra conductor's baton, and then she sent us behind the stage as the guests started to fill the main room. After a few minutes, the head of the Cernosice Red Cross Unit introduced us:

"Comrades men and women, it is a great pleasure for me to present to you Comrade Teacher Humlova and her poetry reciting group!" he said.

Comrade Humlova pushed us onto the stage and we formed a half circle around the microphone. The room was full of flags and old people wearing Red Cross armbands. They sat at their tables as if they were at a pub, and drank lemonade and ate little cakes and sandwiches. It was obvious that they were more interested in the food than they were in our poetry, but they applauded politely after every poem. When it was my turn, I stood on the tips of my toes but was still too small to reach the microphone. I filled my lungs with air and recited loudly:

Across our withered land!
an eastern wind has blown!
in blood red soil, the seeds
of Revolution have been sown!
The Working Class victorious!
its traitors strung up high!
in Leningrad, the fire still burns,
its flame will never die!

A wave of applause almost swept me from the stage. The head of the Cernosice Red Cross Unit was so moved by my performance that he got up and pinned a Red Cross badge to my Pioneer shirt. He complimented Comrade Humlova on being an excellent teacher and invited us to join him at his table while the reunion continued with a demonstration of mouth-to-mouth resuscitation. Two nurses climbed up on the stage carrying a stretcher with a plastic doll, and for the next hour they invited people to blow air into the doll's mouth, making her balloonlike breasts go up and down. Comrade Humlova reached across the table and patted me on the head.

"You made me very proud today," she smiled. "I'd like you to recite at the Great October Socialist Revolution parade."

After my success at the Red Cross reunion, Comrade Humlova invited me to represent the school by reciting poetry at firemen's balls, antifascist conferences, and people's militia reunions. She bought me a Pioneer shirt with her own money, and Comrade Richmanova decorated me with a Pioneer badge (a pin shaped like an open book on fire) in front of the whole class. I was something of a celebrity at school and Mrs. Vincentova had to endure my dirty shoes without comment. But I wasn't too proud of myself. November 7 was approaching, and my father had always said that the people who carried lampions in the Great October Socialist Revolution parade were cowards and collaborators. I didn't want to be a collaborator. I only wore Comrade Humlova's Pioneer uniform to stop Mrs. Vincentova from making me stay behind after class, and I was torn by the conflicting emotions every collaborator must have felt. I liked being a celebrity at school, but I didn't like having to lie to my parents. I hid my Pioneer uniform at school and always asked to read first so that I could leave the recital early and not arouse my parents' suspicions. I made up Pioneer jokes and told them to my sister, and agreed loudly with my dad whenever he complained about the National Committee.

Looking back, I think I must have known that I was going to be caught. Reciting poetry at an antifascist conference or a militia reunion was pretty safe, because the people who went to these functions were the kind of people who went out of their way to avoid my parents. But the Great October Socialist Revolution parade was a public event. It was held in November, because at the time of the Revolution in 1917, the Russian calendar was different from the Western one, and it was first and foremost a children's parade. At school, we would make lanterns to carry in the evening, and after dinner the participating families would gather at the town hall and parade across Cernosice to the Rotten pub. The big room in the back, where the Friday and Saturday night discos took place, would be transformed into a banquet hall, and there would be beer for the parents and lemonade for the kids. It was an interesting example of civic socialism at work. Year in, year out, the Communist families of Cernosice staged an October parade in November, endured the usual speeches, sent their children home early, and then settled down to the important business of drinking. It was through nights of drinking that the town's status quo was maintained. A lot of townsfolk who privately deplored the bad roads and poor public works overseen by the National Committee felt compelled to turn up at all the Communist functions for the simple reason that they didn't want to be excluded. Gossip was rife, and the last thing you wanted was the people in town to start discussing your affairs. My family could be counted on to not attend these parades, but a lot of our neighbors would be there, and the word would quickly spread that Furman's daughter had recited Communist poetry.

I was going to get into a lot of trouble.

As the day of the parade drew nearer, I started willing myself to fall sick. I'd come down to breakfast, complaining of headaches and dizziness, but my mother was impossible to fool. She would take my temperature and put an extra orange in my lunch box, and send me down the hill. I sat in class, glaring at the posters of workers, and was quite rude to Andula Thatcher, whose dad was a policeman. Comrade Humlova must have sensed that something was wrong, because she called me up to the front of the class.

"You seem restless, my dear," she said. "Are you nervous about tomorrow's parade?"

"I'm very nervous!" I replied. "And I think I might be catching a cold! My head hurts and I feel dizzy all the time!"

"You should eat more fruit," Comrade Humlova smiled. "But right now, I'd like you to do me a favor."

"What's that?" I asked.

"We need some cardboard for tomorrow's lanterns, and the art department has run out. Would you be a dear and run to the shop for me? We need ten sheets of orange and ten sheets of purple. You can tell Mrs. Seidlerova to put it on our account."

"Okay!" I said, cheering up immediately.

I went to Mrs. Vincentova and got her to unlock the cage so that I could get my shoes. She was preparing to go out herself, and grumbled and groaned the whole time. I changed out of my slippers and left the schoolyard, walking up the main road to the local shops. There was a newsagent and stationery shop around the corner from the train station, and I felt very important asking Mrs. Seidlerova to give me some cardboard on the school account. She rolled the cardboard up in a tube of butcher's paper and sealed it with sticky tape, and I headed back to school. As I was walking past the long row of notice boards outside the station, a large poster caught my eye. It was a new poster with an old slogan—THE SOVIET UNION: TOMORROW IS YESTERDAY ALREADY!—and it made me remember the parade and reciting Comrade Humlova's poems in front of the whole town. My sister was right. Reciting poetry was stupid, especially since no one believed what the poems were saying. I looked around me at the potholes in the roads and the peeling paint on the buildings and the line of rusting Skodas in front of the town hall, and I realized the poster was right—tomorrow was yesterday already. I snatched it off the notice board and threw it in the bin. I walked back to school and gave Comrade Humlova her cardboard, then I slumped down in my bench and concentrated on my headache. I was definitely coming down with a terrible cold.

A few minutes before the end of the class, Comrade Richmanova made an announcement through the public address system, asking Comrade Humlova to come to her office. The second she left, the classroom erupted into the usual chaos, and for once I joined in. I was out of my seat, helping Honza Tucek throw poor Petr Halbich's slippers around the room, when Comrade Humlova appeared at the door. Mrs. Vincentova was standing beside her.

"To your seats! To your seats!" Comrade Humlova clapped her hands. "Furmanova. Come with us please."

I had no idea what was going on, but the look on Mrs. Vincentova's face made it clear that she had scored some kind of personal victory. I followed them up the stairs to the headmistress's office. The door was open and Comrade Richmanova was standing near the window. This time she wasn't smiling. Sitting on her desk was the crumpled-up poster I had thrown in the bin.

"Would you care to explain this?" she asked me quietly.

My chin started to tremble. How could I possibly explain something so simple and yet so complicated? The conflicting emotions of the past month came flooding back to me, and my eyes filled with tears.

"I saw her with my own eyes!" Mrs. Vincentova hissed. "Willful destruction of state property! That's a serious offense!"

"Thank you, Comrade Vincentova," the headmistress said curtly. "I'd like to hear what Dominika has to say."

"I'm sorry." I sobbed. It was hard to get the words out.

The headmistress's office was very hot. Comrade Humlova pulled out a handkerchief and started to mop her ample bosom.

"I don't understand," she said. "Dominika is one of my best students. She's reciting at tomorrow's parade. This might just be nothing more than a simple case of nerves."

"She knew exactly what she was doing," Mrs. Vincentova snapped. "Her sister was a troublemaker, and her father has well-documented anti-Socialist leanings!"

The tears were spilling down my cheeks.

"I think I've heard enough, Comrade Vincentova," Comrade Richmanova said. "Would you please excuse us?"

The caretaker narrowed her eyes. "As a committed Socialist, I demand to know what you intend to do about this," she said.

Comrade Richmanova walked to the door and pulled it open. Her eyes were very unfriendly. She spoke slowly and her pronunciation was chillingly precise.

"I will punish the girl, Comrade Vincentova," she said. "You've done your duty reporting this matter. You can be assured that we will deal with it appropriately. Thank you."

Once Mrs. Vincentova had gone, the other two women relaxed. Comrade Richmanova handed me a tissue, and asked again why I had thrown the poster in the bin. All I could whisper was "I'm sorry." Comrade Richmanova pulled a detention slip from her desk and sighed as she filled it in, while Comrade Humlova, with real emotion in her voice, told me that I would no longer have the privilege of reciting at the Great October Revolution parade.

"A good Pioneer must never steal or destroy other people's property!" she said, and as punishment, I had to stay after school and write this sentence one hundred times in my exercise book.

I was sad and ashamed, but secretly relieved as well.

Later that afternoon, sunbeams stroked the windows as I sat in the third-grade classroom and refilled my pen with ink. My fingers were dark blue and my eyes were red from crying. I could hear the sound of children outside in the yard. I ground my teeth together, because the nib of my pen was very scratchy on the paper. Every ten minutes, I stopped and counted the sentences. Fifty-five. Fifty-six. I looked at the clock on the wall and watched the minute hand move to a quarter past four. I was thinking about how if I died, Comrade Richmanova and Comrade Humlova would be so upset that they would punish Mrs. Vincentova for pushing me over the edge. My father would rush to the school and yell at the caretaker and maybe even break her broom across his knee. Sixty-six. Sixty-seven. The minute hand moved to half past four, and then the classroom door opened and Comrade Richmanova was standing there, looking in at me.

"You're still here?" She sounded genuinely surprised. "Poor little thing." She handed me a tissue and I blew my nose. "How many have you written?" she asked.

"Sixty-nine and a half," I replied, and covered my face with my hands.

"Well, that sounds like enough," she smiled. "Why don't you pack up your things and go home?"

I took my hands away from my face, and she laughed. "Dear me, you can't go home like that. You'll frighten your parents."

I looked at my reflection in the window and saw that I had smeared ink all over my cheeks.

"Come on," the headmistress said kindly, putting her arm around my shoulders. "Let's get you cleaned up."

We went to the bathroom, and I washed my face with soap. Comrade Richmanova stopped by her office, and when she came back out, she was holding a banana.

"Are you hungry?" she asked. I hesitated, because bananas were very rare in Czechoslovakia at the time, but she gave it to me and patted me on the head.

I took the banana and eagerly started to peel it.

"I'm sorry you won't be reciting tomorrow," she said. "Comrade Humlova says you're very charming."

"I like reciting!" I said with my mouth full. "I just have a problem with all the violence in the poetry."

"Do you now?" Comrade Richmanova smiled. "Your house is right at the top of the hill, isn't it? Why don't I give you a lift in my car?"

Like everyone else in Cernosice, Comrade Richmanova drove a Skoda. Her car was very clean and I liked the way it smelled. I was happy to sit next to her and eat my banana, and even happier to realize that she didn't think I was a terrible person for tearing down the poster. As we drove up the hill, it suddenly struck me that the worst was over. I could stop pretending to be a Pioneer. I could concentrate harder on my ballet lessons. I wasn't going to upset my parents. I felt almost dizzy with relief.

When we arrived at the house a few minutes later, Comrade Richmanova surprised me by unbuckling her seat belt and walking me to the door. She hadn't said anything, in fact. She stood beside me and waited until my mother answered the door, then she quietly asked if there was a place where they could talk for a few minutes. I thanked her for the banana, and she ruffled my hair as she followed my mother downstairs to the kitchen. She didn't seem angry or upset. Her manner could be best described as cautious. I was sent out to play in the yard while the two adults had a cup of coffee and a chat. As I played, I began to understand how dangerous communism could be.

Comrade Richmanova was an important regional official, whereas Mrs. Vincentova wasn't even a party member, but I could see that when Mrs. Vincentova demanded justice "as a committed Socialist," she had made both the headmistress and Comrade Humlova nervous. So nervous that Comrade Humlova was prepared to cut me from her poetry group, even though my recitals had made her look good. My father had warned me about the complexity of the system, but this was the first time it had affected me directly, and I resolved to be more careful in the future.

. . .

FOR THE NEXT THREE YEARS that I attended the state school, Mrs. Vincentova kept a watchful eye on me and was always ready to denounce my bad behavior. Fortunately, I was protected by a handful of teachers who quietly approved of my strong personality. Comrade Richmanova saw that my father's bad papers disappeared from my file, and Comrade Humlova wrote a long report commending me for my stirring poetry recitals. She persuaded me to recite at a few more functions in spite of my fear that my parents would find out, and oddly enough, when they eventually did, the whole thing had a positive outcome. My dad went down to the National Committee one day to renew his license to reconstruct our house, and Comrade Holoubek, the local chief of state and public works, was unusually friendly to him.

"Here's your permission, comrade engineer," the old Communist had smiled. "I have to say, I always thought of you as being the enemy of the regime, but when I saw your daughter reciting at the people's militia reunion, I changed my mind. The way she shook her fist while she spoke! Honestly, it brought tears to my eyes!"

My father was very surprised to hear this, but he was also very glad that he didn't have to pay Comrade Holoubek under the table to have his license renewed. When he came home, we had a friendly chat about politics and art. He told me that if I loved reciting poetry, reciting it for the State didn't necessarily make me a collaborator.

I was a good trumpet. It wasn't my fault that the orchestra was bad.

n i n e

THE LITTLE
YOLK WREATH

 THE FOLLOWING SUMMER was even hotter than the last. Weeds and scaffolding covered the construction site, making our house look like a ruined castle. My father had driven off in search of a job, and my sister had put on a white blouse without a bra and caught the train to Radotin, where she made heaps of money as a waitress. All the children in the neighborhood were away on holidays, and my mother was back at the Economic Institute, working on a new book about the Soviet oil trade. I wandered through the backyard where a spade truck had dug a ditch the week before we ran out of money. I poked the bottom of the ditch with a stick, making clusters of frog eggs float to the surface. Tadpoles swam in the water beneath my feet, and I imagined that the pool was the Mediterranean Sea and the tadpoles were boats sailing from Italy to Greece. I hit the water with my stick, making waves and trying to sink them, pretending to be the goddess of the ocean.

When I finally got bored, I walked down the street to Terezka Jandova's house. Terezka was one of the quiet girls in my class. She had long, braided hair and often brought Comrade Humlova apples. I was never really comfortable visiting the Jandas. The last time I had played in their garden, Terezka's brother Tomas had pissed in my shoes when I took them off to climb a tree. They were devoutly religious, but also kind of mean.

"Hello, Mrs. Jandova!" I called out to Terezka's grandmother, who was reclining on a deck chair beneath a yellow beach umbrella. "Is Terezka home?" Half a sweater hung from the knitting needles she held in her lap. She appeared to be asleep.

"Hello! Mrs. Jandova? Are you asleep?" I tried again.

Mrs. Jandova sat up in her chair. She looked at me without a trace of recognition.

Then she frowned. "Ah . . . you're Furman's little girl."

She lifted her knitting needles up to her nose.

"Terezka's at church," she said briskly. "It's her first communion on Sunday, so she's preparing for it with the other girls and boys."

I looked around the yard. It was full of nice trees and there was a swing hanging from one of them.

"The other girls and boys?" I asked. "I thought everyone was away at Pioneer camp."

"Not at all," Mrs. Jandova replied. "The church has been holding a communion workshop all week. Children have been coming in from as far away as Radotin and Mokropsy."

"Really?" This was very interesting.

Mrs. Jandova began to fiddle with her knitting.

"How many children?" I asked.

"I really don't know," Mrs. Jandova sighed.

"Just a few, or lots and lots?"

"I have no idea," Mrs. Jandova sighed again. "What time is it? Shouldn't you be running home for lunch?"

"There's no one at home!" I complained. "My dad's looking for work and my mother's at the Economic Institute and my sister's making heaps of money at the Portland pub in Radotin. I have no one to play with."

"I see," Mrs. Jandova said gravely.

"But perhaps I could go to church," I pondered. "I've never been to church. Maybe I could go! What do you think? Do you think I could go?"

Mrs. Jandova dropped the knitting into her lap.

"You would like to go to church?" she asked suspiciously.

"Maybe," I said. "I have nothing else to do."

A wince of a smile crept over the old lady's face. She looked up at the sky and made the sign of the cross. Then she climbed out of her chair and folded her knitting on the seat.

"If you are really interested in going to church, I will take you," she said. "But you must promise to behave. And no talking. You're not allowed to talk in church, is that understood?"

"Yes!" I said happily.

And then I talked to Mrs. Jandova all the way down the hill.

The local church was a small, sand-colored building with six vaulted windows and a classic Czech baroque tower. It stood near the Under the Forest pub and the War Memorial, and was surrounded by a wall of boxwoods. There was a small graveyard at the back, where my dad's father was buried. Mrs. Jandova walked me to the ivy-covered balustrade in front of the gate.

"You must be quiet now," she said. "This is God's house. You're sure you haven't been here before?"

"No, never," I replied. "My granddad is buried in the backyard, but I've never been inside."

I hadn't been inside the church, in part because it was rarely open. There was a Mass on Thursday afternoons and a service on Sunday mornings, but the rest of the time, the building was locked. There were many beautiful cathedrals in Prague, of course, such as the Snow Lady, the Saint Martin in the Wall, and the Holy Mother Under the Chain, and my mother and I had often visited them during our long walks around the city. Their cold, silent naves were filled with the smell of incense and mold, and pigeons cooed behind their dusty, stained-glass windows. My mother would lift me up and I'd dip my fingers in the font of holy water, but more often than not the basin would be empty, because religion was discouraged and many people were too afraid to go to church. Most of the city's wonderful cathedrals stood forgotten beneath a permanent coat of scaffolding.

"The Communist Party has liberated the working class from the cage of superstition!" Comrade Humlova would preach from the front of her classroom. "God is the residue of the bourgeois mentality, and the personage of Jesus Christ was invented by priests to fool the working class and steal its money!" A poster with an illuminated head of Karl Marx hung near the door, bearing the slogan RELIGION IS THE OPIATE OF THE MASSES!

AS A LITTLE GIRL, I believed in Heaven and Hell, because the Baby Jesus gave me presents every Christmas, and the devil came to our house every fifth of December. I was very afraid of the devil. His name was Cert (pronounced *churt*), and he accompanied Saint Mikulas as the latter passed through the town. Saint Mikulas had a fluffy white beard and wore a bishop's miter on his head. Every December, he would walk through Cernosice seeking out the girls and boys who had been good for the year, assisted by an angel who carried a basket of sweets. Whenever they visited our house, they would come inside and ask my parents if I had done my homework and been respectful to my teachers, but they would always leave the door open and Cert would sneak in. His face was painted black, and big red horns stuck out of his head. He rattled a chain and made terrible noises as he ran through the house. Every year, my parents would help me find a good place to hide, but no matter where I hid, the devil would find me. He would pick me up and carry me to the living room, and then he would laugh horribly and beg Saint Mikulas to let him take me down to Hell. Saint Mikulas would consider this very seriously. He had a big book with everyone's name written in it, and my heart would leap into my throat as he looked up my behavior. So far, I'd been good. Saint Mikulas would grunt approvingly and tell Cert that he would have to take some other boy or girl this year, and Cert would become so wild with anger my mother would have to fetch him a drink to calm him down. Saint Mikulas would pull some gingerbread from his sack and the angel would give me some sweets from her basket, and then they would take Cert outside and tell him off for sneaking into our house. He never listened to them, though. As long as they kept leaving the door open, he kept sneaking inside. All I could do was be on my best behavior and hope that some other kid in town was worse than me.

MRS. JANDOVA LED ME INSIDE the Cernosice church, and we sat down in a stall next to Terezka. There were quite a few children in the stalls around us, and they were very quiet and looked up from their prayer books when I whispered hello. I wanted to ask many questions, but Mrs. Jandova nudged me with her elbow.

"We have to pray now!" she whispered, kneeling down onto a prayer cushion she produced from her bag. She clasped her hands together and moved her lips in silent prayer.

I lowered my bare knees onto the floor and tried to pray. I hadn't seen the little god since we sold our cottage in Semily, but whenever I was sad or lonely, I talked to him inside my head. I had never officially prayed to him though, and I didn't know any prayers. But I had a good imagination. The flame of the eternal light flickered above me and the pipes of the organ sighed from the balcony. I closed my eyes:

> *Hello, my little god,*
> *I know you are very good and wise.*
> *How are you up there in Heaven?*

I'm sure it must be much better than here in Cernosice.
Down here, we have a broken house and I have nobody to play with.
And I am very worried about my father.
He works too hard and smokes too many cigarettes.
Could you do something nice for him? Please please please?
Thank you. Amen.

"In the name of the Father, the Son, and the Holy Ghost," intoned a voice from the front of the church. I looked up and saw a young man in a black cassock standing next to the pulpit. It was the town priest who had recently been transferred from Prague, and no one was quite sure what to make of him.

"Amen!" the children replied.

The priest laid his Bible on the pulpit. He licked his finger and thumbed through the pages.

"Blessed are they who were persecuted for righteousness's sake, for theirs is the kingdom of Heaven," he said.

The priest was a short fellow with chubby cheeks and a shiny, button-like nose. He didn't look very much like a priest to me, because he had modern glasses with metallic frames and wore a pair of corduroy trousers beneath his cassock. He seemed like a nice man, and I liked him immediately.

"Today, I would like to say a few words about the famous martyrs of the Catholic Church," he announced.

"Amen!" I said loudly. The children in the stalls turned to look at me, and Mrs. Jandova nudged me with her prayer book. But the priest's eyes crinkled with amusement.

"Hello, young lady," he smiled. "I haven't seen you before. Perhaps you can tell me the name of the most famous Czech martyr?"

I didn't have to think for more than a second. I knew the answer. It was one of the first things my mother had taught me.

"Jan Hus!" I said confidently.

Mrs. Jandova let out a soft wheeze. Even the priest looked vaguely alarmed.

"I've seen his statue in the Old Town Square," I continued. "My mother said he was a famous priest who was burned at the stake because he believed that the Church should be poor!"

I looked at the priest with a hopeful smile, but his cheeks had turned red and he burst into a peal of nervous laughter. Then he cleared his throat, pulled a handkerchief from his cassock, and began to wipe his glasses.

"Dear me," he said carefully. "You're not right, but you're not wrong either. Jan Hus is a very famous Czech martyr. He was condemned to death in 1415 for preaching against the Catholic Church. He was burned at the stake and was never officially proclaimed a saint, but I believe he was a good man and a hero of the Czech nation."

He finished wiping his glasses and put them back on.

"But it's another Jan I'm referring to," he continued, this time addressing the whole congregation. "Our holy Saint Jan, who was recognized by the pope as the most famous Czech martyr." And then he launched into a talk about the other Saint Jan—Jan Nepomucky—the most famous martyr of the Catholic Church on account of the fact that it wasn't the Catholics who killed him.

Once the communion workshop was over, the children ran outside to meet their parents. Mrs. Jandova went to have a word with the priest, while Terezka and I walked through the church, looking up at the paintings depicting the Stations of the Cross.

After a while, Mrs. Jandova and the priest emerged from the rectory. The priest had changed out of his cassock and into a timeworn brown jacket that matched his corduroy pants.

"So this is the famous Dominika!" he smiled. "Mrs. Jandova tells me you love to talk."

"Not all the time," I said seriously. "Sometimes I like to listen, too!"

"I see," the priest nodded. "And you know your Czech history, which is very impressive. Tell me, have I met your mother and father? Are they churchgoing folk?"

"I don't think so," I said. "My dad is off looking for work all the time, and my mother writes books about the Russian economy."

"Very well," the priest nodded.

"But my granddad is buried here!" I said. "And I have no one to play with, so I have plenty of time to come to church. I even have a pillow I can bring to kneel on."

Mrs. Jandova and the priest exchanged glances. The expression on Mrs. Jandova's face was that of someone realizing the full consequences of a bad idea that had probably seemed like a good one at the time.

"You would be very welcome, of course," the priest chuckled. "The Sunday service starts at ten in the morning, and I do hope to see you in the congregation. God bless you until then."

THE SMILING PRIEST made such a good impression, I decided to go to church every Sunday. I gave up my morning TV show, *Studio Friend,* and made sure that my favorite purple dress was washed and ironed in time for the service.

Terezka and her grandmother waited for me in front of their house, and we walked down the hill to church together. Old Mrs. Jandova became my custodian in all matters religious. She sat next to me in the stalls and told me when to stand and when to kneel. I was surprised she had become so fond of me, until Terezka confessed that her grandmother was very eager to oversee my embrace of the Catholic faith. She read the Bible the way some people read cookbooks, pouring over its recipes for the best tips on how to get to Heaven, and she was very intrigued by a passage in which Jesus had declared that a single sinner turned into a good Christian was worth more than ninety-nine righteous souls. After my first communion, she gave me a silver necklace with a medallion of the Holy Mary on it, and arranged for me to sing in the choir. I was also a regular guest in the rectory, where I would tell Father Eugene about my adventures at school.

Father Eugene listened patiently, sympathizing with my battle against Mrs. Vincentova and the long hours I spent practicing my *battement tendu* at ballet, and then he would get me to blow out the candles and help him collect the hymn books from the stalls.

"Just out of interest," he asked one afternoon. "What's your confirmation name?"

"My confirmation name?" I was completely puzzled.

"When you were baptized, your godfather or godmother would have given you an additional name," he explained. "You're probably too young to remember, but ask your parents about it."

He made a little cross on my forehead and sent me on my way.

I walked out into the street, where the sound of laughter echoed from the Under the Forest pub, and two stray dogs sniffed each other's bums in front of the War Memorial. There weren't any children around, so I opened the gate to the little cemetery and went to visit my grandfather Emil, who had died before I was born. My grandfather's grave was in the corner of the cemetery. He didn't have a single plot with a headstone, but was lodged in a kind of tower block for dead people. He had a small window in a six-foot wall of small windows, and I had to stand on my tiptoes to see inside. His cubicle was one foot high and two feet deep, and was dominated by a large photo of my grandmother Hilda in an imitation ivory frame. Once or twice a year, she would dress in black and get my father to drive her to the cemetery. Weeping bitterly, she would open Emil's window with a key she wore around her neck and push some more plastic flowers inside. Then she would kiss a small photo of my grandfather and slide it back behind her own. My dad would follow behind as she dramatically crossed the yard, her heaving bosom conveying unspeakable grief to the other widows tending their husbands' graves.

"What are you doing here?" Mrs. Jandova called out across the box-wood trees. She was on her knees, weeding the ground in front of a black headstone covered with ivy.

"Hello, Mrs. Jandova! Can I help you?" I asked.

"Oh, no thank you," she refused. "I need the exercise."

"Well, at least I could bring you some water," I offered, grabbing the handle of her watering can.

"There's really no need," she protested. "I've watered everything already."

I put the watering can back down and sat on top of it. Mrs. Jandova continued to pull dandelions out of the gravel.

"Your grave is much nicer than our grave," I said sadly. "My grand-father is over in that window down there, but I can't make it look nice because I don't have the key."

I put my hands in my lap and sighed.

"Listen," Mrs. Jandova said kindly. "If you go to the other side of the church, you'll find the grave of a little French baby whose parents re-turned to France after the war. It's covered in nettles and briars and could use a bit of work."

The headstone was buried beneath a tangle of weeds, and pieces of shattered plaque were scattered around the site. I had to reassemble them in order to learn the girl's name. A photo of a baby emerged from a thick layer of dirt as I wiped the plaque with my sleeve. There were two inscriptions. The first was an epitaph, *"Et Rose elle a vécu ce que vivent les roses: l'espace d'un matin,"* and the second the baby's name and dates, *"Renée Rose Rouelle, 30 Août 1933–7 Mars 1934."* I counted the years on my fingers. The baby had died forty-one years before I was born. I imagined that she was looking down at me from Heaven, and I waved to her up in the sky.

"Hello, little Rose!" I said. "Don't you worry about your grave. I am going to take care of it from now on. I will fix the plaque on your head-stone and plant you some yellow roses."

I worked in the cemetery until it started to get dark, trimming the bushes with Mrs. Jandova's shears and removing nettles and weeds until my hands were red and itchy. Then I said good-bye to Rose and zig-zagged my way up the narrow lane that twisted and turned around the neighborhood gardens, and could hear my mother calling my name across the valley. As I crested the hill, I caught sight of a lean silhouette holding a greyhound on a leash.

"Hello, Mr. Kraus!" I called out.

Jan Kraus was the subject of even more gossip than the priest. He was the black sheep brother of Ivan and Hugo Kraus, who wielded as much local power as the Communist officials. They were handymen who maintained a network of fellow handymen through regular church services and nights of drinking, and were the people you turned to if your car broke down or your stove needed fixing. The Communist handymen in the region were so bad, even the highest-ranking party officials hated using them, so the Krauses were a valuable resource in Cernosice. The Under the Forest pub was their domain, and their religious status gave them a moral exemption from any Communist activity they didn't wish to participate in. They were untouchable. But they were also rather humorless.

The man with the greyhound was different. He was the well-educated middle son, nicknamed "The Philosopher," because he took great delight in tangling his brothers up in the many contradictions of the Church. He did the same thing with the Communists, and was only tolerated in Cernosice because he was young and handsome, and because no one was sure how much influence he had within his family.

"Hello, Dominika," he said pleasantly. "You're out late this evening. What have you been up to?"

I told him about the French baby's grave, and how I intended to plant yellow roses around it. I also showed him my *battements tendus* and *passés* and *frappés* until he laughed and pointed out that my mother was still calling me home for dinner.

I liked Jan Kraus very much. He was one of the few people in our street who talked to me without the slightest hint of prejudice.

After dinner that night, my mother soaked me in a hot bath and scrubbed the dirt off my hands. I told her about the Baby Rose and the talk I had with Father Eugene.

"What's my confirmation name?" I asked as she rubbed shampoo into my hair.

"You don't have one," my mother said. "You were never baptized."

"Why not?" I asked.

"We wanted to give you the choice," she replied. "If you decide you want to be baptized, you still can. It's your decision. Your sister decided she didn't want to be religious, so she isn't. At the end of the day, what you believe is up to you."

"I believe in my little god," I told her. "But I haven't seen him since we sold our cottage. I'd be very sad if he's gone away."

"If you believe in him, he'll never go away," my mother reassured me. "He'll always be with you, no matter where you are. Now, deep breath—" and she pushed my head under the water.

The following Sunday after Mass, I went straight to Rose's grave, carrying a bucket of cement powder and sand from our construction site. I poured water into the bucket and made mortar, which I smeared onto the headstone with a spatula. Then I reassembled the shattered pieces of the porcelain plaque, tapping them into place with the handle of a hammer. I gave the headstone a good splash with water and wiped it clean with my old pajamas. Rose's grave looked very nice. I could hear someone raking gravel at the back of the church, and I thought it might be Mrs. Jandova or even Father Eugene. I picked up my bucket and skipped around the corner, eager to show someone the good work I had done.

It took me a few moments to locate the source of the noise, because the man doing the raking was on his hands and knees. His head was down and his bum was in the air, and he was meticulously cleaning the white gravel that covered one of the plots. I was about to say hello, when I recognized my neighbor Mr. Caesar's green football socks and jersey. Mr. Caesar didn't go to church. He played soccer on Sundays instead, with the Cernosice team, and must have dropped by the cemetery on his way to a game. I tiptoed back around the side of the church and was about to sneak home, when the rectory door opened and Father Eugene stepped out.

"Hello, was that you I could hear tapping a few minutes ago?" he asked. "I thought we had a woodpecker in the trees!"

He pulled his cassock above his knees and crossed the patch of deep grass at the side of the church.

"I've cleaned the Baby Rose's grave," I said proudly. "Her parents went back to France after the war, so she's all alone. I'm going to plant yellow roses and water them every day."

Father Eugene knelt down to read the inscription on the stone. "Renée Rose Rouelle," he said. "That's a very pretty name. Very French."

"And guess what?" I told him. "You know, my confirmation name? I don't have one. I was never baptized."

"Really?" Father Eugene frowned. "But wait a minute . . . you're confirmed. You've taken communion."

"My mother says that if you're going to believe in something, it's pretty silly unless you're given a choice," I explained.

"Right, but you've taken communion. You've eaten the body of Christ," he said in a serious voice I hadn't heard before. "You're not allowed to do that unless you've been baptized."

"But I can get baptized!" I told him excitedly. "All I have to do is make up my mind."

"No, no, it's a sin for an unbaptized person to take Holy Communion," he said. "It goes against the laws of the Church. Are you quite sure about this?"

"How big a sin?" I asked nervously. "A little one or a very big one?"

Father Eugene shot me a fond but troubled smile. He lifted his cassock and walked back through the grass.

"So let me get this straight," he said at the rectory door. "You haven't been baptized, but you think you might like to be?"

I nodded enthusiastically.

"Ježiš Marja," he sighed. "Let me ask a few questions and see what I can do." He disappeared inside the rectory and latched the door behind him.

A few days later, I was on my way to collect milk from Mrs. Backyard's farm, when I ran into Mrs. Jandova and Mrs. Machova having an over-the-fence conversation on the walking path. Mrs. Machova was a Communist who went to the beauty salon once a week instead of church, but she and Mrs. Jandova loved to exchange gossip from their different communities.

"Speak of the devil," Mrs. Machova said slyly.

Mrs. Jandova glanced up the hill, but instead of smiling and saying hello, she turned her back on me and continued to talk to Mrs. Machova.

"Hello, Mrs. Jandova!" I called out.

Mrs. Jandova ignored me.

I carried my milk pails past the two women, and could feel their eyes burning into my back. They had been talking about the devil, but they might as well have been talking about me. Father Eugene had said that I committed a sin, but he didn't tell me how big it was, and I was starting to think that it might be very big. Big enough to make Mrs. Jandova not talk to me. Big enough to make the whole town talk about nothing else.

Mrs. Backyard had just finished milking when I got to the farm, and she was sitting on her stool looking very tired. A few weeks earlier, she had told me that she was too tired to answer all my questions, so I tried not to talk too much when I came around for the milk.

"Hello, Mrs. Backyard!" I said. "How are things today?"

"Oh, you know," she shrugged. "Everything adds up to an old slipper as usual."

This was a popular Czech expression, but it always made me laugh.

"But what's this I've been hearing about you?" she asked. "According to Mrs. Simkova, they're sending someone from Rome to reconsecrate the church because of this business with you taking communion."

"From Rome?" I gasped. "Someone from Rome is coming here?"

"That's what they're saying," Mrs. Backyard said. "I'll believe it when I see it, but you've certainly managed to set a few tongues wagging. Poor Mrs. Jandova has been crying for days."

"But I didn't know!" I cried. "Nobody told me!"

"Well, exactly," Mrs. Backyard sniffed. "I've always said that your parents let you run wild. Maybe this will give them something to think about."

I left the farm and carried my milk across the hill, and was about to turn into the path next to The Philosopher's house, when I saw Hugo Kraus lurching up the lane. Hugo was the oldest of the three brothers. He had a bristly black beard and wild, seventies-style hair.

"Ah, it's the little blasphemer," he said. "We're going to have to re-build the church because of you."

He paused in front of the fence hedge, panting.

"Do you know what happens to little heathen girls who consume the body of Christ?" he asked. "They go to Hell. Two hundred years ago, they would have burned you at the stake for being a witch!"

He laughed heartily, and I could smell cigarettes and beer on his breath.

I edged around him and then ran home in terror, spilling milk over my dress and shoes. I had been attending church for almost five months, and one of the best things about going was the knowledge that I would be safe in December when Saint Mikulas and the devil came to our house. But now, Hugo Kraus had called me a witch. I had not only committed a terrible sin against the Church, but I'd also been given an after-school detention for tearing down a Communist poster. This was my worst year ever. Mikulas would look up my behavior and surely agree to let Cert take me down to Hell. I would have to say good-bye to my parents and I would never get to dance in *Swan Lake*. I took the milk down to the kitchen and went looking for my mother. But I could hear her and my dad talking quietly in the living room and I understood that they had troubles of their own, so I went up to my room and sat on my bed and cried.

THE FOLLOWING SUNDAY, I put on my purple dress and went to the Jandas' house, but Terezka and her grandmother weren't there. They had gone to church without me. I walked down the path to the War Memorial and sat underneath the chestnut tree, watching the congregation arrive. I could see them and they could see me, but nobody crossed the street to invite me in. Everyone in town was gossiping about me, but no one from the church had come to talk to my parents, not even Father Eugene. It felt like I had been banished. I spoke to my little god every day, but I wasn't sure if he had forgiven me. I needed Father Eugene to tell me what to do.

I sat beneath the chestnut tree for most of the service, then I went to visit the Baby Rose's grave. I hadn't planted any flowers, because I was too scared to go to church, but I tidied up the plot and wiped the headstone with my sleeve. I sat on the edge of the grave and willed Father Eugene to come outside. Then I finally summoned my courage and knocked on the rectory door. After a few moments, Father Eugene unlatched it. He was still wearing his cassock.

"Ah, there you are," he smiled. "You weren't at mass today. I was wondering where you were."

"Mrs. Jandova didn't wait for me," I said in a small voice. "I didn't know if I was allowed to come."

"Of course you're allowed," Father Eugene said. "As a matter of fact, I have some news from the archbishop in Prague."

"It's not my fault!" I sobbed. "I didn't mean for someone from Rome to have to come and rebuild the church! I really didn't know! No one told me I wasn't allowed to have communion! Mrs. Jandova didn't say anything about me being baptized!"

"Someone from Rome is coming?" Father Eugene asked. "I haven't heard about this."

"Mrs. Simkova told Mrs. Backyard," I sniffed. "And Hugo Kraus said that if it was two hundred years ago, they would have burned me at the stake for being a witch!"

"I see." Father Eugene shuddered. He sat down on the rectory steps and motioned me to sit beside him. "I should have talked to you sooner, but I've only just heard back from Prague," he said. "It is a great sin for you to have taken communion, but if you get baptized, God will forgive you"—he smiled ruefully—"and us for this mistake."

"So I won't have to go to Hell?" I asked.

"No, not at all," he replied. "So. Would you like to be baptized?"

"Yes, please!" I said without hesitation.

"Very well," Father Eugene said. "I've taken the liberty of already setting a date. You will be formally baptized on the thirteenth of December."

"The thirteenth?" I said. "But that's too late!"

"Too late?" The priest looked puzzled. "Why is it too late?"

"Because Cert is coming!" I cried. "Saint Mikulas will be here on the fifth and he always leaves the door open! Please, Father Eugene! Please, can I be baptized before the fifth? If you don't baptize me, Cert is going to sneak into our house and he'll take me down to Hell for sure!"

"Ah, of course. Angels and Devils Night," Father Eugene smiled. "I'm sorry, Dominika, but the thirteenth is really the earliest I can manage. Believe me, I want to get this sorted out as quickly as you do, but it takes time to organize a baptism. I'm afraid you'll have to wait."

"But what am I going to do? If the devil finds me, I might not be here on the thirteenth!"

Father Eugene looked away for a moment and I saw his shoulders quiver. When he looked back at me, it was with a perfectly straight face.

He made the sign of the cross on my forehead.

"I will pray for you," he said.

. . .

THE FOLLOWING WEEK was the longest week of my life. Every day
seemed to last forever, and when it was over, I was one day closer to the
Eve of Saint Mikulas. I found it hard to concentrate at school and ballet. I
searched the house for good places to hide, and tried to explain the enormity of the problem to my parents, who somehow didn't seem too worried. My dad even made a few jokes about it until my mother told him to
shut up. I couldn't believe it. This was really their fault, and they didn't
seem to care. I read my bible and asked my little god to protect me, and
whenever I went to collect the milk, I would talk to him as I walked across
the hill. I told him that I was very sorry and that if he would make this one
exception and not let Cert inside our house, I would be good for the rest
of my life. I would continue to get excellent grades at school, and when I
grew up, I would be a kind and noble person. I would fix my parents'
house and buy my dad a new car. Please, please, please. Forgive me just
this once.

"Hello, Dominika," a familiar voice said. "Are you talking to
yourself?"

I looked up in alarm. Jan Kraus and his dog were walking up the path.

"No," I blushed. "I'm talking to my little god."

I liked Jan Kraus so much I was very shy around him.

"Your little god?" The Philosopher smiled. "Are you asking him
to tell the Baby Jesus which presents you would like him to put under
your tree?"

"No. I'm asking him to not let Cert take me down to Hell," I said.

"Really?" Mr. Kraus laughed. "Why do you think Cert is going to
take you to Hell?"

I explained everything as best as I could. When I got to the part where
Hugo Kraus called me a witch, the amused look fell off The Philosopher's face.

"I see," he said quietly.

He walked with me to Mrs. Backyard's gate, testing and rejecting various ideas, trying to devise a strategy for a seven-year-old girl.

"Are you quite sure Cert will sneak in?" he asked.

"He always does," I told him. "He always knows where to look, too."

"Of course. Your parents help you hide."

"My dad helps me, but it never does any good."

"Right. So what can you tell me about the devil? Is there anything he's afraid of?"

"I don't think so," I said. "I don't think Cert is afraid of anything."

"What about holy water from the font in the church?" Mr. Kraus suggested. "He's afraid of that, isn't he?"

"He is!" I said excitedly. "He's not allowed to touch it!"

"Exactly!" The Philosopher grinned. "So if you had some holy water and threw it at him, he would have to run away, wouldn't he?"

"I'm not sure," I said. "Doesn't he burst into flames?"

In the Czech fairy tales they showed on TV, Cert would scream and explode whenever he came in contact with water that had been blessed. People were always throwing it at him. Aside from baptisms, this seemed to be the point of holy water. There was a full font in the Cernosice church.

Mr. Kraus reached down to stroke his greyhound behind the ears. "So here's what you do," he said. "You get some holy water and you wait for Cert to come. When he comes, you throw the holy water at him and say *'Apage, Satanas!'* which means, 'Go away, Satan!' Can you remember that?"

"Apage, Satanas!" I shouted.

"Very good. You throw the water and yell *'Apage, Satanas!'* and then you run and hide, but whatever you do, don't tell your parents where you're going to hide."

"Why not?" I asked.

"Trust me. It'll be a surprise," he smiled. "Do they all come in and have a drink in the living room?"

"I think so," I said.

"Well, try to hide in the living room after you've thrown the holy water. My guess is, you'll never be afraid of the devil again."

And, with his trademark smile, he left me there at the gate. I watched him stroll down the lane with his greyhound beside him.

WHEN THE FIFTH OF DECEMBER finally arrived, I was terribly frightened, but excited as well. I had a little jar of holy water from the church, and knew exactly where I was going to hide. No one would think of looking for me under the couch, because there was hardly any room, but I was small enough to fit. I knew, because I had practiced. I stared at my textbooks and counted the minutes until the end of school, then I came home and had an early supper and refused my dad's offer to help me find a place to hide. Instead, I sat in the stairwell and listened for the sound of footsteps crunching through the snow. Saint Mikulas always started at the bottom of the hill, so we were one of the last houses he would visit. It seemed like an eternity before the bell rang and my father answered the door. I could hear him greeting Saint Mikulas and the angel, while Cert laughed and rattled his chain in the background, and then I distinctly heard my dad tell Cert to take his shoes off. I tiptoed into the corridor with my jar of holy water, and watched in amazement as the devil stepped out of his boots. He was still huge and terrifying, with big red horns and eyes as black as coal, but there was something very wrong about him taking off his shoes.

"*Apage, Satanas!*" I yelled, running up the corridor. "*Apage, Satanas!* Go away, Satan!" I threw the holy water and hit Cert squarely in his chest, and leaped back, expecting him to burst into flames. Instead, he merely looked surprised.

"Why isn't she hiding?" he asked my dad.

"I have no idea," my father replied.

"*Apage, Satanas!* You bad devil!" I cried again, then ran through the house as fast as I could and crawled beneath the couch. After a few moments, Saint Mikulas and his companions followed my dad into the living room. They were talking seriously like adults, and all I could see was their feet. My mother came up with a tray of drinks from the kitchen, and I could hear the clinking of glasses above me.

"Won't you please sit down?" my mother asked. "I'll go and see if I can find Dominika."

Cert and Saint Mikulas sat heavily on the couch, while my dad and the angel occupied the two big lounge chairs. The devil was literally sitting on top of me. His feet were so close, I could have reached out and touched them.

"Your little girl is growing up," Saint Mikulas remarked.

"Yes, she's a handful," my father agreed. "She's keeping them busy down at the school."

"So I've heard," the devil said. "I bet that was holy water she threw at me just then. I've been doing this for six years, and it's the first time anyone's tried a crazy stunt like that! *Apage, Satanas!*" The couch rocked with his laughter.

"Do you have time for a refill?" my father asked.

"Of course!" the three visitors said in unison.

And, right then, I recognized the devil's socks. They were Mr. Caesar's green football socks, and the laugh above me sounded a lot like Mr. Caesar's, too. This was very reassuring, but very troubling as well. Right up until the moment when I realized that the devil was really Mr. Caesar, I had truly believed in Cert and Saint Mikulas. Most children growing up under communism did, because the fifth of December was an evening the community took seriously. It was a Czech tradition that dated back many hundreds of years, and was not commercialized in the same way that the Christian holidays are commercialized in the West. Prior to the Revolution, thousands of parents throughout the country dressed up in homemade costumes and handed out sweets to the kids in their villages. It was one night in the year when neighbors could be neighbors without the illuminated head of Karl Marx looking over their affairs.

I studied Mr. Caesar's socks and thought about climbing out and telling him that I was sorry for throwing the holy water at him, but then my mother's feet appeared and I could hear her telling the neighbors that she couldn't find me anywhere.

"Let's go, Dasha," Saint Mikulas said to the angel. "I need to get home and make some eggnog for the kids."

He stood up and thanked my parents for their hospitality.

"Tell Dominika we'll see her next year," he said. "I guess she's getting a bit old for this, isn't she? Mary doesn't even bother hiding these days. She just asks for her gingerbread as soon as we walk in the door."

I couldn't believe what I was hearing. Could it be true that Saint Mikulas was really Mary Hairy's dad?

"Apage, Satanas!" Mr. Caesar laughed.

The springs creaked above my head and three pairs of socks marched out of the room. My parents escorted our neighbors to the door, then they switched off the lights and went downstairs to the kitchen to sit in front of the warm stove. I lay under the couch in the darkness for a while and thought about my little god.

If Cert and Saint Mikulas were really the neighbors in disguise, then maybe there wasn't any Heaven and Hell. Maybe the posters in the classroom were right. Maybe religion was something that clever men like Hugo Kraus used to frighten people with, just like the Communists. I had spent a whole week being afraid, and neither my parents nor Father Eugene had done anything about it. The whole thing was a game. No wonder my sister didn't take the church seriously.

I suddenly felt very sad.

If my little god wasn't real, whom was I going to talk to when I was lonely? The world would be such a big and scary place without him. I crawled out from the couch and walked over to the window. The sky was dark and empty, and there was no evidence anyone was up there, but I found myself praying to my little god, nonetheless.

Hello, my little god,
I really hope that you exist,
because I would like to continue talking to you, you know?
I like going to church and singing in the choir every Sunday.
It's nice to meet people and it gives me something to do.
And did I tell you that I'm going to plant roses on the
    Baby Rose's grave?
I hope they will make her happy.
Thank you for making me happy.
Thank you thank you thank you.
Amen.

On December 13, 1982, I was baptized in the Cernosice church. It was a quiet service, avoided by most of the people in town. Even Mrs. Jandova and Terezka didn't come. The gossip continued through Christmas and slowly died out the following year, and I was gradually accepted back into the local congregation. I planted yellow roses in the graveyard, and kept my promise to the Baby Rose by watering them regularly for the next seven years.

The Chocolate
Horseshoe

THE NICEST THING about living near a forest is that you really get to see the change of seasons. Leaf raking in autumn was a major event, and in the spring I could look out my bedroom window and watch the whole valley explode with color. The whites and browns of winter were replaced by vivid greens and golds, and the streets and fields were wet with melted snow. The Berounka River, which in winter was a giant ice-skating rink, abruptly came back to life and rolled across the weir like it was making up for lost time.

My favorite part of spring was Easter. In Eastern Europe, the Easter tradition is so ancient that a rational explanation of its origin is hard to come by. Easter Fridays and Sundays are similar to the Christian holidays of other countries, except that on Sunday, the men in the village go down to the river, find a weeping willow, and fashion themselves long canes made of eight braided willow branches, which are later decorated with ribbons.

On the Monday morning, men circulate through town, singing Easter carols and attacking the local women. A group of Czech men would knock on their neighbor's door, and after being invited inside, beat the man's wife and daughters silly with their canes. Young girls caught in their beds would sometimes be splashed with cold water, which would make their nightgowns cling to their bodies. You always knew it was Easter Monday, because the screaming of women could be heard throughout the valley. Fat matrons ran barefoot around their gardens, squealing for the benefit of their neighbors. Despite the flimsy design of the canes, an Easter attack could often inflict spectacular bruises, which the local women would later display as proof of their attractiveness. None of the women was allowed to fight back. In fact, it was the opposite. Visiting men would be rewarded with Easter eggs and candy.

On the Easter Monday after my baptism, I stood in front of the big mirror in our hallway and put my hair up in a bun. I was dressed in a pair of brown corduroy trousers and a miniature men's jacket I had borrowed from the ballet school. To complete the costume, I put on my father's cap, which I had lined with newspaper. I leaned closer and admired the cheeky little boy looking back from my reflection. He was very small but cunning, I thought. I picked up the cane I had made from willow branches and hit the air, making the ribbons smack against the surface of the mirror. My Easter basket was ready. I wasn't going to wait for the boys to catch me. I had no intention of collecting bruises, I was going to collect eggs and candy with the men.

Primroses and daisies sprouted from the lawns, and the sound of birdsong filled the forest. In the distance, I could hear Mrs. Backyard's rooster crowing. It was very early in the morning, and clouds of mist steamed up from the ground. I took my sister's shortcut through the forest and emerged through the hedges two streets below our house, where a group of small boys was hanging around Mrs. Machova's gate. They were summoning up the courage to enter, as the gate was guarded by two yapping dogs.

"Hello!" I called out. "The dogs won't bite! They're very friendly."

The four boys watched with relief as I opened the gate. I called the dogs by their names and they immediately stopped barking and started wagging their tails.

"Here," I said. "You should give them a pat."

The boys hesitantly followed my example.

"Are you from Cernosice?" one of them whispered.

"Yes. Where are you from?" I asked.

"We're from Mokropsy. We rode our bicycles here," the boy replied.

Mokropsy was the next village down the river. Its name translates as "wet dogs," and it was very prone to flooding. It was one of the poorer neighborhoods in the region, and I immediately understood why the boys had ridden their bikes upriver. Their chances of filling their Easter basket were immeasurably better in Cernosice.

"Well, I guess you'd better stick with me, then." I smiled. "I know the best places to look for eggs and candy."

We knocked on Mrs. Machova's door, and she opened it with a big smile on her face. Mrs. Machova had dyed blond hair and wore a purple cardigan over her cupboardlike bosom. Like a swarm of wasps, we surrounded the greengrocer, slapping her legs and bottom with our canes. Mrs. Machova appeared to enjoy the attention. She danced around her front room, squealing and laughing. Then she gave us each a painted egg and some candy called "little strawberries."

"Aren't you a bunch of cute little fellows," she said, chuckling. "If I were younger, I would have given you each a kiss instead of an egg!"

I couldn't believe my luck. Everyone in Cernosice knew me, so I wasn't sure I would get away with dressing as a boy. But the four kids from Mokropsy provided perfect cover. Two of them were even wearing worker's caps that were similar to my dad's. And certainly, they didn't appear to suspect I was a girl.

"What's your name?" one of the boys asked.

I looked down at Mrs. Machova's dogs.

"Ferda," I said. "What's yours?"

"I'm Marek," the boy replied. "This is Honza, Jirka, and Peta."

"Pleased to meet you," I said. "Why don't we go to Mrs. Needy's house next?" I pointed at a yellow villa opposite the town's dilapidated ice-hockey rink. "She works in the pastry shop, so she'll have the best cakes!"

We found Mrs. Needy in her dressing gown and slippers. She was fat yet pretty in a voluptuous kind of way, and favored low-cut tops that showed off her massive bosom. She was a regular at the beauty salon and a popular attendee of the Communist drinking nights at the Rotten pub. Protected from our canes by her formidable girth, she withstood our blows with a serene expression on her face.

"All right, that's enough," she told us. "The cakes are in the kitchen. You may have one of each."

We ran excitedly to the kitchen table, where a pile of hedgehogs and Little Indians sat on crisp white sheets of pastry-shop paper. The Mokropsy boys had only one Easter basket, so they pooled their resources while I kept mine separate. As I carefully put the little cakes in my basket, I caught a glimpse of someone in the living room. I poked my head in the door and saw a man in an undershirt, pouring himself a glass of slivovitz. It was Mr. Lojda, the local maintenance man and plumber, who was known around town as Mr. Fix-it.

"Thank you for the cakes, Mrs. Needy!" I said. "Have your pipes burst?"

Mrs. Needy looked at me blankly. "My pipes?" she repeated.

"Your water pipes!" I said. "Mr. Lojda is here, so I imagine he's going to fix whatever it is that needs fixing!"

Mrs. Needy shook her head in amazement, and then she started to hoot with laughter until her double chin tripled.

"Don't worry, little fellow," she laughed. "Mr. Lojda is very handy indeed."

The next house in the street had a roof covered in lichen and a garden full of weeds. It belonged to Mrs. Kapustova, who was a Jehovah's Witness and a bit of a charity case. Poor Mrs. Kapustova had a schizophrenic daughter who gave birth to two children out of wedlock before her illness was diagnosed. The daughter ended up in an asylum, and the children were eventually sent to reform school. After that, Mrs. Kapustova didn't leave her house very often. When she did, she would carry old copies of *The Watchtower* with her and try to convert everyone she met. She opened her door nervously. Clearly, she wasn't expecting anyone to visit.

"Happy Easter, Mrs. Kapustova!" I cried

Mrs. Kapustova looked at us in surprise. Her body appeared to be mere skin and bones, and none of us had the heart to hit her. Her hands fluttered with excitement as she showed us into her living room, and there on the table was a little basket of eggs. She gave us each a plain brown egg with a premade sticker on each side.

"Tell me, young men," she said earnestly. "Have you met Jehovah yet?"

The boys looked at me for help.

"They don't know anyone around here, Mrs. Kapustova," I explained. "They've ridden their bikes all the way from Mokropsy!"

For the rest of the morning, we worked our way through the streets. I was pretty sure that no one recognized me, although I did receive a few strange looks. It was nice to be invited inside the houses I was usually not welcome to visit, and to see the Communist families in a more friendly light. A lot of them had gone to great trouble painting their homemade Easter eggs. My sister was very good at this, and I always envied her ability to dye her eggs an even color and paint simple, elegant designs on them. My paint jobs were always so sloppy. By midday, the boys and I had filled our baskets and eaten so much candy we could hardly walk. We sat on a bench near the train station and listened to the screams and laughter in the distance. Once the clock struck twelve, there was an official amnesty for the women in town. The men would return home for lunch, and the women would assess their bruises competitively, reasoning that the most attractive women would have received the most attention.

As we sat on the bench, I pulled from my basket the plain brown egg

Mrs. Kapustova had given me. The rest of the eggs I had collected were gorgeous, and I was going to take them home and show them to my parents. The plain egg was ugly and I decided to eat it, so I tapped it against my forehead to break the shell. For some reason, this was the traditional way of cracking Easter eggs. You'd tap them against your head and peel the shell in your hands, and I had done this so often I could remove the shell without looking. But the second I tapped the brown egg against my forehead, I knew that something was wrong. Mrs. Kapustova had forgotten to boil her eggs. The shell cracked against my forehead and raw egg splattered down my face, causing the Mokropsy boys to burst into laughter. I told them to shut up, but they continued laughing, so I wiped the egg off my face and snatched up my basket.

"If you're going to laugh at me, I'm going home," I said with dignity. "You can ride your bicycles back to Mokropsy and tell your parents you wished you lived somewhere nice where it doesn't flood all the time."

"Oh, come on. We were only joking," the boys protested.

"I don't care, I'm going." I sniffed. "And don't expect me to help you next year, either!"

I left the station in a huff and walked around the post office to the narrow laneway that led up the hill. I was halfway up the path when a gang of boys appeared in front of me. There were six of them, and I recognized Tomas Hairy, Mary's brother, at the head of the group.

Tomas was three years older than me, and spent most of his time playing tennis on the public court. I put my head down and tried to hide beneath my father's cap, but it was no use. He had recognized my face. I clutched my basket and tried to edge around him, but he knocked the cap off my head and ruffled my hair until it fell down to my shoulders.

"Dominika Furmanova!" he cried. "You're not allowed to collect eggs! You're a girl!"

"It's past twelve o'clock," I reminded him. "You're not allowed to hit me!"

"Check out her eggs!" One of the boys whistled. "A full basket!"

"It's after twelve," I said desperately. "I'm going home!"

"Not with those eggs, you're not!" Tomas laughed.

He grabbed my wrist and started to pry my fingers loose from the basket. I thrashed and fought with all my might, but Tomas was surprisingly strong. A few summers ago, I had been able to hold my own against him, but now he broke my grip with ease and passed the basket to his friends.

"Give it back!" I shouted. "I worked really hard to collect those eggs!"

The boys surrounded me in front of Mrs. Fejfarova's gate. It was the widest point of the lane and had a thick patch of nettles between the fence and the gutter. They chanted an Easter carol and started to hit me with their canes, beating my arms and thighs until they really hurt. I wanted to cry, but I didn't until they rolled me in the nettles. Then they stole my eggs and left me with the empty basket, laughing as they ran down the hill.

I sat in the nettles, sobbing with anger. The grip of Tomas Hairy's hands and his scornful laughter made me realize that the days when I could fight with boys were over. More humiliating, this was the first time a boy had treated me like a girl, showing no respect for the challenge of fighting me. He only used half his strength to steal my eggs, and this was worse than the sting of the nettles and the loss of the eggs combined.

THE FOLLOWING DAY, I was back at school. I limped up the steps and Mrs. Vincentova blocked my way with her broom.

"What's that on your face?" she asked suspiciously.

"Nettle rash," I replied.

"Nettle rash?" she snorted, leaning down to look closer. "That doesn't look like nettle rash to me. It looks like psoriasis. You've brought another disease to the school!"

"But look at my bum, Mrs. Vincentova!" I said, lifting my skirt to show her my bruises. "A gang of boys hit me with their canes and rolled me in a patch of nettles!"

"Pull your skirt down, young lady!" the caretaker snapped.

"It's true!" I said. "They hit me really hard!"

Mrs. Vincentova gave me a black look. Then she shook her head and swept me inside the building.

In class, I had a hard time sitting on my bench. My legs and bottom were itchy and sore, and I scratched all morning. I noticed that a lot of the popular girls, especially the twin sisters Monika and Alice Rabbit, were looking at me with admiration and envy. They were very jealous of my Easter bruises. Only Marinka Novotna, the third-grade teacher, was not impressed by my scruffy appearance. During the history lesson, she gently tugged one of my pigtails and told me to wait behind after class.

"Listen," she said when the other children had left. "I saw you walking around Cernosice yesterday, dressed as a boy. Look at your legs. They're always covered with adhesive strips. Look at your fingernails. They're always dirty. Do you think any of the boys in the village will want to marry you if you keep fighting with them all the time? You're a young lady now. Isn't it time you started behaving like one?"

"I guess so," I said.

"What you need is some friends," Mrs. Novotna smiled. "How are things working out at ballet?"

"Okay," I replied. "But I'm the only one from Cernosice. Everyone else is from Prague."

"I see," Mrs. Novotna said. "Do you play after school with any of the girls in your class?"

"Not really," I shrugged. Most of the girls were from families that didn't like my parents, and the ones who went to church were still recovering from my baptism scandal.

"Well, you should try," Mrs. Novotna advised me. "There's more to school than just learning, you know. One of the things it teaches you is how to get along with other people."

I loved Mrs. Novotna and wanted to take her advice, but the truth was, it was hard to make friends. I went to ballet three afternoons a week, and had a piano lesson and choir practice when the other children were out playing. All the kids in my street had either outgrown me or were disinclined or not allowed to play with me anymore.

As I peeled my orange during the snack break, I surreptitiously observed the other girls in my class. Many of them were in love with horses, and a few of them went to Mrs. Backyard's farm in the afternoons and helped feed the horses in exchange for the privilege of riding them. These were the tough girls from the bottom of the valley. They didn't want to dance in *Swan Lake*. They wanted to be farm girls and have lots of animals around them.

Dana Bukova was the leader of the horse-loving girls. She was small and willful, with bangs that almost covered her eyes and a mocking smile that she could use to great effect. I watched her enviously during the snack break as she sipped milk from her plastic bag and expertly sketched a horse's head from memory. I couldn't draw a horse's head even when I tried. It always ended up looking like a sausage or a dog.

The bell rang for class, and I got up and walked over to where Dana was sitting with Helenka Vesela.

"Hello, Dana! Hello, Helenka!" I said. "Can I look at your drawings?"

Dana looked at Helenka and grinned.

"I didn't know you liked horses," she said. "I thought you were too busy reciting poetry at Red Cross reunions."

"I love horses," I said. "I ride them all the time at Mrs. Backyard's farm."

This was a lie, but I had a habit of believing my lies as I told them.

"Mrs. Backyard lets me ride the baby horse and the black horse with the white dot on his forehead," I continued. "Do you know which horses I mean?"

"Sure, the black horse is Sandy." Helenka rolled her eyes. "But Sandy's not a he. She's a her."

"Oh," I said.

"And the baby horse is a pony," Dana laughed. "You're a terrible liar."

Her eyes shone bright beneath her bangs and I could see that they were full of scorn. My cheeks burned with embarrassment as I retreated to the classroom, and I distinctly heard Helenka behind me, "I bet she doesn't know the difference between a gelding and a stallion!"

"Are you kidding?" Dana said. "She couldn't tell the difference between a donkey and a goat!"

I felt humiliated and discouraged for the rest of the day, but when the bell rang at the end of school, I hurried home and collected my milk pails. I had been visiting Mrs. Backyard's farm twice a week for the past two years, and it had never occurred to me to ask if I could ride the horses. My Tuesday afternoons had become free, and I was fiercely determined to show Dana and Helenka that I did know the difference between a gelding and a stallion. I was good at schoolwork and dancing and piano. I would become good with horses as well.

I opened the gate to Mrs. Backyard's farm and followed the path down to the stables.

"Hello? Mrs. Backyard?" I called. "Are you in there?"

Mrs. Backyard emerged from behind a pile of hay in her rubber boots.

"What are you doing here?" she asked.

"I've come for the milk!" I said. "I thought I'd come early and have a chat."

Mrs. Backyard looked vaguely alarmed.

"I haven't milked the cows yet," she said.

"I know," I told her. "But I'm free on Tuesday afternoons and I really do like to come and visit your farm, Mrs. Backyard, because I'm very interested in all the animals you have . . . especially the horses."

"Ah." A weary smile appeared on Mrs. Backyard's face. "The horses," she sighed. And without saying another word, she turned around and continued to muck out the stables.

"You know, Mrs. Backyard," I talked as she worked, "I could help out. I'm really very good at shoveling sand into my dad's cement mixer."

Mrs. Backyard didn't answer.

"I'd do it for free," I offered. "And then maybe I could ride the horses with the other girls. What do you think?"

"I don't know." Mrs. Backyard paused to wipe her forehead. "Everybody wants to ride the horses these days."

She lifted her barrow and wheeled it out of the stable. I followed her to the compost heap.

"Please, Mrs. Backyard?" I wheedled. "If I helped you, would you let me ride one of your horses, please?"

Mrs. Backyard shooed a fly with her hand.

"It's not up to me," she said flatly. "You're going to have to ask my daughter. They're her horses. She doesn't ride them much anymore, but we got them for her. Five years ago, she quit ballet to ride them. Now, she's too fat to climb into the saddle."

I found Mrs. Backyard's daughter sunbathing in the small cherry orchard behind the house. She looked like a beached whale in a yellow bikini.

"Hello, Vendula!" I called out. "Are you awake?"

Vendula Backyard stretched and rolled onto her side, moving her sunglasses to the tip of her nose.

"I am now," she yawned. "What do you want?"

"I was talking to your mother and she told me that if I helped you clean the stables, maybe you would let me ride one of your horses," I explained. "She said you used to study ballet. I go to the National Theater Ballet School, but I also want to ride horses like Dana Bukova and Helenka Vesela."

Vendula rolled onto her belly.

"Come here, sweetie," she smiled. "Could you please rub some cream on my back?"

She handed me a bottle of suntan lotion.

"There are too many girls riding Sandy and Bonnie at the moment," she said as I rubbed the lotion into her shoulders. "But if you like, you can ride Nikina the pony. She's a bit frisky, but at least you won't break your leg if she throws you. How does that sound?"

"That sounds great!" I said excitedly.

"And the next time you go to the National Theater, say hello to Professor Paskova from me," Vendula yawned. "She used to say that I had heaps of talent. She should remember me, but if she doesn't, she'll definitely remember my dad."

By the time my classmates turned up, I was feeding sugar cubes to Nikina, who was snorting and licking the palm of my hand. Dana, Helenka, and three other girls entered the stables with one saddle between them, and were clearly not happy to see me there.

"What are you doing here?" Dana shot me a withering look.

"I'm helping Mrs. Backyard," I replied. "And when I'm finished, I'm allowed to take Nikina for a ride."

The girls looked at each other. There were five of them, and they were all wearing jeans and proper riding boots. I was wearing corduroy pants and sandals. The pants were several sizes too big.

"Listen," Helenka said in a reasonable tone of voice. "There are too many of us sharing the horses as it is."

"There's no room for you here," Dana said flatly.

"No way," I shook my head. "Vendula Backyard said I could ride Nikina every Tuesday. I have as much right to be here as you do."

Dana flung the saddle on the ground in disgust. I took two steps forward, clenching my fists. I was the smallest of all the girls in the stable, but I was a tough little customer and all of them knew it. Dana muttered something that made her friends laugh, and after that, they didn't speak to me for the rest of the afternoon. They had obviously decided to kill me with silence.

Dana and Helenka saddled Bonnie the mare, and took her outside without a look in my direction. The other girls grabbed Nikina by her halter and attempted to walk her across the yard. Vendula wasn't exaggerating when she said the pony was frisky. The girls shouted and hit her bum with twigs, but Nikina was sulky and uncooperative. She'd been friendly enough when I fed her sugar cubes earlier, so I dug the remaining cubes out of my pocket and gave them to the girls.

"Here. Try these," I said.

The girls took the sugar and fed it to the pony, and then continued to ignore me after Nikina cheered up. I spent the afternoon waiting for them to let me have my turn, but not being too surprised when they didn't. They decided to go down to the river and I followed from a distance, watching Nikina play tricks on her riders. Whenever the girls said "Trot!" she would immediately stop and refuse to move. Whenever they said "Slowly!" the pony would dart forward like a racehorse and run half a kilometer across the fields. Nikina's favorite trick, however, was to start galloping like mad and then abruptly stop in front of a puddle.

"Noooo!" the girls would scream.

The girls were riding bareback, and Nikina's neck was as slippery as the slide at the public swimming pool. Whenever she stopped and put her head down, the girls would sail over her head and land in the puddle. It was funny to watch, and I was glad I wasn't riding the pony just yet. I would need to make friends with her first. By the end of the afternoon the girls were thoroughly soaked.

I stayed at the stables long after the girls had gone, shoveling dung into the barrow and wheeling it over to the compost heap. Then I brushed Nikina's mane and cleaned and greased her hooves. The sky outside had turned an inky blue, and I could hear Mrs. Backyard talking to her cows. I pressed my face against Nikina's chest. The scent of hay, dung, and the pony's sweat blended together and smelled good.

"I'll be back on Tuesday," I told her. "I'll come early after school and we'll go for a ride. Would you like that?"

Nikina responded by lifting her tail and depositing a fresh load of shit onto the floor of her pen.

In the distance, I could hear my mother calling. I was late for dinner, which always made her anxious. I made one more trip to the compost heap, and then I carried my milk pails to the cowshed, hoping Mrs. Backyard hadn't finished for the day.

"Hello, Mrs. Backyard!" I called out at the doorway. "Can I fill my pails, please?"

A faint rustling from the shed indicated that Mrs. Backyard was still there. I walked inside and there was Mr. Lojda, the plumber, composing himself near the backside of a cow. He had a cigarette and was fumbling for a match. Mrs. Backyard was sitting on her stool, smoothing her shirt. Her boyish hair seemed slightly disheveled.

"You're late," she said. The milk can at her feet was empty, but she quickly started to fill it.

"This will take a few minutes," she told me. "In the future, I would appreciate it if you were here on time."

"I'm sorry," I said. "But I've been making friends with the horses. And I cleaned Nikina's stable twice!"

Mrs. Backyard continued milking in silence.

"Hello, Mr. Lojda," I said to the maintenance man. "I hope there's nothing wrong with Mrs. Backyard's farm!"

Mr. Fix-it put a match to his cigarette and wordlessly strolled outside. I chattered happily to Mrs. Backyard until her can was full, and then she filled my pails with fresh milk. I paid her ten crowns and told her that I would be back on Tuesday to take Nikina for a ride.

"I really did a good job cleaning the stable," I repeated. "From now on, you don't have to worry about Tuesdays. I'll take the very best care of Nikina, and her pen will be spotless."

"I know it will," Mrs. Backyard said dryly.

My mother was waiting for me in front of the house. She held a big wooden spoon in her hand, and the shadow she cast up the road was enormous.

"Where have you been?" she demanded.

"At Mrs. Backyard's farm!" I told her. "I helped clean the stables, and Mrs. Backyard's daughter said I could ride her pony every Tuesday as a reward! Do you think, if we asked Dad, I could have a pair of riding boots as an early Christmas and birthday present?"

"You've just had your birthday," my mother pointed out.

"I know," I said. "But I didn't know I liked horses so much. Horses are great! I think I like horses even more than ballet!"

"Do you now?" my mother said doubtfully. "You're not going to tell me you want to stop dancing?"

"No way! Mrs. Backyard's daughter stopped and now she's too fat to climb into the saddle. Maybe I can do ballet and ride horses! What do you think?"

"Maybe you can," my mother smiled.

She picked up the milk pails and I followed her down to the kitchen. My mother stood in front of the stove, stirring the milk until it slowly began to pasteurize.

"It's actually a lot harder to ride a pony than a normal horse," I continued, "because you have to ride her without a saddle."

The milk started to bubble. The surface was covered with a thick, creamy skin.

"Her name is Nikina," I said, peeling the skin away with a spoon. "I'm going to bring her here on Tuesday so you can have a look at her, okay? She's very beautiful. And I was thinking—"

"I know what you're thinking," my mother said.

"I was thinking that when we finish construction, maybe we could have a pony of our own. They're very small, so a little pony wouldn't take up much space. Do you think? Now that Barry has gone, I mean?"

"Do you miss Barry?" my mother asked.

"I miss him very much," I said sadly.

MY FATHER WAS IN THE LIVING ROOM with Mr. Poloraich, and they came into the kitchen to get some beer from the fridge. Mr. Poloraich had a habit of dropping by unexpectedly. If he arrived when my father was out looking for work, he would follow my mother around the house as she cleaned and washed and vacuumed. I was very impressed by Mr. Poloraich, as he had been a famous Czech spy and always brought exotic presents. There would be flowers for my mother, Swiss chocolate for my sister, and a packet of chewing gum for me. He also brought foreign cigarettes and scotch for my dad. I could tell when he had been to the house, because there would be a pack of Lucky Strikes downstairs where my father was allowed to smoke. My dad smoked two packs of cigarettes a day, but he saved the Lucky Strikes for special occasions. He would carry the pack around with him as he worked his way through vast quantities of cheap Sparta cigarettes, but at the end of the day, or after a particularly good meal, he would light a Lucky Strike with great satisfaction.

"Now, that's a real smoke!" he would sigh contentedly.

Mr. Poloraich had been visiting my father long before I was born, and there was a strong camaraderie between the two men. My dad even helped the former spy find a job at a time when he was having difficulty keeping one himself. When he returned from America in 1969, Mr. Poloraich found himself in similar conflict with the new regime, and it took him a while to find his feet. These days he was doing quite well, and he was one of the few people who came to visit my parents. His unexpected visits were slightly unnerving, however. My sister complained that he stared at her breasts, and my mother expressed her own reservations, pointing out that a lot of Mr. Poloraich's espionage stories involved him sleeping with the wives of his agents and contacts, and he often seemed to arrive on our doorstep the minute my father had left the house. This was one of the rare occasions when he and my dad were in the same room together, and as I hoped, Mr. Poloraich slipped his hand in his pocket.

"A special treat this time, eh?" he grinned. "Had to smuggle this across the border. Very dangerous."

He handed me my very first Kinder Egg.

"Don't eat it all at once." He winked.

I looked to see if my mother was watching, and could tell by the frown on her face that she was. According to Mrs. Saturday, I still needed to lose two kilos if I wanted to be accepted by the State Conservatory, and my mother had taken it upon herself to police my eating habits. I quickly unwrapped the Kinder Egg while Mr. Poloraich was in the room, knowing that she wouldn't reproach me in front of a guest. I was surprised to discover that there was a plastic toy inside it. I made a lot of fuss over the toy, hoping it would distract my mother from the chocolate eggshell, but she knew all my tricks.

"Dominika." She smiled sweetly. "Would you care to share your chocolate with our guest?"

My shoulders slumped. "I guess so."

"Oh, please, not for me." Mr. Poloraich shook his head gallantly. "Much too old for candy these days."

"What was that? Oh, no thanks," my dad growled, a cigarette in his mouth and a bottle of Pilsner in his hands, but before I could follow him out of the room, my mother pounced.

"Well, I'd like a piece," she said, smoothly intercepting me at the doorway and relieving me of the larger half of the egg. This was my mother's classic sacrifice. She wasn't a big eater of sweets. She was breaking her diet to save me from breaking mine.

"Did you say thank you to Mr. Poloraich?" she asked.

"Thank you, Mr. Poloraich," I said glumly.

"And who was it telling me she didn't want to become too fat to ride horses?" she teased.

"Does that mean we're getting one?" I cried, offering my mother the rest of the Kinder Egg. "You can have my chocolate if we get one! If we get a pony, just a little pony, I'll never eat chocolate again, I swear!"

My mother looked at my father and shook her head in amusement.

"An interesting moral dilemma," she observed.

. . .

THE FOLLOWING TUESDAY, I ran home from school and changed into my corduroy pants. I felt slightly ashamed of my corduroy pants, the same way I felt slightly ashamed of my mother's homemade ballet costumes. The pants were brown and very fuzzy around the knees, and the horse-loving girls looked so professional in their jeans. It was difficult enough having to compete with a whole group of girls; the fact that my clothes weren't right made things even harder. Still, I knew that I was good with animals. The other girls didn't know how to talk to Nikina, and she had treated them roughly in spite of their clothes. I was confident that I could make friends with Mrs. Backyard's horses. They didn't care if I was wearing jeans or not. They went by tone of voice, and I was very good at talking.

I went down to the kitchen to get some sugar cubes, only to discover that my mother was cleaning. She did this twice a year and was very meticulous about it. The sugar cubes were buried beneath a big pile of boxes, and I knew better than to disturb her system, so I collected my milk pails and went to Mrs. Backyard's farm, gathering fresh grass along the way from the neighboring lawns. I said hello to the dogs and Lisa the goat, and hurried over to the stables.

"Hello, Nikina!" I called out. "I've brought you some tasty grass! It's not as nice as sugar, but it's better for you. Nikina?"

The stable was silent.

All three horses were gone.

I ran around the farm in a panic, trying to find the missing horses, but already despairing because I knew what had happened. Nikina's halter was missing from its peg on the wall. Dana and her friends had come early.

I found Mrs. Backyard in the cow shed, hosing down an enormous cow.

"Mrs. Backyard! Mrs. Backyard!" I cried. "It's my turn to ride Nikina today, but she's gone! The stable is empty!"

Mrs. Backyard looked as weary as usual.

"Why are you telling me this?" she asked.

My eyes immediately filled with tears. "Because it's my turn." I sobbed. "I don't have any free time except for Tuesdays, and I told my mother that I would bring Nikina over so she could see if we could have a pony of our own. Everyone knew that today was my day. I told everyone a hundred times!"

I bit my tongue to stop myself from crying.

"Come on, sweetie." Mrs. Backyard patted me awkwardly on the shoulder. "It's just a pony. She'll be here next week."

"It'll be too late!" I sniffed. "My mother will have lost interest by then!"

I walked out of the shed, feeling betrayed. I was so looking forward to walking the pony up our street, and now my afternoon was ruined. And to make matters worse, I still had a couple of hours to wait before Mrs. Backyard milked her cows. In the back of my mind, I could hear Dana Bukova laughing, and I resolved to never speak to her again. I walked up the path from the shed to the house and was greeted by Lisa the goat, who started sniffing my pockets.

"That's right. I was going to bring you a snack," I remembered.

Lisa bleated hopefully and stared at me with her watery blue eyes. The grass around her was overgrazed, and it occurred to me that a nice thing to do would be to take her to the forest. The forest was full of things a goat might find tasty. I cheered up a little bit as I realized that this would give me something to do. I would take the goat for a walk. What a good idea! Perhaps I could even show her to my parents.

I untied Lisa and led her out Mrs. Backyard's gate. The little goat turned out to be surprisingly strong, and I had to really struggle to keep her under control. We walked up the narrow lane and then turned into my street, which was the quickest way to the forest. Lisa's hooves clicked along the road as we walked, and I saw Mrs. Jandova hurry over to her fence and watch us disapprovingly until we turned the corner.

We continued up the road to the forest, but I had to keep stopping because Lisa ate everything around her. She ate weeds and thistles, and even started to nibble at a bag of cement that was sitting outside Mr. Acorn's garage. Once she decided to eat something, it was very hard to make her stop, and I was completely exhausted by the time we reached my house. Taking Barry for a walk was much easier. I led Lisa around the side fence and tied her to the generator at the top of our garden. My father's recent attempts to find a job had been thwarted, so he was working by himself in the yard, laying the cement foundation of what would later become a large retaining wall. Many empty Pilsner bottles sat on top of the generator, along with a pack of Spartas and his beloved Lucky Strikes.

"You're back," my mother greeted me as she came out into the yard. "Did they let you ride the pony?"

"The pony wasn't there, so I took a goat instead," I told her. "She's a very nice goat and I've brought her home to meet you."

I pointed to Lisa, who was sniffing around the generator.

"You took a goat? Does Mrs. Backyard know you have her?"

"Yes," I lied. "And next week, I'll definitely have the pony. But see how happy Lisa is in our garden? She really likes it here! There's plenty of room, and a pony is really only a little tiny bit bigger than a goat, so there's not much difference, and I was thinking—"

A look of horror appeared on my mother's face. And when I turned to see what she was staring at, I was confronted by the most terrifying sight in the world: Lisa the goat had her head above the generator and was eating my dad's Lucky Strike cigarettes!

"Nooooo!" my mother and I screamed in unison.

We ran across the yard, but it was too late. Lisa had chewed her way through the whole pack, and had wisps of tobacco all through her beard. She smiled and stamped her hoof with pleasure.

"Ježis Marja!" my mother gasped.

"Goats aren't supposed to eat cigarettes!" I wailed. "Oh, Lisa, you bad goat! You naughty goat! My dad is going to be so angry with you! It's not my fault, Mum! Really!"

My mother salvaged the pack of Spartas, knowing that this would be small consolation.

"If I were you, I wouldn't be here when he finds out."

"It was an accident!" I cried. "You have to tell Dad it wasn't my fault! I only brought Lisa because Dana Bukova and Helenka Vesela came and took Nikina early to stop me from riding her. Mrs. Novotna says it's time for me to behave like a real girl, but none of the girls in my class want to let me. I really am trying very hard."

"I know you are, sweetie," my mother sighed. "Take the goat back to Mrs. Backyard, and I'll have a word with your father."

"I hope so," I said ruefully.

I dragged Lisa away from the generator and hurried around the house. There was no point in going to the forest. I had fed Lisa the most expensive snack in Cernosice, and I was going to get in lots of trouble. My heart sank as we walked back across the hill. I secretly knew that we would never get a pony, the same way I knew that I was not the kind of girl who would ever end up on a farm. My reality was different. I was clever and I tried very hard, but this seemed to count against me for some reason. My sister didn't seem to try (even though she was clever), yet people seemed to like her, especially the boys. My mother often said that these things would sort themselves out when I got older, but it wasn't much comfort now. Lisa and I were halfway to the lane when the town's public address system came to life.

"*Prosim! Pozor!*" a voice crackled across the valley. "This is an urgent message for Comrade Lojda! We have an electrical fault in the stationmaster's fuse box. Comrade Lojda! Can you report to the National Committee right away?"

A long burst of marching band music concluded the message.

Lisa and I continued down the road, and were just about to turn into the lane when Mrs. Fejfarova's gate flew open and Mr. Fix-it hurried out to his car. Mrs. Fejfarova was a widow who lived in a tiny cottage at the end of our street. Her plumbing and heating must have been really bad, because a lot of work seemed to go on at her house and Mr. Fix-it was a regular. He walked over to his rusty Skoda, but instead of driving to the National Committee building as requested, he leaned against the door and leisurely lit a cigarette.

"Hello, Mr. Lojda!" I called out as I led Lisa past him. "Would you like to pat my goat?"

Mr. Fix-it's eyes twinkled. "No," he replied. "But I'd pay a thousand crowns to pat your sister's."

He drew on his cigarette and smiled mysteriously.

"My sister doesn't have a goat," I said. "The only person who has a goat is Mrs. Backyard."

Mr. Fix-it laughed and opened his car door.

"Mrs. Backyard's goats are pretty exceptional," he said, cupping his hands over his chest. "But your sister's are right up there with Sophia Loren's."

Then he tossed his cigarette into the gutter, climbed inside his car, and drove away in a thick cloud of dust.

I looked down at my chest, slowly processing the double meaning of *koza*, the Czech word for "goat." My sister did have big goats, and her popularity was in no small way due to their appearance. The bad things in Klara's life had really improved with age, and maybe I could look forward to the same kind of changes when I was older, as my mother promised. But it all seemed so insultingly simple. I led Lisa back down the path to the farm, and understood that in order to be a real girl you didn't need to be determined or clever. You didn't need to ride horses or dance in *Swan Lake*.

All you needed was a great pair of goats.

e l e v e n

THE HEDGEHOG

 OF ALL THE TEACHERS at the Cernosice state school, I liked Eugina German the best. Mrs. German was a tall woman with permed hair and glossy lipstick, who had recently moved to Prague from South Moravia. She spoke in a Moravian "long beak" accent, which was the opposite of my grandmother's "short beak" accent from the north, and I couldn't help smiling when she swept into the classroom and introduced herself.

"Good morning and welcomes to grade four," she said. "My name is Mrs. German, and I will be your teacher this year. And this"— she tilted her head toward the door, where a young boy was standing nervously— "is my son!"

Her cheeks glowed with motherly pride.

"But I wants you to forgets that I'm his mother while we're here," she continued. "I treats my students equally, and I'm much more severe with my son than I am with my ordinary pupils. Isn't that right, Eugene? Please, takes a seat."

Mrs. German pointed in my direction, and the boy obediently put his satchel on the hook beneath my bench and sat down on the empty seat next to mine. The girls behind us immediately started whispering. "Silence!" Mrs. German ordered from the front of the room. She sat down on the corner of her desk, which was a strange and modern thing for a teacher to do, and started to take a roll call. Once she had checked off all our names, she put her clipboard away and took off her jacket.

"We will begins the lesson with a five-minute warm-up," she said. "It is good to exercise your body before you exercise your brain, so I would likes you to stand up now and stretch your arms and legs, and then we will brush up on our multiplication tables."

A screeching of chairs swept through the room as we stood up and waited for Mrs. German to tell us what to do. She took a deep breath and planted her feet wide apart.

"How many of you are training for the Spartakiada?" she asked.

Monika and Alice Rabbit immediately put up their hands, along with a few other girls from Communist families.

The Spartakiada was a mass exercise that took place in Prague's Strahov Stadium every five years. Hundreds of thousands of flag-waving families performed synchronized gymnastics in a huge demonstration of the collectivist spirit. The event was very much like an Olympic Games opening ceremony (only ten times bigger), and was broadcast on both channels of Czech TV. It was without question one of the most exciting events in the Communist calendar, and, predictably enough, I was forbidden to join in.

"Excellent," Mrs. German nodded approvingly. "We will begins!"

For the next five minutes, our unusual new teacher took us through a series of light aerobic exercises. Mrs. German was very fit, and most of the class had a hard time keeping up with her.

"You move well," she told me. "You're not training for the Spartakiada?"

"No," I said. "But I study ballet three times a week."

"Very well," Mrs. German smiled. "Perhaps you would likes to lead the class in our morning exercises from now on?"

"Yes, please," I said eagerly. "I would likes this very much!"

We returned to our seats and I spent the rest of the day with my hand in the air, fighting to answer all of Mrs. German's questions. She made a very strong first impression upon me, and I could tell that her son was clever in a shy and quiet way. I was glad, too, that I had someone nice to sit next to. Monika and Alice Rabbit were glaring at me again, which meant the popular girls would soon be giving me a hard time as usual.

After school, I caught the train to Radotin, for my piano lesson with Mrs. Lake. Mrs. Lake was a young and enthusiastic woman who was fond of children and loved to talk. With a bit of prompting, I could get her to tell me all about the in-fighting between the teachers at the music school, or how things were coming along with her new mother-in-law. I would sit at the piano with my fingers on the keys, pretending to study the sheet music I hadn't bothered to practice, then I'd waylay Mrs. Lake into talking for an hour. The next thing we knew, the lesson would be over. There was one year where I managed to keep the Twelfth Etude by Carl Czerny on the music stand for twelve consecutive lessons. Despite my reluctance to practice, piano came relatively easily to me, and my afternoons with Mrs. Lake were a small source of pleasure in an otherwise hectic week. On Mondays, Wednesdays, and Fridays, I had ballet practice. Mrs. Saturday may have made an exception by taking me despite my size, but she made it very clear that she expected this favor to be repaid in sweat and tears. The fact that I was regularly late on Mondays didn't help, and I sometimes wished I could skip my piano lessons entirely, as the pleasant hour spent chatting with Mrs. Lake was immediately followed by the ordeal of my father racing against the clock to get me to the National Theater on time.

My dad loved to drive. Seven years of driving taxis had honed his already reckless skills, and there was nothing he enjoyed more than driving my mother and me around Prague at high speeds. He would insist on picking me up from my piano lesson at the very last minute, and then we would hurtle into town in his yellow Skoda 120, weaving in and out of traffic and ignoring road signs.

On the Monday after I first met Mrs. German, I sat on the railing in front of the Radotin music school and waited for my dad, who was even later than usual. By a quarter past four, I had counted more than thirty yellow Skodas, but none of them belonged to my father. Finally, his car appeared in the distance. I could tell it was my dad. No one could quite make an engine howl like he could. He thundered up the road and screeched to a halt in front of the music school.

"Get in!" he growled, swinging the back door open.

I dove inside, banging my head against the ceiling.

"Dad, we're really late!" I cried.

"I know! Shut the door and let me concentrate!" he ordered, turning the steering wheel and stepping on the accelerator. The tires squealed and I was thrown to the other side of the car.

"How long have we got?" he asked.

"Ten minutes," I said, reading the clock on the dashboard.

This was our usual ritual, but we had never cut it as close as this before.

"What have you been doing?" I asked. "You know how much trouble I get in when I'm late!"

"I've spent the afternoon with Dr. Ulbert," my dad replied. "He has a new invention. It's a device for measuring electricity in the air. I just know we're going to make a lot of money with it!"

Dr. Ulbert was a physicist my father had worked with briefly at an agricultural cooperative. They had formed an immediate friendship, which had survived my dad's dismissal. The doctor had stayed in touch, largely because my father was very impressed by his many disastrous theories about electromagnetic energy. Dr. Ulbert had tufty white hair, like

Albert Einstein, and an endless stream of ideas for inventions which my father attempted (and failed) to turn into patents. His last invention had been a crop-watering machine that was designed to fly above the fields on an electromagnetic current. My father had assembled a team of engineers and paid them out of his own pocket to build a prototype in our garage, but the device had steadfastly refused to fly. When it became obvious that the problem was in the design, not the engineering, my father had a long talk with Dr. Ulbert, in which the inventor grudgingly admitted that he had underestimated the force of gravity in his calculations. The amount of energy required to keep the device in the air turned out to be many times greater than the cost of watering crops by conventional means, and the project was ultimately scrapped. Strangely enough, despite having lost a lot of hard-earned money in Dr. Ulbert's inventions, my dad continued to have faith in his friend, while my mother privately referred to the physicist as "Dr. Stein-Ein."

"This new invention is an absolute winner!" my father said enthusiastically. "We'll sell it to the Germans and make a pile of deutsche marks; then we'll throw this rotten Skoda onto the trash pile and buy ourselves a brand-new Mercedes!"

"A Mercedes?" I protested. "You said we were going to buy a BMW."

"I've looked into it," my dad replied. "It turns out that a Mercedes has a much better engine than a BMW."

"Last month, you said BMWs were better."

"Well, that was last month! I've just read an interesting article on the subject. Medveds have better engines, end of story." (*Medved,* the Czech word for "bear," is the widely used Czech nickname for a Mercedes-Benz). My father and I loved to discuss the merits of Western cars, despite the fact that we hardly ever saw one, and my dad's biggest ambition was to one day buy himself a really nice German car. In a funny kind of way, he deserved it. He frightened my mother to death on a regular basis, but he really was an excellent driver.

"How long have we got?" he asked.

I looked at the dashboard. "We haven't!" I said desperately. "We're three minutes late!"

The traffic lights changed, and my father drove up the tram tracks to overtake a row of cars. This was completely illegal and was the kind of thing that would have his fellow drivers writing down his license plate and denouncing him. We zipped around the yellow barricade and back out onto the road.

"You still want me to drop you off around the corner?" my dad grinned.

"No time!" I cried. "Let me out right here!"

I opened the door and leaped out onto the sidewalk. Another part of our Monday afternoon ritual was my dad dropping me off around the corner from school, because I had somehow tangled myself up in a huge lie wherein my father actually owned all the cars we liked to talk about. At the last count, we had a white Mercedes, a blue BMW, and a red Volvo in our garage. None of the girls believed me, of course, and catching me out had become a major pastime at the school. I just prayed that Mrs. Saturday had started the lesson already. The trouble I would get into for being late was nothing compared to the embarrassment and shame of being seen climbing out of a rusty Skoda.

I crossed the street and pushed my way through the big revolving doors. The glamorous mothers were already in the cafeteria, smoking foreign cigarettes, and I ran up the stairs to the junior studio, where I found my classmates shivering in the unheated dressing room. They wore white or pink leotards that their mothers had bought from Tuzex, along with thick woolen socks that had been cut into leg warmers. Their shoulder blades jutted out from their backs and their arms and legs were as thin as broomsticks.

"Hello, Bara!" I called out to a fragile girl in an expensive leotard who was standing by herself. "How was your holiday?"

"Boring," Bara sighed. "Mum dragged me to Italy and I spent two weeks lying on the beach."

"Really?" I said, as though I couldn't imagine anything more boring than going to Italy.

Bara Fisherova was my only friend at school. Her father was a successful painter who had a private agent and sold his paintings in the West, and her mother wore extravagant outfits and drove around Prague in a brand-new Fiat Uno, which was the only Fiat Uno in the country. But Bara was struggling in class as much as I was. She had never wanted to be a dancer. Her body was wrong for ballet, but her mother had pulled a lot of strings to get Mrs. Saturday to accept her, and the other girls teased her mercilessly. I was a good but unpopular dancer, so we usually stood next to each other. Whenever the class picked on Bara, I would try to stand up for her. Whenever the class picked on me, Bara would usually join in.

"It's the first class of the year and you're late," Bara whispered.

"I couldn't help it," I whispered back. "My father was busy inventing a device to detect electricity in the air, and he forgot to pick me up."

Renata and Ilona Walnut were stretching near the window, and they moved in closer to disrupt our conversation.

"Your father drives a yellow Skoda, admit it," sneered Renata, whose eyes were slightly crossed.

"No, he doesn't," I said coolly. "He drives a blue BMW."

The younger Ilona put her hand in front of her mouth to hide her braces. "We saw you out of the window!" she cried. "We saw you! You ran across the street!"

I smiled as though I wasn't concerned. "That's because our car is at the garage," I said. "The mechanics lent us the Skoda to drive while they're fixing the BMW."

"I thought you said you would never be caught dead in a Skoda," Bara laughed. "Why didn't your dad take one of his other cars?"

I glared at her.

"Yeah, why didn't you take the Mercedes?" Renata grinned.

"I don't know," I blushed. "Ask my dad."

Ilona and Renata shook their heads in disbelief and went back to their stretching exercises. Like most of the other girls, they were from a rich Communist family that lived in beautiful Old Town Prague. They wore new leotards every year, and also owned a lot of *sedgeka,* which were little plastic letters you could connect on a chain and wrap around your waist like a belt. In 1984, *sedgeka* were the big craze in Czechoslovakia, and you could really buy them only in Tuzex or on the black market. I had five *sedgeka* letters, which I had found at school the previous summer, and my ballet costume was the ugliest in the class. My mother had made it out of an old tank top and it was sewn together with big, irregular stitches. As I hurriedly put it on, I heard Mrs. Saturday bellowing my name. I stuffed the wooden tips of my ballet shoes with pieces of cotton wool, tied the laces around my ankles, and hurried out of the dressing room.

In the studio, the girls were already kicking out from the bar and Mrs. Saturday was pacing around them. She wore an orange-and-blue dress that looked like an apron.

"Furmanova!" she said as I entered. "You're late!"

When I opened my mouth to explain, she silenced me with a wave of her hand. "No excuses!" she snapped. "While we all admire your vivid imagination, you're not here at this school to tell stories. You're here to dance! And dance you will!"

The class drew in a collective breath. Mrs. Saturday's temper was legendary.

"Move to the bar!" she ordered.

I trotted to the wall and squeezed in beside Linda Linkova, who was the daughter of a popular country music singer. I drew my legs together, set my feet into fifth position, and started to kick my right leg in the air. Bohunka, the fat piano player, continued with her regular waltz, while Mrs. Saturday stalked around the room clapping her hands. *"Un, deux, trois!"* she cried. *"Grand battement! Piqué! Grand battement! Piqué!"*

I swung my leg up and down, tapping the floor with the tip of my toe. It hurt, but I gritted my teeth and swung as high as I could.

"See, now here's how you do it." Mrs. Saturday grabbed Klara Kutilova's leg and lifted it so high it touched her ear. She looked like a marionette in Mrs. Saturday's hands, and smiled beatifically throughout the demonstration.

This went on for two hours. The minute hand traveled slowly around the clock on the wall until class was almost over. Finally, Bohunka pulled a packet of biscuits out of her bag, and Mrs. Saturday put a disc on the ancient record player. The needle scratched across the vinyl, and the "Song of the Dying Swan" crackled out from the speakers.

"Five minutes of improvisation!" Mrs. Saturday ordered, and everyone hesitantly stepped away from the bar. Without instruction, they didn't know what to do. All the girls were tremendously afraid of making a mistake, so they turned, as they always did, and waited for me to start dancing. I listened to the music, and the dying swan's melody filled my heart with sadness. I experienced a strange sense of tranquility when I was allowed to move freely. I didn't see the studio with bars and mirrors, I moved and was moved in a different space. I was a swan and not an ugly duckling, and as the moonlight glittered on the surface of the lake, I spread my wings and began to fly.

The next thing I knew, Mrs. Saturday was clapping her hands.

"Very good," she said. "Girls rehearsing for *The Nutcracker*, please stay in the room. Everybody else is excused. See you all on Wednesday."

A group of older girls who were dancing in *The Nutcracker* were standing at the door. They remained silent until I had taken my last steps, then they burst into the room, filling it with chatter. I took off my ballet shoes and walked alone into the dressing room. I was the only girl in my class who wasn't in *The Nutcracker*. Mrs. Saturday hadn't given me a role on the grounds that I was too small for the costumes.

I changed into my street clothes and walked up the empty corridor, wishing that there was some kind of magic potion that would make me taller. My big dream was to dance Odette in *Swan Lake,* but I was willing to settle for the tiniest role in *The Nutcracker.* I could do a much better job than Bara Fisherova, who hated dancing and couldn't even do the splits, but I knew she was given roles because her mother bought Mrs. Saturday presents whenever they traveled to the West. My dad couldn't do this. His papers were bad and he drove a rusty Skoda. Once again, I was having trouble fitting in.

I was so depressed, I almost collided with a small woman who had just walked out of the main studio where the National Theater Ballet Company was rehearsing *Sleeping Beauty.* A young ballerina rushed out of the room behind her.

"Hold your thumbs for me tonight, Mrs. Paskova!" she begged, which is the Czech way of asking someone to cross their fingers.

The small woman smiled and put her arms around the girl. "Ptui, ptui, ptui!" she said, pretending to spit on the floor, which is a more intimate way of wishing someone good luck.

"Break a leg, my dear. I'm sure you'll be wonderful," she said.

The ballerina blushed and disappeared inside the room, and Mrs. Paskova continued up the hallway. I wandered along behind her, and as I did, I suddenly realized that this was the woman Vendula Backyard had told me to say hello to. She was obviously a very important person at the school, and I picked up my pace and trotted up behind her.

"Hello, Comrade Paskova!" I called out. "Comrade Paskova! Hello!"

The woman stopped and turned to face me.

"Can I help you?" she asked.

"Vendula Backyard told me to say *ahoj!*" I exclaimed. "Do you remember Vendula? She is my friend and she said you used to be her ballet teacher. She said that you would remember her, but in case you didn't, I should mention her father, Doctor Backyard, who is a very famous surgeon."

Mrs. Paskova looked down at me and smiled. "Of course I remember Vendula. How is she?"

"I think she's very happy," I replied. "Whenever I see her, she's sunbathing in the orchard and eating chocolates, and she has two horses and a pony and a goat!"

"I see." Mrs. Paskova looked vaguely amused. "And who are you and what are you doing in the hallway by yourself? Shouldn't you be rehearsing for *The Nutcracker?*"

I smiled and tried to make up an excuse, but my eyes filled with tears. Before I knew it, I was pouring my heart out to Mrs. Paskova. I told her that I didn't have a role in *The Nutcracker* because I was too small, and that I never got any roles. I was afraid that I would never get to dance in any of the big productions. Mrs. Paskova put her arms around me and gave my shoulders a friendly squeeze.

"Well, that's no good," she said. "As is happens, I'm looking for a little girl to carry a candleholder across the stage in *Rigoletto*. Do you think this is something you might like to do?"

I nodded so hard I nearly sprained my neck.

"Very well," she said decisively. "If you come to the lobby at seven o'clock tomorrow evening, I'll have a word with the casting director and we'll try you out for the role. Bring your parents with you. If it all works out, you can alternate with one of our junior cast regulars."

I let out a squeal of delight and shook her hand vigorously.

"Thank you, Comrade Paskova! Thank you!" I exclaimed.

"It's only a little role," Mrs. Paskova smiled, pausing at the foot of the stairs. "But it's a start. All the great dancers carried spears when they were young. It's part of the tradition. Oh, and do say hello to Vendula for me the next time you see her. Her father is a great surgeon. He saved my life, as it happens."

THE NEXT DAY in class, I squirmed triumphantly on my seat, wanting to tell everybody about my role in *Rigoletto*. Mrs. German sat on the corner of her desk, dictating an article about Comrade Yuri Gagarin, the first man brave enough to orbit the Earth in a Soviet-made spaceship. She carefully enunciated the difficult words like "cosmonaut" and "atmosphere," repeating each sentence three times while we wrote it down in our notebooks. Her son, Eugene, was as quick at transcription as I was. Between sentences, he would stare out the window, biting the end of his pencil and humming to himself. He had sandy blond hair, and I thought he was even more handsome than Mr. Slavicky from *Swan Lake*. I pretended that I wasn't looking at him, but I secretly was. After half an hour, I finally nudged him with my elbow.

"What do you wants?" he whispered.

Eugene's accent was even thicker than his mother's. The troublemaking boys at the back of the class mimicked it, yelling "Fucks you!" at each other during the snack breaks.

"Would you hold your thumbs for me tonight?" I asked him. "I'm going to dance in *Rigoletto* at the Smetana Theater, which is very exciting, but I'm also a bit scared, too, you know?"

"Okay," Eugene whispered back, hiding behind his notebook. "What time do you wants me to holds them for you?"

"Eugene!" Mrs. German slapped the blackboard with the palm of her hand. "Is that you I hear whispering?"

"It wasn't me, Mum." Eugene looked up with a innocent expression.

"What do you mean, it wasn't you? I knows it was you!" Mrs. German's accent grew thicker as her voice rose in volume. "Put that notebook down! And off you goes behind the door!"

Eugene's face turned red. He climbed to his feet and the whole class roared with laughter. He looked at me bitterly and clenched his fists.

"It's not his fault," I blurted. "It's my fault, Comrade German! I asked Eugene to hold his thumbs for me and he did. See, look—" I pointed to her son's clenched fists.

"And just why were you asking him to holds his thumbs?" Mrs. German demanded.

"Because I have a role in *Rigoletto* and I'm going to dance in the Smetana Theater tonight," I explained. "And I need someone to hold their thumbs for me. I'm very sorry. I was trying not to ask, but I couldn't help it. It's the first role I've ever got!"

"You're dancing at the Smetana Theater tonight?" Mrs. German was very impressed. "How absolutely wonderful! I'm sure the whole class will holds their thumbs for you if you ask them. Shall we holds our thumbs for Dominika, class?"

The class groaned and made a sullen display of holding their thumbs.

"Very well!" Mrs. German said approvingly. "I've always wanted to goes to the Smetana Theater. It's supposed to be one of the nicest theaters in Europe, but it's practically impossible to get tickets to it these days. You need to have very good connections. I hears the shows are sold out three years in advance!"

"Do I still have to goes behind the door?" Eugene asked.

"I'll lets you off this time," Mrs. German said sternly. "But if I catches you again, you can stay behind after class!"

Eugene glared at me as he returned to his seat.

"I'm sorry," I whispered, trying hard not to smile.

AT SIX O'CLOCK that evening, my mother and I stood next to the big pile of sand inside our front gate and waited for my father to return from town.

I was dressed in my best clothes, and my mother was wearing high boots, a leather coat, and a black cowboy hat. I had butterflies in my stomach and my mother was tense. Not only was Dad late but my sister had made a scene during dinner, refusing to come to *Rigoletto* on the grounds that she had to write a letter to an Italian man she had met during her summer holiday in Hungary. Klara had gone to Budapest on a youth exchange program, and had met a handsome young man at the famous Vidampark. She assumed he was Hungarian, while he thought she was an American actress or model, and they had somehow struck up a conversation in English, which Klara had studied along with Russian in high school. The young man's name was Renzo, and he was an engineering student in Florence. After a romantic afternoon at the amusement park, he had followed her around Budapest for the rest of her vacation, begging for her address until she finally gave it to him. After that, his letters regularly appeared in our mailbox and Klara became very interested in Italy. These days, her standard way of getting out of doing something was to say that she had to write a letter to Renzo. It was an inspired excuse, because if my parents refused to let her, she could (and would) accuse them of trying to break her heart. She would burst into tears and lock herself in her room, and after the usual shouting and banging, my parents would eventually leave her alone. I was sad my sister was going to miss my first performance, but I was secretly excited about her Italian romance, so I told my mother that I really didn't mind.

The sky turned dark as we waited. It was now half past six and my mother's face was very grim beneath her hat. Finally, the yellow Skoda roared up the hill. My dad threw the gears into reverse, but midway through his three-point turn, his engine cut out.

"Ježis Marja!" my father exploded. "Stupid piece-of-shit car! Sorry girls," he growled apologetically, "I'm going to have to ask you for a push."

This was another one of our routines. We put our hands against the trunk and pushed the Skoda through my father's three-point turn. The car started to roll down the hill and we ran behind it, faster and faster until the exhaust pipe spewed a cloud of smoke in our faces. The engine shuddered to life and we scrambled inside, brushing soot off our clothes and scraping mud off our boots. When we finally arrived at the theater, Mrs. Paskova was in the lobby, anxiously checking her wristwatch. It was five past seven. My father led the charge through the big revolving door, pushing so hard that my mother and I were spun around twice.

"You must be the parents of this charming little girl," Mrs. Paskova smiled, presenting my dad with two *Rigoletto* tickets.

"Sorry we're late," my father said gruffly. The whole way into Prague, my mother had fulfilled her part of the routine by screaming even louder than his Skoda's noisy engine.

"Really, it's not a problem. I hope you enjoy the show," Mrs. Paskova replied. "Your seats are upstairs, third balcony on the left, and be sure to watch out for your daughter in scene five."

She took my hand and led me down the passage that connected the Federal Parliament building with the ancient Smetana Theater and into a labyrinth of dimly lit corridors. In one of the dressing rooms, I glimpsed a group of medieval knights sitting around a small television set, puffing away on their cigarettes while a lady dressed as a queen idly flipped through the pages of a magazine. Men in overalls pushed huge props around on wheels, and the floor was a complex network of rails. The Egyptian pyramid from last week's *Aida* had been wheeled aside to make way for a huge cathedral that was going out onstage. Mrs. Paskova steered me into a room that was crowded with women wearing big Italian wigs. "Fifteen minutes," a speaker crackled overhead. Talcum powder flew in the air as the wardrobe assistants bustled around their ironing boards. In the distance, I could hear the orchestra tuning up.

"Take your clothes off," Mrs. Paskova said as a woman wheeled in a rack of junior costumes.

"What's your size?" the wardrobe lady asked.

"I don't know," I replied. My size was so small I wasn't even sure if it had a name or number. Whenever we went shopping, my mother always bought the smallest size in stock, and even then she would usually have to alter my clothes at home.

The wardrobe lady rattled the hangers. "This is the smallest I have," she said, handing me a black velvet jacket with beautiful sleeves and a lovely starched collar. I put it on and buttoned it up, desperately trying to make myself look taller. I craned my neck and stood on the very tips of my toes, but the costume was still several sizes too big.

"Hmm. That's not going to work," Mrs. Paskova said. "You really don't have anything smaller?"

I looked pleadingly at the wardrobe lady, until she sighed and disappeared into a nearby storage room. I listened hopefully to the clattering of hangers, but the woman returned empty-handed.

"I'm afraid not," she told Mrs. Paskova. "That's definitely the smallest jacket we have. You're going to have to find yourself another girl."

She collected my costume and went back to her ironing board as though nothing had happened. It took me a moment to realize that I had just lost the role. I started to sob uncontrollably.

Mrs. Paskova took my hand and whisked me from the room.

"Now, don't you worry," she said, leading me back toward the Parliament lobby. "I'm sure we can find something else for you. How about one of the little hedgehogs from Janáček's *Smart Fox*? The costumes are simple and I'm sure they'll fit you." She gave my shoulder an encouraging squeeze. "Besides, the candleholder is quite heavy and you would have had a hard time carrying it across the stage."

I blew my nose into a handkerchief. "No, I wouldn't," I sniffed. "I can carry twelve liters of milk across the hill!"

Mrs. Paskova took me to the cafeteria and bought me a lemonade to calm me down. She ruffled my hair affectionately and wrote the rehearsal details for *The Smart Fox* on the back of a napkin. Then she rushed back to the Smetana Theater, looking for a taller girl to fill my position.

I sat in the cafeteria and waited for my parents. The overture from *Rigoletto* started up in the distance, and a tired-looking waitress wiped her counter with a sponge. In a nearby booth, a group of old firemen were playing *mariash*, the Czech version of penny poker. I looked at the piles of change in front of them and wished that I had thirty *halir*s to buy myself half a slice of bread with mustard. This was not only the cheapest meal in the cafeteria but one of the few a dancer could eat on the premises without being yelled at.

"I'll see your twenty," an old firemen wheezed, pushing some coins out on the table, "and raise you fifty!"

"I'll see your fifty and raise you a crown!"

Two hours later, after the sound of applause finally died inside the theater, my parents walked out into the crowded foyer. I ran over and met them with the bravest face I could manage.

"You were wonderful!" my dad exclaimed. "I nearly cheered out loud when you walked across that stage!"

"It wasn't me," I said, biting my lip. "I was too small. They said I was too small for the costume."

My mother and father exchanged looks. Before I knew it, my dad had swept me up in his big miner's arms.

"Just as well," he growled. "The girl who did carry the candleholder was awful. She walked like a chicken." He gave me a conspiratorial wink. "It's not the costume that's too big. It's the role that's too small."

"But guess what?" I sniffed, holding up the napkin. "Mrs. Paskova said that I can play a hedgehog in *The Smart Fox*."

"A hedgehog? Well, now we're talking!" My father balanced me on his hip and pulled out his wallet. "That sounds like a serious role for a serious actress! What do you think, Honza? I think this calls for a celebration!"

He carried me back to the cafeteria and plonked me down on the counter.

"What can I get you?" he asked.

"Half a slice of bread with mustard," I said happily.

THE FOLLOWING MORNING, I came in to class at the last minute and hid behind a wall of books I piled up on my bench. Eugene sat next to me in silence. He was obviously curious but too shy to speak. Dana Bukova and her horse-loving friends were watching me with interest, and seemed to have picked up on the fact that I hadn't said a word about my theatrical debut. Unfortunately, I didn't escape Mrs. German's attention.

"The reviews were good!" she told the class. "I read them this morning. So how was your scene, Dominika? Were you scared?" She deposited our marked-up Yuri Gagarin transcriptions on the top of her desk and smiled at me expectantly.

I peeked up from behind my wall of books.

"To tell you the truth, Comrade German," I said, "I didn't get to dance in *Rigoletto* last night, because . . . because I was given a new role at the last minute!" I held my chin up with some difficulty. "My new role is actually much better than the old one! I'm going to play a hedgehog in *The Smart Fox*!"

"A hedgehog?" Dana Bukova snorted. "What a pity they didn't let you play a goat!"

The class roared with laughter, with the puzzled exception of Eugene and his mother.

"Silence!" Mrs. German snapped. "There are no goats in *The Smart Fox*! Only animals from the forest."

She studied the class, and then walked back to her desk and retrieved our transcriptions.

"*The Smart Fox* by Leoš Janáček," she said quietly, "is a wonderful opera by one of our greatest composers. It's one thing to listens to Mozart or Tchaikovsky, but this is an opera written in our own language." She threw me a sympathetic glance. "I think it's charming that you've been given this role," she told me.

And then her face became serious.

"But on the subject of goats, many of you will have extra homework this evening," she declared. "Your classwork leaves a lot to be desired."

She quickly began to distribute the transcriptions, and most of the class groaned as they received their marks. When she was at the back of the room, Eugene nudged my arm.

"I held my thumbs for you," he blushed. "Would you likes me to holds them again?"

"Yes, please," I said. "That would be very nice."

. . .

THE FOLLOWING WEDNESDAY, I walked alone through the backstage corridors of the theater. A group of deer were smoking cigarettes and watching TV in the men's dressing room, while a female squirrel, who looked suspiciously like the queen from *Rigoletto,* poured herself a cup of coffee from the communal urn. A huge mushroom was being rolled out onstage, and I hurried around it, darting into the dressing room, desperately hoping my costume would fit. I didn't need to worry. The hedgehog costume was a piece of cloth covered in foam-rubber needles, which was attached to my body by four elastic bands. A makeup lady blackened my nose and drew whiskers on my cheeks, and sent me out to join the other girls and boys.

There were twelve children in the junior chorus. Four mice, three hares, three squirrels, and two hedgehogs, played by Bara Fisherova and me. We ran around the giant mushroom, which took up most of the stage, and watched the set designers as they surrounded it with a forest of cardboard trees. I was surprised (and slightly frightened) to see Mrs. Saturday in the wings.

"What is she doing here?" I asked Bara.

"She's the assistant director," Bara shrugged. "What are you doing here? I thought I was the only hedgehog."

"I was supposed to be in *Rigoletto,* but it changed at the last minute," I said. "So I get to be a hedgehog instead."

"*Rigoletto?* That show just finished," Bara frowned. "And aren't you a little late for *The Smart Fox?* It starts tomorrow and I've been rehearsing all week."

"Is there much to do?" I asked nervously.

"Not really," Bara sighed. "We stand around at a wedding, and then, in the last act, we get to dance a little bit and sing a song."

"So, it's not difficult?"

"No. Mostly, we sit around and wait."

There were many questions I wanted to ask, but right then, Mrs. Saturday clapped her hands.

"Can everybody hear me?" she asked. "As you know, this is a dress rehearsal for tomorrow's premiere, so we're going to do the whole opera from the beginning to the end. The junior chorus is here, so I want the baby animals to stand near their mothers and fathers. Take your positions on the stage according to the marks on the floor. And please remember, children"—she glared at us for emphasis—"the dress rehearsal is as important as the premiere. Whatever happens, there will be no stopping!"

The curtains closed, and the cast scurried backstage as Mr. Volleman, a tiny conductor with a famously bad temper, entered the orchestra pit. I watched from the wings as he raised his baton and tapped the musicians to silence. With his knees bent and his hands in the air, he looked like a cat about to pounce. He nodded at the director, made a brisk movement with his baton, and the orchestra surged to life. The curtains drew back and a spotlight appeared in the middle of the stage, illuminating the Smart Fox as she trotted out from behind the mushroom, sweeping the floor with her tail.

For the next hour, I sat in the wings and listened to *The Smart Fox*. I loved the opera and knew most of it by heart. Janáček was one of my mother's favorite composers, and I had grown up listening to his music. The wedding sequence went smoothly, and before I knew it, the final act had arrived. A lady dressed as a hedgehog grabbed my hand and led me out onto the stage. Squirrels and mice ran into the clearing and started to dance around the giant mushroom. Mr. Hedgehog put his arm around Mrs. Hedgehog's shoulders, and they started to sway to the music of the finale. Bara and I swayed along with them, and as the opera climaxed with the *Smart Fox* theme, I looked around for Mrs. Saturday to see if I was allowed to sing along with the chorus. No one had told me not to, and I knew the melody and all of the words. The other baby animals were pretending to sing, but it seemed silly to pretend when I actually could. So I started to sing, softly at first, but louder and louder as the music built in volume. It was nearly the end of the finale when Mr. Volleman silenced the orchestra by throwing his baton across the pit.

"Stop!" he screamed. "Will someone shut that little girl up!"

Mrs. Saturday hurried out from the wings to talk to Mr. Volleman, and the next thing I knew, I was back in the dressing room, listening to the chorus finishing the opera without me. I had no idea what was going to happen, but my heart grew heavier with every passing minute.

Finally, Mrs. Saturday reappeared.

"Take your costume off," she ordered. "Mr. Volleman has banned you from the production."

"But I won't sing next time!" I squealed. "I won't! I promise!"

Mrs. Saturday had an uncompromising look on her face. "There won't be a next time, my dear," she said. "Mr. Volleman is like this whenever he has to work with children. He has insisted that we only go out with one hedgehog. There's nothing more I can do."

"But nobody told me," I pleaded. "I came in late!"

She shook her head. "There's nothing more I can do," she repeated.

I looked at her with my mouth open but I couldn't even cry. As if in a dream, I removed the elastic bands and started to take off my costume. My hands were shaking so badly, Mrs. Saturday had to help me undress.

"Listen, Dominika," I heard her say. "I'm opening a new production in a month. It's a children's ballet called *The Ant Ferda*. I could use someone very small to dance an ant."

"An ant?" I came back to life.

"It would actually be a double role," Mrs. Saturday added.

"A double role?"

"Yes, a very important role." She widened her eyes to emphasize the point. "You start out as an egg and then you turn into a baby ant." She pointed to a box in the corner of the dressing room. "See? These are the costumes." The box contained a number of black bicycle helmets with fuzzy antennae glued on top.

"And since Professor Paskova believes that you have heaps of talent, and since I can see that you're trying very hard"—she paused dramatically—"I have decided to give you one more chance."

"Thank you, comrade professor," I stammered.

"Don't thank me," she said gruffly. "Just make sure you're on time for the rehearsals. The premiere will take place in the National Theater in less than a month, and I can't afford to lose another minute with you."

She thrust her hands into her pockets and strode out of the room without saying good-bye.

THE NEXT DAY AT SCHOOL, I watched Eugene play "the line" during snack break. The line was a popular gambling game played with *sedgeka*. A group of boys and girls would throw their plastic letters between two white lines on the basketball half-court, and whoever managed to land their letter the closest to the farthest line would win all the *sedgeka* the others had thrown. Seeing as I had only five *sedgeka*, I stayed out of the game, because I was afraid to lose them. I held my thumbs for Eugene instead, and it seemed to work, because he won several games in a row. By the time the bell rang, he had collected more than twenty plastic letters, some of which were rare and sought after.

"Gosh, you were lucky!" I said when we were back in class. "Maybe it's because I held my thumbs for you. See?" I showed him my hands.

"Thanks you," Eugene blushed. "And I'm going to holds my thumbs for you tonight!"

"Oh, no." I gestured that he should bring his head closer to mine. "There's been a change in plans," I whispered. "I'm not going to play a hedgehog anymore. I'm going to play an egg and a baby ant instead. It's a double role, and the premiere will take place in the National Theater, which is much better than the Smetana Theater!"

"Wow," Eugene whispered back. "How come you don't haves any *sedgeka*?" he asked suddenly.

"*Sedgeka* are okay. I'm just too busy to collect them," I lied.

Eugene studied me with his wide-spaced eyes, and then he separated a dozen from his pile. "You can haves some of mine if you likes," he said.

"Are you sure?" It was my turn to blush. "You don't want them?"

He shook his head. "I likes you!" he whispered.

"I likes you, too, Eugene," I whispered back.

That night, I told my mother I was in love with Eugene German. I wrote his name in red wax pencil on the wall above my bed, and wrapped the *sedgeka* he had given me around my wrist like a bracelet. The girls in ballet school wore their *sedgeka* around their hips, and laughed at my bracelet until I convinced them it was a new fashion in the West. After that, they took to wearing *sedgeka* around their wrists as well. My status at school was finally improving after four years of struggle. I had my first role, and Mrs. Paskova had told the teaching staff to keep an eye out for me.

A week before the *Ant Ferda* premiere, Mrs. Saturday took the whole class to the National Theater to watch the dress rehearsal. The famous Golden Chapel had been under reconstruction for the best part of a decade, and its completion was the source of great excitement in Prague. The scaffolding had been removed, and the front of the building looked like a huge ship anchored at the Vltava quay. Its roof was surrounded with golden railings, and sculptures of winged horses jutted out from its prow. There were so many incredible buildings in Prague, but it was as if the Communists had trained us not to see them. As I walked around the National Theater that day, I couldn't help thinking that the building really glowed, as though someone had taken a huge cloth and wiped it clean for the first time in forty years.

We followed Mrs. Saturday through the huge stage door, and found the cast and crew of *The Ant Ferda* getting ready for rehearsal. Bees and grasshoppers swarmed through the lobby, and beetles sat in the cafeteria's plush leather armchairs. Mrs. Saturday stopped a ladybird and asked her to take the girls and boys playing ants up to the dressing room. I felt very proud as I hopped in the elevator and went to the third floor with the rest of the junior cast. The National Theater dressing rooms were much nicer than those at the Smetana Theater. There were floor-to-ceiling mirrors, and the clothing racks were made of polished chrome. I searched quickly through the children's racks and was incredibly relieved to find my name written inside one of the eggs. The egg was blue and made of foam rubber. There were no holes for my arms, but my legs poked out through two holes in the bottom and I could look out through a small hole at face level. I climbed into it with difficulty, and a wardrobe lady zipped me up. Then I joined the rest of the eggs onstage, where we stood around the giant anthill that was the set for the first act.

I had assumed we would be running the play from beginning to end, but instead we worked out the choreography. The choreographer was a tall, cheerful man called Mr. Blazek, who wore a turtleneck sweater. He stood in the middle of the orchestra seats, chewing on a pen, and called out instructions to Mrs. Saturday on the stage.

"Put the blue egg in front of the bottle fly!" he would suggest, and Mrs. Saturday would push us into position. "No, no, no!" he would shout. "Swap the pink egg with the blue egg in front of her!"

When he was finally satisfied, he got Mrs. Saturday to mark our positions on the floor with tape. Then we had to do it all over again for the next scene. We didn't get to dance. We just baked in the glow of the reflectors. By the end of the afternoon, I was drenched with sweat. It was really hot inside that foam-rubber egg.

After the rehearsal, Mrs. Saturday sent the class home and told the junior cast to meet her in the orchestra seats. She was in a good mood and had a stack of envelopes in front of her.

"Here are your tickets to the premiere," she said, handing us the envelopes. When she gave me mine, she smiled unexpectedly. "You're a good kid," she said. "If you promise not to sing, I might be able to give you a few more roles. Luisa Podarilova is moving on to the conservatory, which means I'm going to have to find a replacement dancer."

"What?" I cried out. "Do you really mean it?"

Luisa Podarilova was a tiny girl who performed children's lead roles in many of the big productions. In *The Smart Fox*, she had played the Smart Fox as a baby. She was a good dancer from a well-connected family, and her sister had been a huge star at the ballet school. It was inevitable that Luisa would join her sister at the State Conservatory sooner rather than later, and I had secretly prayed that this would happen. I was just the right size to replace her.

I leaped over the table and sent Mrs. Saturday's envelopes flying.

"Thank you, comrade professor!" I exclaimed.

"*Ježis Marja*, girl!" she snapped. "You're going to destroy the tickets! I don't need to tell you how precious these tickets are! They're impossible to get, because they've all been reserved for party members and their families!"

I took my envelope and scampered away in delight. Out on the street, I looked up at the National Theater and wished again that my grandfather could see me dance. I peeked in my envelope and discovered there were four tickets inside. I pulled two out and put them in my pocket. I would tell my parents that I only had two tickets, and secretly send the other two to my grandparents. Even though *The Ant Ferda* was a children's ballet, maybe I could warm their hearts by inviting them to see me in the famous Golden Chapel.

That evening, my parents and my sister and I sat down to eat dinner. My mother served the "Spanish bird," which was little rolls of meat stuffed with sausages and pickles.

"Mrs. Saturday wants to give me some more roles!" I announced. "Luisa Podarilova is going to the conservatory, which means they might let me dance the little girl in *The Nutcracker* the next time they put it on!"

"What do you mean?" my father asked. "We thought you would go to the State Conservatory as well."

"I would like to," I said. "But it's very hard to get in. Mrs. Saturday says they take twenty girls out of the five hundred who audition. Even if they don't take me, I can still make lots of money playing children's roles at the Smetana Theater. *The Nutcracker* pays fifty crowns a performance and I'm already getting thirty-five for *The Ant Ferda*!"

"Fifty crowns!" my mother whistled. "You'll soon be making more money than me!"

"Of course they'll take you at the conservatory!" my father growled. "You have more talent than the other girls put together. You can dance and act and sing. Like Barbra Streisand."

My sister choked on her Spanish bird. Barbra Streisand was one of my father's recent obsessions. My dad loved nothing more than to speculate at length about my future as an actress. The Iron Curtain would fall and I would go to New York and perform in Broadway musicals. After which he would throw his Skoda on the trash pile and go out and buy himself a new Mercedes. Or a BMW. Or a Volvo. Or all three.

"Guess what?" I said, changing the subject. "I've invited someone very special to the premiere!"

"And who would that be?" my mother smiled.

"I'm not telling," I said mysteriously. "It's a surprise!"

The morning of the premiere, there was a letter addressed to me in our mailbox. The handwriting on the envelope was unfamiliar, but when I opened it, I discovered that it was from my grandparents. I read the letter slowly and then took it down to the kitchen and showed it to my mother.

Dear Dominika,

Thank you for inviting us. We will not attend the premiere and we return your tickets. Your mother has renounced us in writing and destroyed our relationship with some of her other actions. This is why we request that you leave us in peace and stop bothering us.

The Cermaks

Two tickets to *The Ant Ferda* fell out of the envelope and fluttered to the floor. I had sent them to my grandfather five days earlier, along with a friendly letter it took me half a day to write.

"Oh, Trumpet," my mother sighed. "I'm so sorry. You should have told me you were going to invite them."

"I wanted it to be a surprise," I said sadly.

I picked the tickets up from the floor and wondered what I should do with them. They were very valuable, and it would be a pity to throw them away.

I thought about this for a moment, and then I had a very good idea. I would invite Eugene and his mother to the show! They were from Moravia and didn't have party connections, and it was obvious that Mrs. German really loved the theater. A ticket to the Golden Chapel would be something they would appreciate much more than my grandparents, who were so used to the privileges of their Communist lifestyle that they didn't even go to half the things they were invited to.

"We could invite Eugene and Mrs. German!" I said. "Eugene is going to hold his thumbs for me, so maybe he can hold his thumbs and watch me at the same time."

"That's a good idea," my mother agreed. "Would you like me to call them?"

"Yes, please!" I said. "And afterward, maybe we can go to Slavia as a special treat. What do you think?"

Slavia was an expensive restaurant directly opposite the National Theater. Whenever the secret police were making my dad's life misery, he would take us to Slavia for dinner to show them that his spirit wasn't broken. He couldn't afford to do this, of course, but I didn't know that at the time. Those special dinners at Slavia are some of my fondest childhood memories.

"I don't know about that," my mother smiled. "We'll have to ask your father."

At a quarter to seven that evening, I stood in the wings of the Golden Chapel with the other junior dancers. This was it. I was finally going to perform in front of an audience. The theater was empty, but the orchestra had started to tune their instruments in the pit. Suddenly, Mrs. Saturday clapped her hands and told us to take our positions. She was wearing her very best apronlike dress, and pretended to kick our bottoms as we ran onto the stage.

"Ptui, ptui, ptui," she whispered to each of us. "Let the devils take you!"

The doors swung open and I heard the audience rumble in. It was exciting, but terrifying as well. There's nothing quite like an opening night to set your nerves on edge. I took my position and waited for the conductor to tap the stand with his baton, and, as the curtain drew open, I swarmed around the anthill with the other eggs and ants. Mrs. Saturday had cast me as a naughty egg, so I got to disobey the ant who played our nurse. I hopped gleefully up and down and danced deliberately out of time, and by the end of the scene, I had annoyed the nurse so much that she pretended to spank my bottom before pulling me offstage.

During the intermission, I took the elevator up to the dressing room, exchanged my foam-rubber egg for a black leotard and a plastic helmet with antennae, and then went backstage and quietly waited for the final scene.

Like so many Czech plays produced during the Communist regime, *The Ant Ferda* was a children's tale festooned with political ideology. Ferda, a single-minded ant (who reminded me of my father), decides to leave the colony and set up shop on his own. He goes out into the world and has many adventures before ultimately realizing that he's better off in a collective. In the final act, he returns to the colony and all the ants rush out to greet him. The whole cast ran onstage and we formed a giant circle around Ferda, waving red handkerchiefs above our heads as we danced. The music swelled and the dancing became more triumphant, and then the conductor struck the air with his baton and everybody froze.

After a moment of silence, the theater shook with applause. The curtain closed and then opened again, and the cast took turns bowing. A ticket lady ran onstage with a basket of flowers for the lead ballerina, and a minute later, the junior chorus and I lined up to take our bows. I heard my father yelling, "Bravo!" and looked into the orchestra seats in time to see Mrs. German lifting Eugene up to the balustrade. She called my name, and Eugene threw a rose in my direction. I tried to catch it, and would have fallen into the orchestra pit, had someone not grabbed me from behind. The stem of the rose brushed the tips of my fingers and then fell down into the horn section. The junior chorus bowed once more and was hurried off backstage. The curtain closed for the final time and the applause died away.

I went up to the dressing room and changed out of my costume, and was walking back to the elevator when a man wearing a black tuxedo stopped me in the hallway. He was carrying a black trumpet case in one hand and a white rose in the other.

"Are you Dominika?" he asked me. "If you are, I've been told that this might belong to you."

He offered me the rose and I accepted it eagerly.

"Thank you very much!" I exclaimed.

"Don't mention it," the trumpet player laughed. "I'm just glad you're not the lead ballerina. Your flower landed on my head. I don't think I would have survived the whole basket."

He smiled at his own joke, and we rode the elevator down to the lobby together. I clutched the rose and felt unbelievably happy. I had danced in my first ballet and received my first flower. I pressed the petals to my nose and took in the sweet fragrance, not minding its broken stem and battered appearance. It was mine and I had earned it, and I carried it delightedly out of the elevator and down into the lobby where my parents were waiting.

THE LITTLE TUBE

 IN 1985, FOUR DAYS after I turned ten, Mikhail Gorbachev became the General Secretary of the Soviet Communist Party. A feeling of liberation swept through Czechoslovakia. Even the monotone of the Voice of America's broadcaster, Karel Jezdinsky, started to crackle with hope. My father was beside himself. He was convinced that Cold War communism was finally coming to an end, and took to wearing the Solidarnosz pin Mr. Poloraich had given him as a joke. Whenever he was interviewed by the secret police, he pinned it to his lapel to let them know that the times were changing. Still, nothing much changed. After one particularly heated interrogation in which he told the STB that it would be they, not he, who would soon be unemployed, he was fired from his job and threatened with prison for vagrancy under article 203 of the criminal code.

"The bastards are becoming desperate!" he'd exclaim in the mornings. "I can hear the Politburo grinding their teeth!" He would rub his hands gleefully and wolf down his breakfast, and then he would throw on his jacket and drive away in search of work.

One day in early April, he came home very late with a sack of potatoes and a barrel of wine in his trunk. He had found a job at an agricultural co-operative in South Moravia, near the famous fields of Austerlitz where Napoleon had defeated Austria and Russia. The chief of the cooperative was a short, temperamental man called Comrade Maxian, who liked to think of himself as a modern-day Napoleon. He was a Communist with strong capitalist leanings, and cleverly used ideology to run his coopera-tive in the style of a land baron. Comrade Maxian recognized a fellow en-trepreneur in my father and cheerfully overlooked his bad papers. He took my dad on a tour of his private wine cellar, where they quickly fell into a long discussion about Gorbachev and the changes he was likely to make in Eastern Europe. By sunset, my father had pitched Comrade Maxian two of Dr. Stein-Ein's inventions, along with the concept of turn-ing ideas into patents and selling them in West Germany. The agricultural chief was very impressed. Uncorking the fourth bottle of wine for the evening, he authorized my father to develop ideas and build prototypes for the cooperative. Comrade Maxian would finance these inventions and provide political cover, while my father would assemble the necessary teams of scientists and technicians. They shook hands on what would be-come the first stage of their collaboration—a small chemical factory in our garage.

By the time Gorbachev had appeared on Russian television, my father, in the true spirit of perestroika, had turned our garage into a medium-sized laboratory. Bags of cement and boxes of tiles were hauled out and deposited into the backyard, where they slowly disappeared into a jungle of weeds, and the huge pile of sand that had been sitting in front of our driveway for two years was shoveled over the fence, only to be replaced by barrels of lye and epichloride.

A few days later, the first laboratory truck showed up in our street. Mr. Simek lingered over his lawn clippings as my father helped the driver unload his equipment. These deliveries became a weekly occurrence, and the Simeks, Acorns, Caesars, and Haseks watched with interest as boxes and barrels were carried into our garage. Soon afterward, strange vapors began to emanate from the house. The smell of ammonia was quite over-powering, confirming the neighbors' suspicions that whatever it was my father was up to, it must be illegal.

In our garage, a team of technicians was assembling the *aparatura*, which was Dr. Stein-Ein's latest invention. It was a high-tech chemical distillery, connected to a state-of-the-art computer the size of a wardrobe. The computer looked like something out of a fifties science fiction film, and was made by TESLA, the state-run electronics factory. The name TESLA was the subject of an old and bitter joke in the scientific community. It was said to stand for *TEchnicky SLAba*, which translates as "technically weak," but Dr. Stein-Ein was very proud of his computer. "It may be slow, but it's un-breakable!" he would declare. My mother, Klara, and I watched nervously as he tried out his invention for the first time. My mother was very tense, and told me in a low voice that along with the lye and epichloride, some of the barrels in the garage contained highly toxic nerve gas and contact poisons.

"If you ever hear an explosion or smell almonds, you must jump out of the window and run away from the house," she warned me on many occasions. Which was funny, because for the next three years the smell of cyanide in our yard was almost as constant as the smell of ammonia. In fact, compared to the ammonia, the almond smell was quite pleasant, and after an apprehensive period, we did what we always did with my father's crazy projects.

We learned to live around it.

As spring gave way to summer, I discovered that I had grown two centimeters taller. My costumes started to fit, and I performed in chil-dren's ballets three times a week and deposited my earnings into my sav-ings account. By the end of June, I had saved 2,650 Czech crowns, which was more than my mother's monthly salary at the Economic Institute. More exciting, I had passed three rounds of auditions for the State Conservatory, and was on the short list for next year's students. When the summer holidays began, I found myself nervously awaiting a letter from the conservatory. Every morning, I would sit on top of a barrel of lye and listen for the sound of Mrs. Rufferova's bike. Mrs. Rufferova was the Cernosice postmistress and something of a town legend, as she had delivered the mail for the past twenty years on her husband's old motorcycle. She rode incredibly fast and was very hard to catch. She would speed up and down our street, stuffing *Red Right* newspapers into our neighbors' mailboxes, and I would have to dash out onto the road and wave my arms to make her stop.

"Hello, Mrs. Rufferova! Do you have anything for me today?" I would ask her.

"Not a thing, sweetie!" she would bellow over the sound of her engine, although sometimes she would have a letter for my sister. Without braking, she would execute a sharp turn in front of our garage and toss me a foreign-looking package with an Italian stamp. I'd watch her zoom off down the street, then take the letter up to Klara's bedroom. During the summer holidays, my sister spent a lot of time in bed.

"Is it for me? Is it for me?" she would scream. "It is! It's a letter from Renzo!" She'd snatch the package from my hand and glare at me until I left her to read it in peace. Bringing Klara her letters was often more stressful than waiting for mine.

On the days when there was no mail, I would pluck a bunch of daisies from Mr. Simek's gutter and despondently pull off their petals.

"Yes, they'll take me. No, they won't," I'd whisper as I stripped each daisy. My heart would sink with each unfavorable answer, and I'd toss the bad daisy into the drain and grab a new one. The gutter would slowly fill up with petals until my mother called me in for lunch.

A week after I'd given up waiting, Mrs. Rufferova parked her scooter in the driveway and rang the front doorbell. I ran upstairs and watched in fascination as she fished a certified mail envelope out of her bag. She asked me to sign a delivery form and gave me a broad smile as I filled out the paperwork. "Ptui, ptui, ptui!" she said, pretending to spit on the floor. I was too scared to open the envelope, so I took it downstairs to my father. I handed him the letter with trembling hands and he called my mother and sister into the room. We stood around him as he cut the envelope open with a kitchen knife.

"Dear Dominika," he read. "We are pleased to announce"—he paused dramatically—"that you have been accepted to study at the State Conservatory in Prague!"

I cried with relief and my mother swept me into her arms. My father was delighted, and even my sister, who tended to take a dim view of anything requiring discipline or exercise, seemed happy for me. We had a wonderful lunch, and later in the afternoon I ran around Cernosice, attempting to share the news with anyone I could find. The streets were hot and dusty, and the town was deserted except for a handful of weekenders from Prague who hung around in front of the pastry shop. Everyone else was away on vacation. Terezka Jandova had gone to Bulgaria with her parents, Eugina and Eugene German were visiting their relatives in Moravia, and Dana Bukova and the other horse-loving girls were away at the Pioneer camps. I was disappointed but not surprised. Traditionally, my family was the only family in town that didn't have the time or money to go on holidays.

Sometimes I wished that my father would take us to a nice place where we could eat ice cream and lie on the beach, but I knew it would never happen, because he was very restless and would somehow manage to turn the holiday into a business trip. Also, my mother had used up all of her vacation time helping my father build his factory. She was due back at the Economic Institute the day after Comrade Maxian had signed the contract my father had prepared. The problem was, there was no guarantee that Comrade Maxian would sign it. He wanted to see the *aparatura* in action first, he unexpectedly told my father a month after they had made their agreement, and an inspection was scheduled for the fourteenth of July. My father was optimistic about the outcome, but my mother was worried to the point where she was having difficulty sleeping. One night, when I crept out of bed to go to the bathroom, I overheard her telling my dad that if Comrade Maxian didn't sign the contract, we would have to sell our house to pay Dr. Stein-Ein's expenses.

The next morning, I went to church and prayed to my little god.

Hello, my little god.
I'm really trying to do my very best to please you,
and I'm grateful to you for helping me to get into the State Conservatory.
But could you also please make Comrade Maxian sign my father's
  contract?
So we don't have to sell our house? Please please please?
Thank you. Amen.

For the next two days, I helped my mother in the kitchen, where she was preparing a delicious meal in the hope of feeding Comrade Maxian into signing the contract. I cooked caramel, which my mother used to make homemade rum out of the pure alcohol my dad had used the *aparatura* to distill while Dr. Stein-Ein wasn't looking. I also picked juniper berries in the forest, which we used to flavor the alcohol so that it tasted like gin. We put the rum and gin in the empty bottles left by Tomas Glatz and Mr. Poloraich after their frequent visits.

"We shouldn't be doing this, you know," my mother told me. "It's illegal to make your own alcohol. If the neighbors denounced us, we'd be thrown into prison."

She flared her nostrils to emphasize the gravity of her statement. "You must never tell anyone!" she said. And then she went back to whisking egg whites for her famous apricot cake.

THE DAY OF THE VISIT, our house was bustling with activity. My mother had risen at the crack of dawn and was stuffing an enormous goose in the kitchen, while my father polished the *aparatura* and Dr. Stein-Ein fine-tuned the computer. At ten o'clock, I volunteered to go outside and wait for Comrade Maxian's car. I sat on top of a lye barrel and listened for the sound of approaching engines, but with the exception of Mrs. Rufferova's scooter, the town was silent. After a while, I realized that Mr. Hasek was watching me from his kitchen window. Shortly afterward, he ventured outside his front gate. He performed his usual ritual of looking up and down the street, and then made his way over to where I was sitting. I knew what he was up to. He was going to ask me, yet again, what was inside our garage and why my father wasn't looking for a job. Mr. Hasek was a notorious gossip, but I didn't have to worry too much about him informing on us as he was very old and had Alzheimer's disease. By the time he returned home, he would not only have forgotten what I told him, but that we had even talked in the first place. If I stayed outside in the street long enough, he would see me from his kitchen window and come back out and ask me the same questions all over again.

"Goodness me! Haven't you grown up!" he would say. "And what is your father up to? I keep smelling ammonia and almonds. What's going on inside your garage?"

Mr. Hasek always looked up and down the street because he wanted to avoid Mr. Simek, the other neighborhood gossip. Poor Mr. Simek had a terrible speech impediment that made him very hard to understand, and his snooping technique consisted of him coming out of his garage with a rake and pretending to rake the leaves beneath his walnut tree. He did this in all seasons, even when the snow was thick on the ground. He'd rake for a while and then suddenly pretend to see me. Then he'd shuffle over for a neighborly chat, hoping to learn what Mr. Hasek had learned.

"Hello, little girl. Haven't you grown up?" he would say. "I hear that your father has been busy building some kind of chemical factory in your garage. Is it true?"

Actually, I had no idea what he said. Apart from the speech defect, he also spoke too fast, running his words into each other. It often sounded like he was speaking Hungarian.

"*Huurgleh. Granneh? Iceland yer gargoyle magland hallelujah.* Goulash?" he would ask. Our conversations were very strange. The fortunate thing was that no matter what I told him, he could never really repeat it to anyone. Even his wife had trouble understanding him.

As Mr. Hasek left and Mr. Simek appeared, a black Tatra 613 drove up the street. The Tatra 613 was a government car, an East European Cadillac. Cars like this were only driven by high-ranking Communist officials, because no one else could afford them. They consumed so much gas, you had to fill the tank every hundred kilometers. Mr. Simek's jaw dropped as he saw the car coming, and he hurriedly raked his way back to his garden.

I jumped down from the barrel and rang the doorbell.

"Dad! Dad! This is it! They're here!" I cried.

The Tatra rumbled to a halt, a little flag with the Austerlitz coat of arms fluttering on its hood. Behind me, the garage door flew open and my family and Dr. Stein-Ein came out wearing white lab coats. A short, energetic man leaped from the car and made a huge show of kissing my mother's and sister's hands. This had to be Comrade Maxian. Despite the fact that his Tatra (and his shoes) were covered in mud from our construction site, he really did seem like an aristocrat. Two men climbed out of the car behind him, and he introduced them as Comrade Drapal and Comrade Fejk. Comrade Drapal looked like a big, sleepy bear in a gray suit, whereas Comrade Fejk reminded me of a ferret. The three men spoke in the same "long beak" dialect as Mrs. German, and I had to stop myself from giggling. Comrade Drapal made small talk with Dr. Stein-Ein, and Comrade Fejk made eyes at my sister, while in the background, Mr. Simek raked his invisible leaves and Mr. Hasek loitered in the street, struggling to memorize Comrade Maxian's plates.

"Who ares these people?" Comrade Maxian demanded. "Ares they friends of yours, or neighbors?"

"They're neighbors," my father said. No other explanation was necessary. Everyone knew exactly what he meant.

"Well, then," Comrade Maxian said cheerfully. "You must takes us inside and shows us this machine!"

Dr. Stein-Ein's cheeks flushed with pride as he led the comrades into the garage. He launched into a long speech about electromagnetic energy, using technical terms that no one understood. He was tiny and intense, and with his mane of white hair, he really did look like a mad scientist. He switched on the computer, and the *aparatura* came to life. Comrade Maxian put on a pair of glasses and smiled with anticipation, while my mother pulled me toward the door. My father stood beside the machine, pointing out the different kettles and tubes as the pressure slowly built inside the distillery. The thermometer climbed past seven hundred degrees, and the smell of ammonia was so strong you could taste it. Comrade Drapal collapsed into a chair and mopped his forehead with a handkerchief. Comrade Fejk looked like he was going to faint. Twenty minutes later, a rich, honeylike liquid poured into a test tube at the bottom of the *aparatura*.

Dr. Stein-Ein handed the test tube to Comrade Maxian.

"What we have here is an antifriction lotion capable of attracting molecules of water from the air," he said excitedly. "By applying it to any synthetic surface, you can neutralize the antistatic charges caused by friction. Nylon threads won't snap while running through a loom, and vinyl plates in a press won't attract dust from the air!"

Comrade Maxian dipped his finger in the test tube.

"Incredible," he said politely. "So how does we makes money with this, exactly?"

"Well, for a start, we can sell it to the textile industry as a prevention against combustion," my father explained. "This is a serious problem in Russia. Factories burn down all the time because of the sparks generated by static electricity and friction."

Comrade Maxian looked at the yellow goo on his hands.

"I see," he said doubtfully.

There was an awkward pause. My mother tightened her grip on my hand while my sister unbuttoned her lab coat and started fanning herself like Marilyn Monroe.

"It's hot in here," she moaned. "Can't anyone open the window?"

Comrade Fejk leaped to attention. He strode manfully across the laboratory, leaned forward, and reached over a row of bottles sitting in front of the window. He pulled the window open, knocking the stopper out of a large bottle of alcohol that my father had recently distilled.

"I'm so sorry!" he exclaimed. "I hopes this is not some kind of—"

His face changed.

"Good Lord," he sniffed. "This smells like booze!"

Comrade Drapal bounced out of his chair and immediately joined his comrade at the window. Comrade Fejk lifted the bottle and inspected it against the light.

"Oh, that," my dad said nonchalantly. He tilted his head toward the door, indicating that the neighbors might be out there listening, and then he whispered something in Comrade Maxian's ear.

"Really?" Comrade Maxian's eyes lit up. "In this garage?" My father nodded, and the agricultural chief burst into laughter. "What an interesting machine," he said, patting my father on the shoulder. "Shows us more!"

My father demonstrated the *aparatura*'s versatility, filling test tubes with homemade gin and handing them to everyone except me. "To perestroika!" he declared. "To the successful harvest!" Comrade Drapal responded, draining his tube in one gulp. "To your beautiful wife and daughter!" Comrade Fejk exclaimed. Comrade Maxian tasted the gin like a connoisseur, swishing it around in his mouth until the strength of the alcohol made his eyes bulge, and then he shot my father a conspiratorial smile.

"Very promising, this invention of yours," he said gleefully. "Perhaps we coulds discuss the technicalities in a less formal environment?"

My mother could barely conceal her relief as she escorted the comrades into our dining room. She filled our best glasses with gin and told my sister to carve the goose. My sister took off her lab coat, revealing a white stretch top without a bra, and leaned low over the table as she carved, much to Comrade Fejk's delight. I ran in and out of the kitchen, carrying bowls of steaming cabbage and dumplings. The room quickly filled up with cigarette smoke. The comrades drank and ate heartily, paying little attention to Dr. Stein-Ein, who kept trying to redirect the conversation to the more important subject of electromagnetic energy. Suddenly, Comrade Maxian slapped his forehead with his hand.

"*Ježiš Marja!*" he cried. "I nearly forgot! We haves brought you a present from Moravia."

"Oh, you shouldn't have," my mother smiled. "You have given us so many sacks of onions and potatoes, we really have nowhere to put them."

"This one you must puts in your freezer," Comrade Maxian said seriously. "It is the finest product the Austerlitz Cooperative has to offers the top members of its scientific community."

We followed the agricultural chief outside and watched him unlatch the trunk of his Tatra. A sweet smell wafted out of the trunk, making my mother cover her mouth with her hand.

"His name was Pepa," Comrade Maxian said proudly, pulling a sheet of blood-soaked newspaper off what appeared to be a headless pig. "He wons the Pig of the Year contest! But we only gives you half, otherwise you will be eating him past Christmas!"

Comrade Drapal hoisted what was left of Pepa onto his shoulder and carried it down to the kitchen. He threw it onto the counter and went back to the dining room, where my father had cracked open another bottle of gin, and was toasting the pig and Mikhail Gorbachev's health. My mother was shocked by the huge amount of work the meat represented, but she didn't complain. She armed herself with a cleaver and a carving knife and began to disassemble Pepa before the smell became too bad. My sister sullenly threw on an apron and started cutting chunks of pig fat into small pieces. I was in charge of the big pot. Wielding the wooden spoon my mother used to pasteurize milk, I stirred the melting fat until it turned into lard. Then I poured it into jars, securing them with pieces of cellophane and rubber bands while my sister refilled the pot with more cubes of fat.

By the time the comrades had started to sing Moravian folk songs, I had prepared twenty-five jars of lard and my mother had frozen more than fifty pork chops. It was seven o'clock in the evening and Dr. Stein-Ein had finally left the comrades to drink in peace. Comrade Fejk wobbled down into the kitchen, carrying a bottle of homemade gin. He proposed yet another toast to my mother's and sister's beauty, and insisted on kissing my sister's greasy hand. Halfway through kissing it, however, he passed out. We had to ask the agriculturalists to come and rescue their fallen comrade, which they did, dragging the semiconscious Fejk out of the kitchen in much the same way they had hauled Pepa in.

At four o'clock in the morning, after the last chop had been thrown into the freezer, my father walked the comrades to the door and we were relieved to hear the Tatra 613 roaring down the hill. My mother collapsed into a chair and stared at the pile of dirty plates and glasses. She poured herself a glass of gin and told me to come and sit on her lap. She was exhausted and I could tell she was close to tears. She told me that she was sad she had to go back to the Economic Institute. She didn't like her job, but was afraid to quit because my dad's work was unsteady and she was worried we might end up losing the house.

A heavy stomping echoed down the stairway and my father burst into the kitchen with a huge smile. His hair was messy and his shirt and trousers were covered in cigarette ash.

"A triumph!" he laughed, waving the contract above his head. "Everything is signed, sealed, and delivered!"

He threw his arms around my mother's waist and squeezed her breathless. "Five thousand a month, full time!" he declared. "And the first thing I'm doing is hiring you as my assistant!"

My mother pushed him away and burst into tears.

"Are you mad?" she sobbed. "What if the comrades change their minds? What if they refuse to pay you? A contract means nothing in this country and you know it!"

"Come on, Honza," my father smiled. "Try to be an optimist!"

"An optimist?" my mother exploded. "You know what an optimist is? An optimist is a pessimist without information!"

She started to pace the room like a tiger. "I can't sleep because I'm so worried," she cried. "My hands shake. My parents don't speak to me. My boss publishes my work under his name. I haven't had a holiday in five years!"

I had never seen my mother so upset. Her voice spiraled so high, she sounded like an ambulance.

"I don't get to go to the hairdresser!" she wailed. "I don't get to go to the theater! I work like a donkey and get nothing in return except half a pig and a pile of dirty dishes!"

And with that, she grabbed a plate and threw it onto the floor. It shattered loudly and her anger immediately disappeared. She looked shocked and vaguely surprised. She knelt on the floor and gathered up the shards of porcelain as though they were pieces of her own broken heart.

My father threw his big arms around her.

"Shhh," he whispered tenderly. "Tomorrow you'll quit your job and we'll go on holiday." He kissed her forehead like he was putting a stamp on a contract. "We'll go to a nice place where you'll have nothing to worry about except the weather."

My mother wiped her eyes with her sleeve. She was never very good at staying angry. She put her arms around my father's neck, and I put my arms around both my parent's knees. The three of us stood in the middle of the kitchen, which was cozy and full of steam. My sister had vanished as soon as the pig was in the freezer, so I was the only sober person in the room.

"Where will we go?" I asked. "Terezka Jandova's parents had to put their name on a waiting list for two years just to go to Bulgaria! All the seaside holidays are sold out."

My father considered this for a few seconds.

"I have an idea," he said. He tapped his nose with his forefinger, suggesting he had just thought of something extremely clever. "I know exactly where we'll go. We'll go . . . to Poland."

My mother looked up in horror.

"Poland?" she said. "No one ever goes to Poland."

"Exactly," my father smiled. "That's why it won't be sold out."

NONE OF US BELIEVED MY FATHER was serious until he turned up the next day with a brochure from Cedok, the state-run travel agency. The brochure displayed a photograph of a Polish four-star hotel and a pleasant-looking beach dotted with sunbathers and umbrellas. The hotel was called the Hotel Romance, and my dad had already made a weeklong reservation. I couldn't believe he had found such a nice place on such short notice. He sent our Skoda to the garage to be serviced, and bought two additional tanks of gas to keep in the trunk in case of emergencies. The big Michelin map of Europe was spread across the kitchen table, and a pyramid of canned food was piled up across it. There apparently wasn't much to eat in Poland, so we would take our own supplies.

"There is no way I am going on this trip," my sister declared. "The Poles are so religious and poor, all they eat are communion wafers! I have no intention of starving! I'm staying right here!"

"No, you're not, young lady," my father growled. "You're going to lie on a beach and have a wonderful time if I have to drag you there with my own hands, or else!"

My sister burst into tears and fled the kitchen, and my father stormed after her. We could hear them shouting all the way up the stairs.

I looked at my mother. My mother looked at me.

"Perhaps we'll let them sleep on it," she said.

Two days later, my parents and I arose at four in the morning and loaded our luggage into the car. My sister stayed in bed. She had won again, and had arranged to keep working at my grandmother's buffet while waiting to see if Renzo would visit. Renzo had written her a letter saying he was thinking about coming to Prague in the summer, and wanted to know if he should bring his own food. The Italians obviously had the same preconceptions about Czechoslovakia as we had about Poland—preconceptions that Klara was in no hurry to change. "Yes. Absolutely. Bring Italian food," she had written, along with a detailed list of suggestions. I noticed that she had stockpiled several bottles of gin. Her private holiday was shaping up nicely.

It had been Hilda who had really pushed for my sister to stay at home. The idea of Klara and an Italian man occupying an empty house was something she found enormously appealing, and she made my father's life hell until he finally gave in. Hilda was hoping that Klara would become pregnant and that Renzo would be her ticket out of Eastern Europe. This sounds terrible, but it was the private fantasy of hundreds of thousands of Eastern Bloc families. At any rate, Klara was allowed to stay at home, and I think my parents were secretly relieved. Driving with my sister was never much fun, and my father's optimism was contagious. We were really looking forward to our Polish vacation.

It was dark and misty when we left the garage. The car was loaded with cans of baked beans and sausages, two crates of beer, and thirty frozen pork chops in an ice chest. Six bottles of gin had been hidden in the backseat upholstery, and three thousand Czech crowns had been wrapped in aluminum foil and glued to the bottom of the engine. As we rolled out of the driveway, I saw Mr. Hasek staring out of his bedroom window. He was dressed in his black-and-white-striped pajamas and looked a bit like a prisoner of war.

"*Ahoj*, Mr. Hasek!" I rolled down my window and waved at him. "We're on our way to Poland!" I knew he wouldn't remember, but it was nice to let someone know that we were finally on holidays.

We drove down the hill and across the fields, watching the sun rise slowly in the eastern sky. We got on the D1 (the only highway in Czechoslovakia at the time), and my father floored the accelerator. We made good time to Ostrava, which I was looking forward to seeing, as it was the place where my dad had spent his childhood. We passed through the desolate landscape of smoking chimneys and mining towers, and I couldn't help marveling at a huge concrete sculpture that dominated the skyline. It was a monument to the Russian Army, which had liberated Ostrava from the Nazis.

"Do you remember the Nazis, Dad?" I asked.

"Of course I remember," he said. "I was about your age when the Russians drove them out."

"Was it exciting?" I asked. "Were you happy when the Russians came?"

"No," my father said grimly. "The Russians were worse than the Germans. They would point their rifles at Czech civilians and yell, '*Davay cziasy!*' If you didn't understand and didn't give them your wristwatch, they'd shoot you on the spot." He shook his head. "I saw them do this a few times. Some of the soldiers had their sleeves rolled up, and their arms were covered with watches right up to their shoulders. I saw a lot of things in Ostrava I'd rather forget. Living in Prague is much nicer."

It was forty years after the war, and no one had bothered to fix up the town. Many of the public buildings were still dotted with bullet holes. I couldn't believe that my father had grown up in such an ugly place. Everything was covered in thick layers of soot, and the only decorations were the Communist posters in the shop windows: HONOR YOUR FATHER-LAND! they exclaimed. WORKERS UNITE TO BUILD A BETTER WORLD!

I was glad when we arrived at the Polish border, even though the checkpoint was very frightening. We stopped at a red-and-white-striped gate that was made from the barrel of a tank. Two Polish soldiers pointed Kalashnikov rifles at our car while my father handed a third soldier our passports. My mother shaded her face beneath her hat and started to fan herself with a road map. She knew we would be in serious trouble if the soldiers caught us smuggling Czech money across the border.

"Off on holidays?" the Polish soldier asked, smiling. "I hope you've brought your own food with you." And he stamped our passports without looking in the trunk. The tank barrel rotated slowly to the side, and my mother let out a deep sigh of relief.

"I told you!" my father laughed. "You could emigrate to Poland for all the Communists would care! It would be like trying to sneak into a concentration camp!" He kissed my mother, knocking her hat off. "And now the fun begins! If we make good time, we should be able to see the Baltic Sea by sunset!"

There were no highways in Poland, so we traveled along a two-lane road that was wide and straight and flat. Fields of green and gold crops stretched as far as the eye could see, and cows with horns as large as handlebars grazed contentedly in the meadows. Everywhere I looked, I saw corn and barley. Wild cherries and apples hung from the trees.

"Why are the Polish people starving?" I asked. "There's food everywhere."

"It would be stealing from the State," my father explained. "All this food goes straight to Russia. After the Solidarity uprising in 1981, Russian tanks threatened to roll into Warsaw. Everyone thought they were bluffing, but they weren't, and when it became clear that the Americans weren't going to intervene, the Polish Communist Party was forced to cut a deal in which they agreed to export their crops to Russia immediately after the harvest."

"Would the Polish people be starving if they hadn't stood up to the Russians?" I asked.

"Probably not," my dad replied. He tapped the Solidarnosz pin on his suit. "Mr. Poloraich may think it's a joke, but you have to admire a nation that's prepared to fight for its freedom. The Poles may have nothing to eat, but they still have their pride."

I was very impressed by this, and started waving at all the Polish cars we overtook. Most of them were tiny Fiats overloaded with large Catholic families. I waved at all the children in these cars and they waved back at me. A road sign informed us that we had 350 kilometers to go before we reached the Baltic Sea. It was a beautiful day and we were making good time. Then my father changed gears to overtake a tractor, and the Skoda's engine began to shudder. A cloud of steam billowed from the hood, and the temperature needle climbed high into the red. We pulled off the road and the car spluttered to a halt. It was a familiar situation in an unfamiliar environment. My father leaped out of the car and popped the hood. The engine sizzled like a pressure cooker, and I could hear my father yelling in the background.

"*Do prdele!*" he roared. "*Na hovno!*" He kicked the front tire viciously.

My mother walked around the front of the car and handed him a rag so he could unscrew the radiator cap. Boiling water spurted out of the pipes.

"The money!" my mother cried, jumping back.

"*Kurva fix!*" my dad hissed as he dove beneath the hood. A second later, he had the aluminum package in his hand.

"Run to the river and bring some water!" he told me, pointing to a creek two hundred meters away. I took two empty bottles, filled them with water, and ran back to the car. I handed them to my dad and watched as he poured the water onto the radiator. The cloud of steam cleared and the engine cooled down. My father bent down to inspect the damage, and when he stood up, his face was white with anger.

"Those bastards in the garage!" he said grimly. "They've swapped my engine for an older one! This one has a crack. We're going to have to drive very slowly from now on."

The practice of switching car parts was common in Eastern Europe, but my father was not only on friendly terms with the mechanics in the garage, but he had paid them under the table to do a good job. He glared at the engine for a long time, and then we rolled up our sleeves and push-started the car. My dad put his shoulder to the door frame and his hand on the steering wheel, while my mother and I pushed the car from the trunk. We pushed the Skoda until it gathered momentum, then my father jumped inside and hit the gas. The exhaust pipe spewed a cloud of smoke across my mother's favorite dress.

"Hurrah!" my father cheered.

We jumped inside and no one said anything for a long while. Eventually, my father attempted to make lemonade out of the lemon we were driving.

"I've switched on the heating to cool the engine," he said cheerfully. "But if we roll down our windows, we can imagine we're driving somewhere exotic and warm. Like Italy."

We didn't have to stretch our imaginations much. For the remainder of the trip, it felt like we were driving across the Sahara Desert. Our average speed was twenty kilometers an hour, and when the engine died (which it did often), we would push the Skoda past dunes of barley and corn. We ate and slept in the car and bathed in the various creek beds we were able to find. It took us a day and a half to push the Skoda to the resort town Miedzyzdroje. We were dirty and hot when we arrived, and wasted no time in running down to the beach. We dove into the water and swam for less than a minute. I now understood why there was no waiting list for the hotels in Poland. The Baltic Sea was freezing and full of jellyfish. The other beachgoers wore sweaters and scarves, and watched us dive into the surf with openmouthed amazement. They sat in old-style canvas beach stalls, watching the cold waves and drinking hot tea out of plastic cups.

We warmed ourselves up by pushing the Skoda to the Hotel Romance, which was a handsome art nouveau building with lovely wrought-iron balconies. We lodged the car between a BMW and a Mercedes, and carried our luggage up to reception. The clerk studied our passports and his warm smile became slightly forced. "Your suite will be in the Friendship Pavilion," he said. "It's a hundred meters up the beach. Go out the back door and turn right."

He kept our passports and handed us the key.

"I can't wait to take a hot bath!" my father exclaimed.

He grabbed our suitcases and carried them through the lobby. We followed him out the back door of the hotel, smiling with anticipation, and then our jaws dropped. The Friendship Pavilion was an ugly cement tower block covered in miniature blue tiles.

"Wait a second," my dad growled. "This has to be some kind of mistake!"

He spun on his heel and went back to reception. We could hear his voice thundering in the distance. After a while, he returned with a defeated look on his face.

"Romance is offered exclusively to the Germans," he said, crumpling up the Cedok brochure and throwing it into a bin. "Friendship is the best they have to offer us Czechs."

We carried our luggage to the Friendship Pavilion. It was a classic, Soviet-style *panelak*. The front door was missing the handle, and the lock was stuffed with matches to keep it open. Half the tiles in the lobby had fallen off. The elevator smelled faintly of urine, and most of the lightbulbs in the hallway had been stolen. Our suite was a small room crowded with two beds, a closet, and a dining table. A noisy fridge hummed in a tiny kitchenette, and an even smaller balcony offered a view of the back of the Romance Hotel. We were disappointed, but far too tired to complain. We ate sausages and beans from a can and went to bed without the hot shower we'd been looking forward to all day. Cold water ran from both the red and blue faucets.

I awoke in the night to the sound of thumping. The lights were on and my father was crawling around the room with one of his shoes.

"What are you doing, Dad?"

"I'm killing earwigs," he whispered. "This room is infested!"

I looked under my bed and saw a couple of fast-moving insects scuttling around in the shadows. They looked like tiny, armor-plated centipedes.

"Why are they called earwigs?" I asked.

"Because they crawl inside your ears and lay eggs in your brain," my father grunted, pounding the floor with his shoe. I had no idea whether he was joking or not.

I pulled the blanket over my head and tried to go back to sleep, but the thought of tiny insects laying eggs in my brain was absolutely horrifying. I huddled under the bedclothes, and tried to fall asleep with my fingers in my ears. An hour later, I was still awake, listening to the sound of my father snoring. I climbed out of bed, tiptoed to the bathroom, and found my little overnight bag. Inside was a tube of my favorite strawberry-flavored toothpaste, which I carefully used to plug up both my ears. I waited until it had hardened, and then I crawled back into bed and promptly fell asleep.

The next morning, my parents shook me awake. The sun was up and they were already dressed.

"We're going to town," my mother seemed to be saying. "Hurry up, it's almost ten o'clock."

I went to the bathroom and attempted to dig the toothpaste out of my ears, only to discover that the paste had hardened into cement. My balance was slightly off and my parents sounded like they were talking underwater. I tried to tell my mother I had a problem, but my father was in his usual hurry, and before I had time to explain, we had push-started the car and were on our way to Szczecin, a big seaport town on the Polish-German border. As we drove, I began to understand what my father was up to. He intended to exchange our Czech crowns for Polish zlotys on the black market, and use them to pay for our car to get fixed.

We arrived on the outskirts of Szczecin and drove past many kilometers of barbed-wire fence surrounding the port. The bay was narrow and dirty and full of rusty boats and cranes. We eventually found the city center and parked our Skoda in the old town square.

"Why can't we just go to a bank?" my mother asked nervously. "I'd hate to spend my holiday in jail!"

"Come on, Honza," my father said patiently. "The bank will give us two hundred zlotys a crown, which is less than a quarter of its market value. Never mind that the weekly exchange-allowance for a family of three is five hundred and fifty crowns."

"All right," my mother sighed. "Ptui, ptui, ptui!" She grabbed my hand and we followed my dad across the square.

I imagined we would find the black market hidden in one of the town's narrow streets. The stalls would be made out of black canvas, and there would be Barbie dolls and Swiss chocolate stashed underneath the counters. A barefoot boy would look out for the police, and the whole thing would be very dangerous and exciting. But we crossed the town many times and all we found was a greengrocer selling potatoes and apples that no one could afford to buy. Eventually, we came back to the square where our car was parked.

"Exchange? *Wechsel?* Exchange?" A man in a blue denim jacket appeared at my father's elbow. "Where are you from?" he asked.

"Prague," my dad replied. "What's the going rate for Czech crowns?"

"One thousand zlotys a crown."

The man had a shifty expression and a thick gold chain around his neck.

"Sounds about right," my father said nonchalantly. "Can you handle three thousand?"

The man's eyes lit up. He smiled, revealing several gold teeth. It was like he was carrying his bank in his mouth.

"Follow me," he said, and quickly darted through a passage leading into the courtyard of an old building. My mother sat on a bench and started to fan herself with her hat.

"I'll wait for you here," she said apprehensively. "For heaven's sake, Jarda, be careful."

"I can take care of myself," my father growled.

"I'll come!" I said. "I want to see the black market!"

I was excited that something was finally happening, but I was also slightly afraid. My ears were hurting because of the toothpaste, and I didn't like the man with gold teeth. He seemed like a bad person. I tightened my grip on my father's hand, and we walked through the little passage together. We came out into the courtyard and the Polish man looked around furtively, even though there was nobody there except me and my dad. He gestured that we should follow him inside a half-open doorway where there was a spiral staircase, and the man motioned us into an alcove under the stairs. My father showed him our money, and the Polish man unzipped a kidney-shaped bag he wore under his jacket. He pulled out a thick roll of zloty banknotes, licked his thumb, and started to count them one by one.

"Fifty thousand. One hundred. One fifty. Two hundred," he said in Polish, which sounded like someone lisping in Czech. He was very quick and professional, like a magician handling a deck of cards. He separated sixty banknotes from his roll and folded them into a little tube. He wrapped an elastic band around the tube and handed it to my father.

"Three million zlotys," I heard him say.

My dad blocked the man's exit from the alcove, removed the elastic band, and recounted the money. The Polish man bristled with indignation, but my father silenced him with a glance. I had never seen my dad look so tough. He pulled his cigarette lighter out of his pocket and told me to hold it up so he could see what he was doing, and then he counted his way through the tube of zlotys. The man with the gold teeth looked annoyed but not nervous. He waited patiently until my dad had finished counting.

"Three million zlotys," my father said decisively. "Forgive me for checking. You can never be too careful."

He shook the man's hand and gave him our three thousand crowns, and we went our separate ways. I ran unsteadily across the square to tell my mother the good news.

"Guess what?" I cried. "We're millionaires!"

My mother heaved a huge sigh of relief.

"Not a problem," my father said as he walked over. "I used to deal with *Wechsel* men all the time when I was driving taxis. The trick is to let them know that you're on to them. *Wechsel* men will only rip you off if they're sure they can get away with it. If you put up a good front, they won't bother, and besides"—he winked at me—"Dominika was there for extra protection. Weren't you, honey?"

"I have toothpaste in my ears," I finally said.

My parents looked at me strangely.

"I put toothpaste in my ears because of the earwigs," I explained. "But now it's gone hard and I can't get it out!"

My mother inspected my ears and told my father that we needed to find some hot water. So, with his usual logic, my father drove us around Szczecin in search of a garage, reasoning that we could wash my ears and fix the engine at the same time. The successful currency exchange had put him in a particularly good mood, and we eventually found a garage on the outskirts of the town. It was a small barn crowded with broken Trabants and Fiats. The mechanics were friendly but unable to fix our car. Skodas were rare and expensive in Poland, they explained, and parts were hard to come by. The best they could do was refer us to a big garage in Gdansk, a large seaport three hundred kilometers up the coast. They had no hot water for me to clean my ears with, either, but as a gesture of solidarity, they offered to help push our car out of the yard.

"I always wanted to go to Gdansk," my dad said cheerfully as we drove back to the Friendship Pavilion. "Solidarnosz was founded there. Lech Walesa worked in the dockyards before they threw him in prison."

"Who is Lech Walesa?" I asked.

"He's a Polish trade union leader," my father replied. "If there's one thing the Communists hate more than capitalists, it's workers who want to form trade unions. The Solidarity uprising happened because a bunch of dockworkers from Gdansk refused to comply with Russian shipping regulations. They thought they were being treated unfairly, and stood up for their rights. Walesa was their leader. He's a very brave man."

"What's he doing now?" I asked.

"Well, the police have been chasing him since 1981, so he's in hiding," my father said. He shook his head in admiration. "They've had his house under constant surveillance, and yet he still manages to make his wife pregnant every year!"

. . .

BACK AT THE FRIENDSHIP PAVILION, my mother boiled a pot of hot water and tried to remove the toothpaste from my ears. She wrapped a piece of cotton wool around a match and gently prodded and poked until I started to complain.

"It's never going to come out!" I said. "I'm going to have toothpaste in my ears for the rest of my life!"

"No, you won't," my mother sighed. "You're going to have to wait until we're back in Cernosice, though. I'll take you to Dr. Polakova."

My dad came in from the balcony where he had been drinking a celebratory glass of gin.

"I have a terrific idea," he said. "Why don't we go to the Hotel Romance for dinner? We have enough zlotys to fix the car, have an expensive meal, and—" he slapped my mother on the bottom, "buy your mother a new summer dress!"

My mother's favorite dress had been completely ruined by two days of car pushing.

"Well, that would be nice," my mother said. "Do you think we'll be able to find a nice dress in Poland?"

"A nice dress? We have enough zlotys to buy you an entire new wardrobe!" my father laughed.

"Can I play outside before dinner?" I asked.

"Of course," my dad winked, pouring my mother a gin and tonic. "What a good idea! You go outside and play for a few hours and then we'll have the most wonderful meal!"

"Back at six!" my mother called out as I left.

I wandered down to the sea, looking for someone to play with. A sharp wind had made the waves choppy and there were lots of dead jelly-fish washed up on the beach. Some of them were as big as pizzas and had bright purple veins running through their bodies. I stepped around them as I walked across the sand, until I encountered a group of Polish kids who were picking them up and throwing them into the sea.

I walked over and introduced myself.

"Hello! My name ith Dominika!" I said, lisping in Czech to try to make it sound Polish. "I'm on holidath from Prague. Ith it thafe to touch the jellyfith? They're not going to thting you?"

The Polish kids were very friendly. One of the boys picked up a jelly-fish and turned it upside down.

"They can't sting you if you hold them like this," he said. "But it doesn't matter, because whenever you see a jellyfish washed up on a beach, it means it's already dead. You want to throw one?"

"Yeth, pleath," I said.

He handed me the jellyfish. It felt like I was holding a big see-through pudding.

"Now throw it so it hits the face of a wave," the boy said. "If you do it right, it will explode like a grenade."

I threw the jellyfish into the sea and watched it splatter against the water. It really did explode like a grenade. For the next hour and a half, the Polish kids and I gleefully blew up all the jellyfish we could find, until the one girl who owned a wristwatch announced that it was time to go home for *"kolace."* This was very interesting. *Kolace* was the Czech for "cakes."

"You have *kolace*?" I asked.

"Yes, of course," the Polish kids replied.

"Wow," I said. "I'm going to have a yummy dinner ath well. My dad ith taking uth to the Hotel Romanth."

The Polish kids were very impressed.

"Why are you lisping?" one of the boys asked me.

"I'm trying to make my Czech thound Polith," I told him.

"Well, don't. It sounds ridiculous," the boy said. "We can all under-stand you. Would you like to come and see our apartment building?"

"Yes, please," I said.

The Polish kids lived in a big concrete *panelak* half a kilometer down the beach. I didn't think it was possible, but their house was even uglier than the Friendship Pavilion, and a lot of people lived in close proximity to each other. My new friends invited me inside, but I had to go home for dinner, so I told them that I would see them tomorrow and sprinted home to change.

At seven o'clock, my parents and I walked through the lobby of the Hotel Romance. My father was in an excellent mood and my mother looked very pretty. She wore a tight-fitting dress and a hat, and turned the heads of many German businessmen. The restaurant had high art nouveau ceilings and plush red carpet on the floors. A waiter in a white tuxedo ushered us over to our table. He wore white velvet gloves and had a napkin folded across his arm. With a flourish, he handed us the menus, which were bound in brown leather. All of the meals had French names.

I ordered the *soupe royale* and had *médaillons de jambon glacé à la Monte-Carlo* as an appetizer. For the main course, I chose the *soufflé de poisson*. A piano tinkled away in the background as the waiter uncorked an expensive bottle of wine and poured a small amount into my father's glass. My father inspected its texture against the light and made a show of tasting it. He nodded approvingly, and the waiter poured wine for both my parents as a bowl of soup materialized in front of me. It was then that we discovered the full extent of the food shortage in Poland.

The *soupe royale* was a pink cherry soup. It was served cold, and tasted horrible. I took two mouthfuls and pushed it away. The appetizer was similarly unappealing. It came in a majestic silver serving tray, and I removed the lid with anticipation, only to discover that the *médaillons de jambon* were a roll of fatty ham in aspic that reminded me of the jellyfish I had thrown into the sea. I poked it with my fork and quickly put the lid back on the tray. My parents also left their food untouched, and I noticed that many Germans weren't eating, either. It was heartbreaking, because the waiters behaved with such dignity. They were serving us the best food their kitchen could produce. The *soufflé de poisson* turned out to be a dish of mashed herring in a watery tomato sauce. It was difficult to eat, but I ate without complaint. I listened to the piano and watched the waiters fuss over the Germans, but I was secretly relieved when our waiter brought the little basket with the check, because I wanted to go home and eat some baked beans. The meal came to four hundred and eighty thousand zlotys. My father nonchalantly peeled ten notes from his tube and put them in the basket.

"Keep the change," he told the waiter, who bowed and walked away.

"The Polish kids have cakes for dinner," I said loudly.

"Really?" My mother looked doubtful. "I had no idea the food situation was this bad. These poor people."

"They have cakes!" I exclaimed. "Do you think there's somewhere around here where we could get cakes?"

"Shh. Keep your voice down," my mother said sternly.

"Excuse me, sir." The waiter came back to our table. "I'm terribly sorry, but you've only given me two hundred and seventy-five thousand zlotys. You've probably mistaken the five thousand notes for the fifty thousand ones. This happens all the time."

He was very apologetic. He put the little basket back onto our table and waited for my dad to recount the money.

The blood drained from my father's face. He verified that he had underpaid the bill, and then pulled the roll of zlotys from his pocket and unwrapped the little tube. He examined the money the *Wechsel* man had given him, counting the zeros on the side of the banknotes.

"Oh, dear," he said calmly. "You're right. It is hard to tell the difference." And as we watched, he peeled another forty-five notes from his tube and handed them to the waiter. With the tip, the meal had cost us almost all the money my father had exchanged.

Nobody spoke for a very long time.

I listened to the piano, while the cigarette in my father's hand burned down to a long stick of ash. The *Wechsel* man had used a very old technique to cheat us. Polish money was issued in multiples of thousands, and was similar to American money in that the different banknotes were the same color and size. The man with the gold teeth had put a small number of fifty thousand zloty notes on top of a large pile of five thousand zloty notes, rolling them into a tube so that the last zero was obscured. He then calmly watched my father (and me) count three million zlotys, when he had, in fact, given us less than half a million.

We were now completely broke in Poland.

My mother's eyes were very wide and her mouth began to quiver, and then she unexpectedly let out a high-pitched giggle. My father and I looked at her with amazement. She was trying not to laugh, but was soon laughing so hard that tears were streaming down her cheeks, and I couldn't help but join in. Pretty soon, my father was roaring as well. The German businessmen looked up from their tables as we left the restaurant in semi-hysterics, and we laughed all the way to the Friendship Pavilion. None of us mentioned the money from that moment on. We just laughed until we cried, which is the Czech way of dealing with disaster.

FOR THE REST OF OUR VACATION, we ate baked beans for lunch and pork cutlets for dinner. My mother soaked her summer dress in Ajax and washed it by hand until it was as good as new, while my father spent a lot of time in front of his car, staring wistfully at the crack in the engine. Everything had gone spectacularly wrong, but we still managed to have a good holiday. I became friends with the Polish kids and spent my after-noons throwing jellyfish into the sea, and even started speaking a little Polish. It was very similar to Czech. I would say *"Dzienkujemy bardzo"* in-stead of "Thank you," and *"Dowidzenia"* whenever I had to go home for dinner. After dinner, my new friends and I would meet in a public play-ground near the Friendship Pavilion, and stay outside and play games un-til it got dark.

"Did you have cakes for dinner?" I would ask.

"Tak," they would reply. *"U nas kolace."*

"And you have cakes every night?" I would shake my head enviously. I was really sick of baked beans.

"Of course." The Polish kids seemed puzzled by the question.

"I love cakes," I said, after dropping many hints. "Do you think you could bring me one?"

The Polish kids looked very worried.

"Okay," they agreed after conferring between themselves. "The problem is, we don't have much to bring you. We have only very little cakes."

"A little cake would be great!" I said happily.

The following morning, I wolfed down my breakfast and ran down to the beach.

"*Dzien dobry!*" I called out when I saw them. "Did you bring me a cake?"

A tiny girl called Kaczya, who was even smaller than me, smiled weakly and pulled a boiled egg out of her pocket.

"I'm sorry," she said. "This is the best we could do."

"An egg?" I said. "I thought you would bring me *kolace.*"

"*Tak jest,* we brought you what we had for *kolacja* last night," the kids said. "*Zalujemy bardzo,* but we don't have much to eat."

I suddenly understood that I had misheard them saying "*kolace.*" My ears were still blocked, and I realized with deep embarrassment that *kolacja* meant "dinner" in Polish. My friends were eating boiled eggs for dinner, and even so, they had brought me what little food they had.

I didn't want to offend them, so I said, "*Dzienkujemy bardzo,*" and accepted the egg. I tapped it on my forehead and started to peel it, when I suddenly had a very good idea.

"Listen," I said. "We have tons of food at our place! Why don't you come and have lunch at the Friendship Pavilion!"

It was the Polish kids' turn to look embarrassed, but I was already leading them up the beach. I knocked on our apartment door, and my mother opened it and smiled at the pack of scrawny boys and girls behind me. I introduced my new friends and explained that I had invited them for lunch. "*Dzien dobry,*" my mother said to them in Polish. She invited them inside and told them to sit at the table, and then she opened the refrigerator and pulled out our remaining pork chops. My dad came in from the balcony and joined her in the kitchen, opening many cans of baked beans. The smell of food quickly filled the room. The Polish children were very polite. They called my father "sir" and mumbled answers to his questions, but when my mother handed them each a big plate of pork and beans, their eyes lit up and they ate with relish, telling us about their lives in Miedzyzdroje. Most of their fathers worked in the dockyards and most of their mothers were pregnant. They went to school on Saturdays and church on Sundays, and dreamed of becoming astronauts or emigrating to America. After they cleaned their plates, my mother served them a second helping, and when they had finished, my dad gave each of them a bottle of Czech beer to give to their fathers.

My new friends were very sad when I told them that we had to go home to Prague in the morning. They insisted on swapping addresses, and we ended up writing to each other for many years on.

THE NEXT MORNING, my parents and I drove to Gdansk. It was only three hundred kilometers away, but it took us the whole day to get there. It was long after sunset when we finally arrived. We drove around and around, looking for the garage the mechanics in Szczecin had told us about, until we took a wrong turn into a narrow cul-de-sac that ended right at the dockyards. My father changed gear and attempted to execute his famous three-point turn, but the engine spluttered to a halt as usual. Push-starting the car without help was impossible. We sat in exasperated silence, staring at the sea. A searchlight cone randomly pulsed across the water, and the sound of police sirens echoed in the distance. It was nearly midnight and we were completely exhausted.

My dad opened the door and climbed out of the car.

"I'm going to ask for help," he said wearily.

A nearby house had a light in the window, and my father paused in front of the high wooden fence. He rang the bell on the gate, and a couple of dogs started to bark in the yard. After a few moments, a man unlatched the window.

"*Kto tam?*" he called out. "What do you want?"

"*Dzien dobry,*" my father said. "I'm sorry to disturb you, but my family and I are from Czechoslovakia and our car broke down in front of your house. Do you know if there is any kind of hotel or a hostel around here?"

"Wait a minute," the man said.

He shut the window and appeared at the gate a few minutes later. We could hear him talking to my dad, and he cautiously stuck his head outside the fence to verify that two women were sitting in a broken Czech Skoda.

"Honza, Dominika, come here!" my father called.

My mother and I climbed out of the car and ventured over to the Polish man's gate.

"These are my wife and daughter," my father explained. "Don't worry, I understand your concern."

The Polish man was a stocky, tough-looking fellow. He looked us up and down suspiciously, registering our exhaustion and my mother's beauty. Then he checked the street to see if there were any suspicious cars parked nearby. When he was satisfied that our plight was genuine, his face relaxed.

"You'll have to forgive me. But when a stranger turns up in the middle of the night wearing one of those"—he pointed at my dad's Solidarnosz pin—"you immediately assume he's with the secret police. Why don't you get your things and follow me inside?"

We were greeted by a plump woman whom he introduced as his wife. She had no idea who we were or why her husband had invited us in, but she led us into the kitchen and offered us a cup of tea and biscuits. She also brought a jar of pickled fish from her pantry, along with a loaf of chewy black bread.

"We'll put you up in our spare room," the man said. "The child looks like she's about to fall asleep, and there are no hotels around here you'd want to go to. This is a dangerous town. You hear those sirens? The police cruise the bay looking for people trying to jump a boat to Sweden. It would be hard to make them believe your car just happened to break down near the water."

My dad was very grateful for the Polish man's offer. He opened his suitcase and produced the last bottle of homemade gin, which my mother had hidden in her nightgown. The Polish woman brought four glasses from her cupboard, and my father filled them and passed them around.

"My name is Jarda. This is Jana and Dominika," he said. "I worked for the Czech government during the Prague Spring. The Communists have been on our case ever since."

The Polish man snorted with amusement. "No kidding?" he said. "I'm Tadeusz, this is Elena. We worked with Walesa organizing the strike of '81. The Communists have been making our lives hell for the past four years as well."

"Really?" my father said. "You're with Solidarity, then?"

"*Tak jest,*" the man nodded. "I'm a dockworker. It comes with the territory."

The adults drank their gin, and my father cheerfully poured a second round. The kitchen, like so many kitchens I sat in as a child, was quickly filled with cigarette smoke and laughter. I ate my pickled fish and struggled to keep my eyes open until suddenly my dad was carrying me upstairs. He tucked me up in a strange bed and kissed me on the nose, and then I heard him creaking back down the staircase. I fell asleep listening to voices floating up from the kitchen.

". . . becoming desperate!"

". . . heads will roll like cabbages!"

". . . can hear the Politburo grinding their teeth!"

The following morning, I woke to the sound of my parents carrying our bags down the stairs. "Hurry up." My mother poked her head inside my room. "Tadeusz has made an appointment at a garage. He knows a mechanic who might fix our car for free!"

We spent the morning at a small garage in Gdansk, where Tadeusz's friends did their best to fix our car. My father handed out his remaining beers, and the Polish mechanics filled the crack in the engine with some kind of silicon glue. They treated Tadeusz with great respect, and later on, my father told me that he was an important member of the Solidarity movement. He had gone to a lot of trouble to help us get home safely. He had even taken the morning off from work.

"This is only a temporary solution," the mechanics told my dad. "You can drive at normal speed, but whatever you do, don't let your engine die or you might not be able to start it again. When you get back to Prague, you had better get your mechanic friends to give you back your old engine. This one's ready for the scrap heap."

"Don't worry," my father snorted. "I'll be paying their garage a visit as soon as I get back."

We said good-bye to Tadeusz and gave him our address in Cernosice. He and his wife would be welcome to stay with us whenever they came to Prague.

My father turned the ignition and the engine came to life. It sounded strong and confident. The mechanics looked pleased.

"Remember. No stopping between here and your front door!" Tadeusz grinned.

"Dʒienkujemy bardʒo!" I called out as we drove away. *"Dowidʒienia!"*

WE HAD A SEVEN-HUNDRED-KILOMETER drive in front of us, no money, and almost no food. Fifty empty beer bottles rattled in our trunk. Our financial situation was so bad that my father intended to return the bottles for their deposit once we were back in Czechoslovakia. Each empty bottle was worth one crown, and fifty crowns would buy us a cheap meal at a pub across the border. As we drove out of Gdansk, the sky became over-cast. It started to rain, and the rhythm of the window wipers made me sleepy. I snuggled up in a blanket and felt warm and safe.

"I can't wait to get home," I declared. "I'm going to have my ears cleaned out, and then I'm going to eat something yummy. Maybe Renzo will have some Italian food left over!"

"Don't get too excited," my mother said from the front seat. "You're going to the conservatory, remember? You don't want to end up like Vendula Backyard."

"She gets to eat chocolates and ride horses all day!" I pointed out.

"Yes, she does, but she doesn't get to dance in *Swan Lake*. You still want to dance in *Swan Lake*, don't you?"

"I guess so," I sighed.

"Well, now," my father said with his usual optimism. "This was a bit of an unusual holiday, but everything turned out okay in the end. Next time, it's going to be really great! Once we make some money with the *aparatura*, we'll buy a new car and drive to Italy!"

"But we're not allowed to travel to the West," I reminded him.

"Says who?" my father demanded. "With Gorbachev in power, the Iron Curtain has got to fall. I bet all my money we'll be seeing some serious changes in the future!"

"You don't have any money to bet," my mother smiled.

"Not yet, I don't," he growled. "But just you wait!"

WE ARRIVED AT THE BORDER at nine in the evening. I woke up as my father jammed on his brakes. He really had managed to drive the whole way without stopping. I sat up and pressed my nose to the window, and recognized the red-and-white-striped tank barrel blocking our path. The Polish border guards waved us through, and then a Czech policeman in a green uniform came out of his office.

"Your passports!" he said harshly.

My father rolled down his window and gave the policeman our passports. He kept his engine running and the man waved his flashlight over the documents. Then he shone his light inside the car.

"Engineer Jaroslav Furman and Engineer Jana Furmanova!" he said in the sneering tone Communists often used to address white-collar workers. "And what are two university-educated people like yourselves doing in Poland? Studying their agriculture?" He snorted and swept his light across my face. "Open your trunk!" he ordered.

"Excuse me, comrade." My dad stuck his head through the window. "We have a problem with our car. The mechanics in Gdansk have fixed it so that we can get back to Prague, but they told us not to switch off the engine. I can't open the trunk unless I pull the key out of the ignition."

The policeman shrugged.

"Open your trunk!" he repeated.

"Comrade, please," my father said humbly. "If I stop the car, it's not going to start again. I assure you, we have nothing in our trunk except dirty clothes and an empty ice chest."

The policeman shook his head in disgust and walked back inside his office. A moment later, he reappeared with two Czech soldiers who pointed their rifles at my dad.

"Open your trunk, comrade engineer," the policeman said quietly. "I'm not going to ask you again."

My father sighed and switched off the ignition. The engine shuddered to a halt. He climbed out of the car and opened the trunk, and the policeman shone his flashlight over the empty beer bottles. He knocked the lid off the ice chest and halfheartedly unzipped our suitcases, and then he stepped away from the car and stamped our papers. Guessing from his expression, he was both satisfied and disappointed.

"Welcome to Czechoslovakia," he said, handing my father our passports. He waved at the soldier who was in charge of the gate, and the tank barrel rotated to the side. The policeman disappeared inside his office.

The soldiers lowered their rifles and watched my father repack the suitcases. He shut the trunk and climbed inside the car, but when he turned on the ignition, the engine let out an ugly wheeze. My mother squeezed his hand and told him to try again. He switched the ignition off and on, and the engine kept coughing until the battery was out of juice.

We climbed out of the Skoda and looked at the soldiers.

"You want to give us a hand?" my father asked.

The soldiers looked at each other and retreated to the office. The windows were made of one-way mirror glass, but we could see the soldiers and the policeman watching us from inside.

My dad put his shoulder to the door frame and my mother and I took our positions at the trunk. Then we counted, "One, two, three!" and pushed the car into our country.

It was a mild summer night. The sky had cleared and the air smelled faintly of hay and fresh rain. We push-started the car and drove across the countryside all the way back to Prague. Poplar trees lined the roads, and the towers of the baroque churches slanted up from the hills. We were too tired to talk, too hungry to sleep. I pressed my face to the window and watched the world go by. The crumbling facades and peeling paint on the houses, the potholes and dirt and barbed-wire fences, and the Communist posters were now hidden in the dark. All I could see was the outline of a poor and generous soil that was my home.

This was the country of little cakes and sausages. This is the memory of my childhood. Driving back home in our old, rusty Skoda; my father's big hands steering us safely through the night; the soft touch of my mother's hand on my head. This was the happiest time in my life. The time when we had no money, no choice, and no chance.

It would take me another eighteen years to realize that what we had back then was as much as anyone on earth would ever need.

We had each other, and plenty of love in our hearts.

ADDITIONAL
ACKNOWLEDGMENTS

I am very grateful to my little god for sending many nice people my way. I would never have been able to complete this book without their help. Elvira Schejbalova, Vaclav Jakubec, Petra Stypova, Eva Splichalova, Romana Krenkova, Martina Matouskova, Petra Langerova, Christine Williams, Brett Cheney, and Tanya Wolfe read my pages, comforted me when I was sad, and helped me in every way. My parents held their thumbs for me and provided me with a roof, bread, and butter. Dominic Buchta gave me love and hope when I needed it the most. Susanne Harrer, Pavel Konecny, and Martin Tucek scanned many photos and pictures and printed out numerous copies of the manuscript. Shannon O'Keefe and Julie Barer from Sandford J. Greenburger went out of their way to help me. Wendy Carlton from Riverhead did a great and thorough job editing the manuscript. Stephanie Huntwork designed the interior, Honi Werner is responsible for the beautiful book jacket, and Beth Krommes for the illustrations of the little cakes. Alexandria Morris was very lovely and worked hard to accommodate my needs and wishes. I really was fortunate to have had such great friends and collaborators.

ABOUT THE AUTHOR

DOMINIKA DERY was born in Prague in 1975. As a young girl, she studied at the State Conservatory in Prague, and danced and performed in the National Theater Ballet Company and later performed in the National Theater as an actor. In 1994, she was awarded a French government scholarship to study theater at the Ecole Internationale de Théâtre Jacques Lecoq. She is the author of four collections of Czech poetry and a play. *The Twelve Little Cakes* is her first book in English.